Primitive Renaissance

PRIMITIVE RENAISSANCE
Rethinking German Expressionism

DAVID PAN

University of Nebraska Press

Lincoln and London

© 2001 by the University of Nebraska Press
All rights reserved
Manufactured in the United States of America
♾
Library of Congress Cataloging-in-Publication Data
Pan, David, 1963–
Primitive renaissance : rethinking
German Expressionism / David Pan.
p.   cm. — (Modern German culture and literature series)
Includes bibliographical references and index.
ISBN 0-8032-3727-8 (cl.: alk. paper)
1. Aesthetics. 2. Expressionism. 3. Primitivism—
Germany. 4. Germany—Intellectual life—20th century.
I. Title. II. Modern German culture and literature.
BH301.E9 P36   2001
111′.85′0943—dc21
00-062028

For my parents

Contents

Illustrations

Acknowledgments

I would like to thank the Council for European Studies, the German Academic Exchange Service, the Getty Grant Program, and Washington University for their generous financial support, without which I would not have been able to complete the research and writing of this book. I would also like to thank Jean Kisling, Liliane Meffre, Klaus Siebenhaar, Hermann Haarmann, the Carl-Einstein-Archiv in Berlin, the Bibliothèque St. Geneviève in Paris, the Galerie Leiris in Paris, and the Getty Research Institute Library in Los Angeles for granting me access to archival materials. I would like to thank the Städtische Galerie im Lenbachhaus in Munich and the Guggenheim Museum in New York for permission to reprint photos of works from their collections. I would like to thank Russell Berman, Ute Berns, Charles Haxthausen, Andreas Huyssen, Klaus Kiefer, Anna Marie Medina, Paul Piccone, and Holmer Steinfath for their comments and criticisms regarding earlier versions of the material in this book. Finally, I would like to thank my wife, Muriel Pan, for her support, insight, criticisms, and patience during the years spent preparing this book for publication.

INTRODUCTION

In the "Sirens" episode of *The Odyssey*, Homer would have us believe that Odysseus, relying on nothing more than the wax in his sailors' ears and the rope binding him to the mast of his ship, was able to hear the song of the sirens without being drawn to his death like all the sailors before him.[1] Franz Kafka, finally giving the sirens their due, points out that Odysseus's "childish measures" were obviously insufficient to escape the sirens.[2] Their song could certainly pierce wax and would lead a man to burst all bonds. Instead of attributing Odysseus's survival to his cunning use of technical means, Kafka attributes Odysseus's survival to the sirens' use of an even more horrible weapon than their song: their silence. Believing that his trick had worked, Odysseus did not hear their silence but imagined he heard the sound of their singing. For no one, not even Odysseus, could resist "the feeling of having triumphed over them by one's own strength, and the consequent exaltation that bears down everything before it."[3] The sirens disappeared from his perceptions, which were focused entirely on himself. Kafka concludes: "If the sirens had possessed consciousness they would have been annihilated at that moment. But they remained as they had been; all that had happened was that Odysseus had escaped them."[4]

Max Horkheimer and Theodor Adorno have argued that this ancient epic clearly demonstrates the inseparability of myth from Enlightenment thought. Homer's Odysseus is the model of an Enlightenment optimism and faith in human technology: through clever technical means he is able to escape the injunctions of a mythic fate, creating an exception to the mythic law and thereby destroying it and replacing it with a new law of human technical mastery over nature.[5] In Kafka's account, however, the fascination of the story does not stem from Odysseus's cunning but from the naive optimism that could place so much trust in "his handful of wax and his fathom of chain."[6] This interpretation changes the character of the exception to the rule of fate that the story of the sirens presents. Instead of being the first instance of a new law of human sovereignty over nature, Odysseus's escape is an exception to the law of mythic fate that only affirms fate's power to capriciously grant survival as well as ordain death. His actions prove the degree of his self-delusion, and his refusal to recognize the power of the sirens has no effect on these impersonal manifestations of the forces of nature. The punishment that they have prepared for him is far worse than the physical death other sailors had found. In contrast to his predecessors, Odysseus, mesmerized by his faith in his own technical powers, has been rendered deaf to the voice of fate and dead to the world of the spirit. The song of the sirens becomes an invention of his own mind that, in its inconsequential entertainment, diverts him from the silence that surrounds him. His survival in the epic depends upon the silencing of the myth; but the fate that lies behind the myth continues to exist, though he is oblivious to it.

In this example, Kafka has taken the epic modernity of Homer's story and reinterpreted it so as to reveal once again the primitive mythic power that Horkheimer and Adorno seek to deny. If, in their reading, Homer's text struggles to overcome a mythic fate, Kafka's text struggles to revive it. The contrast between the Frankfurt school's modernist reading and Kafka's primitivist one does not demonstrate the regressive implications of progress, as Horkheimer and Adorno argue.[7] Rather, it reveals an alternative to the twin notions of progression and of regression in history. The progressivist position is not a new one. It is simply the latest version of the kind of cultural chauvinism that motivates the episodes of *The Odyssey* in which Homer describes how Odysseus's cleverness ultimately overcomes various instances of a backward or barbaric primitivity (for example, the Lotus Eaters or the Cyclops).[8] When Kafka reads the opposition between myth and Enlightenment as part of a continuing conflict in human culture between piety and pride, he defends the coherence and relevance of a primitive perspective.

In presenting this perspective, Kafka does not close off all possibility for Odysseus to succeed in his struggle against the sirens. He merely redefines the criteria for determining this success. Kafka notes in an addendum to his story that Odysseus's only hope of outwitting the sirens, "although here the human understanding is beyond its depths," is by hearing their silence, thereby recognizing their power, and then feigning a feeling of victory.[9] This chance to effect a true escape from the sirens' trap does not lie in Odysseus's own technical abilities but rather in his ability to maintain an inner consciousness of their sovereignty.

The opposition between a modern belief in human achievement and a primitive reverence for mythic fate provides the two basic categories defining the development of German culture in the twentieth century. Both perspectives coexist, often within a single text. Yet this conflict between two perspectives should not lead us to define expressionism as ambiguity.[10] Rather, it should be interpreted as part of the struggle of a primitive perspective to assert itself in art and literature after a prolonged suppression of primitive forms. According to this interpretation, "modernism" is a misnomer for early-twentieth-century aesthetic movements. The idea of progress and the opposition to the notion of tradition embedded in this word do not describe but rather contradict the motivating impulses of this "primitivist" movement.[11]

The confusion is not simply due to an interpretive fallacy but to the historical situation of modernization against which the expressionists were revolting. The artists and writers of this period were deeply affected by the rapid pace of industrialization, which had transformed Europe from a traditional agrarian to a modern industrial society.[12] Yet, twentieth-century aesthetic movements did not develop as an accompaniment to modernity but as a reaction to and revolt against it. The age of industrialism institutionalized an aesthetics of autonomy in the nineteenth century, and the twentieth-century avant-garde attempt to merge art with life that Peter Bürger has described sought on the one hand to overturn this Enlightenment aesthetics of autonomy and on the other hand to critique so-

cial modernization.[13] This double revolt against modernity leads to
the development of a perspective on culture that does not supplement or accompany but contradicts and replaces a modern perspective. Rather than subsuming twentieth-century art within a larger
process of modernization, understanding this art as fundamentally
primitivist serves to emphasize the polar opposition between the
modern and the primitive.

The equation of expressionism with primitivism brings with it a
reinterpretation of the former's historical context. It makes expressionism on the one hand a result of the imitation of primitive art
forms rather than the creation of the radically new and, on the
other, a part of a cyclical rather than evolutionary European development. Primitive art, including the art of Africa and the South
Seas as well as medieval and twentieth-century European folk and
religious art, played a crucial role in the development of twentieth-
century European art, one analogous to the important influence
Greek classicism had on the Renaissance. In both cases, art from
other cultures inspired and impelled a radical shift in the development of Western art.

Yet both the classical Renaissance and the rise of primitivism
were also integral parts of an inner-European movement between
the two poles of progressivism and primitivism. In fact, the
twentieth-century primitive renaissance to be delineated in the following pages was described by expressionists such as Franz Marc as
the completion of a cyclical trajectory that began in the Middle
Ages, moved through the Renaissance and Enlightenment, and
ended with a return to the aesthetic forms of, among others, the
pre-Renaissance Italian primitives.[14] Thus, the first formal definition of primitivism, published in France at the turn of the twentieth
century, designated it as "imitation des primitifs," where the word
primitif referred to pre-Renaissance European art.[15] This initial understanding demonstrates that the primitive did not simply invade
the European cultural tradition from outside but rather developed
out of the European critique of a Renaissance-oriented aesthetic.
The primitive does not designate something foreign but familiar,
though perhaps repressed. It is true that the receptivity of European artists to the primitive art of Africa and the South Seas some-

times reverted to an exoticizing attitude.[16] However, the underlying impulse of primitivism was determined by a coincidence of the goals pursued by these European primitivists and the tribal primitives they imitated.

Defining expressionism as a primitivist critique of modernity does not limit the heterogeneity of positions encompassed by this movement. Rather, the idea of primitivism provides the explanation for the explosion of new and varying artistic practices and goals that characterizes late-nineteenth- and early-twentieth-century European culture. The examples of primitive art from Africa, the Americas, and the South Seas that expressionists used as models for their work all came from cultural situations in which no unifying, imperial culture was dominant. Instead, they came from cultural environments in which the art of each particular tribe or community was allowed to develop on its own, leading, for example, to the varied array of artistic forms and styles characteristic of African art. Primitive art implies a local art, and the primitivism of expressionist art becomes evident not only in the stylistic affinities between expressionist and African art but also in the genesis of expressionism in a series of local groups of artists in separate centers such as Berlin, Dresden, Munich, Vienna, and Prague. One of the main characteristics of primitivism is thus the elimination of a unifying "imperialist" or "nationalist" perspective and a consequent multiplication of local aesthetic possibilities.

The aesthetic multiplicity of primitivism also corresponds to a political heterogeneity. The political allegiances of expressionist writers and artists are notoriously difficult to typify. Yet when considered as political primitivists, writers and artists with such varying political sympathies as the communists Johannes Becher and Max Pechstein, the anarchists Carl Einstein and Franz Kafka, and the protofascists Gottfried Benn and Emil Nolde all suddenly appear as presenters of variations on a single political theme.[17] Though the specific characteristics of each variant, whether communist or anarchist or fascist, were to have dire consequences for the political history of Europe, the primitivist political outlook they shared clearly links these figures to each other as expressionists.[18]

But if primitivism is linked to such aesthetic and social variety, how can we define a specifically primitivist perspective? What do all of the competing primitivist aesthetic forms share? Determining what primitivism excludes is a first step toward the answer. The immediate answer is one we have already suggested, that primitivism excludes the idea of progress, along with aesthetic forms based on this idea. Progressivism and primitivism can be distinguished according to their view of the possibilities of human endeavor in light of recent advances in science and technology. While a progressivist view discerns in modern, rapid technological development a fundamental change in the parameters of human existence, the primitivist critique of science emphasizes that technological progress does not change the existential situation of the modern compared to the primitive.[19]

We need to demonstrate this distinction in perspective further and to sketch out a preliminary definition of primitivism and the primitive viewpoint that it seeks to recover. To do so, it will be useful to contrast the critique of modernity developed by the German Jewish writer and art historian Carl Einstein (1885–1940) with that of his contemporary Walter Benjamin (1892–1940). A comparison between the two is pertinent in the first place because of the similarities in their biographies.[20] They were both German Jews with secular educations who nevertheless became interested in the relationships between art and religious forms. Neither of them held any academic or official positions, and they lived by writing books, reviews, and articles for journals and newspapers. They spent most of their adult lives in the two cities Berlin and Paris, writing and publishing in both German and French. Finally, they both committed suicide in southern France in 1940 shortly after the German invasion. But though Benjamin has enjoyed a healthy revival in the postwar era, Einstein's work still remains largely unknown outside of a small albeit growing circle of specialists.

The reasons for the previous underappreciation of Einstein's work and the current increasing interest coincide. While his political affinities placed him in the same category as leftist and anarchist intellectuals such as Walter Benjamin, Ernst Bloch, Gustav Landauer, and Franz Kafka, his theories contain an unmistakable metaphysical element that ultimately lines up closer to conservative figures such as Gottfried Benn, Ernst Jünger, or Carl Schmitt. As a testament to the unsettling affinities between left-wing and right-wing critiques of modernity between the wars, Einstein's work was unassimilable by a Cold War, liberal academic perspective. As a consequence of the end of the Cold War and a renewed postmodern critique of Enlightenment it has now begun to reemerge. Add to this the current trend toward interdisciplinary work, and this art historian-writer-philosopher-ethnographer-political activist becomes a key figure in the current theoretical debates on culture.

Einstein's innovation as a thinker becomes immediately evident when his work is compared with Benjamin's. Though Benjamin is known for being a critic of the idea of progress, his conception of modernity is nevertheless founded upon a progressivist consciousness that believes in an evolution from a traditional to a modern world. By contrast, Einstein's primitivist refusal to accept the validity of an evolutionary understanding of the distinction between tradition and modernity leads him to view these two terms as opposite poles of a constant conflict within human society. The strength of Einstein's view lies in his ability to delineate a distinction between rationalist and mythic modes of relating to nature. By the same token, the weakness of Benjamin's argument stems from his inability to recognize that myth and ritual are still crucial for human experience because rational critique remains an imperfect tool for organizing cultural life.

Commentators have noted in Benjamin's work an ambivalent attitude toward tradition and ritual.[21] He affirms the hypothetical value of aura and ritual for maintaining the possibility of coherent, communal experience in the modern psyche, but at same time he argues that traditional forms dependent on aura and ritual can no longer function in the modern world.[22]

He voices his regret at the loss of the cult ritual when he recognizes, both in "The Storyteller" (1936) and "On Some Motifs in Baudelaire" (1939), that the aura of the cult object is the prerequisite for genuine experience: "Where there is experience in the strict sense of the word, certain contents of the individual past combine with material of the collective past. The rituals with their ceremonies, their festivals (quite probably nowhere recalled in Proust's work) kept producing the amalgamation of these two elements of memory over and over again. They triggered recollection at certain times and remained handles of memory for a lifetime."[23] In contrast to modern genres such as the novel, traditional forms such as oral storytelling presuppose the audience's embeddedness within a collective cultic experience. Benjamin's mourning of the end of storytelling is based on his recognition of the need for cultural constructs that integrate individual experience with collective memory.

But though Benjamin's nostalgia for traditions and rituals such as storytelling may be read as a celebration of tradition, his work is built on the antitraditionalist assumption that culture evolves as a progression from a traditional world to a modern one. He attributes the causes of this evolution to advances in technology that create an incommensurability between a modern situation and traditional modes of human experience. Describing a modern situation inaugurated by World War I in which communicable experience is no longer possible, Benjamin writes: "For never has experience been contradicted more thoroughly than strategic experience by tactical warfare, economic experience by inflation, bodily experience by mechanical warfare, moral experience by those in power. A generation that had gone to school on a horse-drawn streetcar now stood under the open sky in a countryside in which nothing remained unchanged but the clouds, and beneath these clouds, in a field of force of destructive torrents and explosions, was the tiny, fragile human body."[24] In this passage, Benjamin depicts the modern decline of human experience as an incommensurability of the human body (the measure of experience for the individual) with the landscape in which it exists. He blames this incommensurability on the scale of modern structures, which have replaced familiar human contexts. In Benjamin's account, the conflict between the individual and the outside world is a specifically modern dilemma that results from new technology and mass systems of government and economy.

This decidedly progressivist vision of a world that has advanced beyond the capacities of traditional culture undermines any recognition of the value of rituals for constituting human experience. Because he believes that modernization has made the decline of tradition irreparable, he argues that collective experience can no longer be transmitted, as before, in the form of stories, and "the art of storytelling is coming to an end."[25] Benjamin's affirmation of the possible value of ritual is thus conducted with the consciousness of its obsolescence.

Because he views the liquidation of tradition as an irreversible progression, he turns to modern methods to dispel the alienation that he describes. The solution he offers is to create new hybrid forms such as "profane illumination," which he sets up as a replacement for religious illumination: "the true, creative overcoming of religious illumination does not lie in narcotics. It resides in a *profane illumination*, a materialistic, anthropological inspiration, to which hashish, opium, or whatever else can give an introductory lesson."[26] Such new secular forms do not create auratic or cultic experience; rather, they foster rational critique and reflection. In contrast to the attitude of submission to a collective past that Benjamin sees in the ritual, his ideal art is a kind of "shock defense" that transforms potentially traumatic experiences, which much like rituals would affect the very structure of consciousness, into everyday events that are assigned a specific place in the memory: "Without reflection there would be nothing but the sudden start, usually the sensation of fright which, according to Freud, confirms the failure of the shock defense."[27] To cultivate the reflection necessary for a successful "shock defense," Benjamin seeks (in "The Work of Art in the Age of Mechanical Reproduction" [1936], for instance) to develop in the film audience a critical attitude toward the outside world. He looks to film as montage rather than as storytelling to find the essential aesthetic objects of the twentieth century. Such a replacement of ritual with reflection is only possible if one, on the one hand, affirms the capacity of human consciousness to plumb the depths of experience through rational means and, on the other hand, denies that nature can present a tragedy-producing opposite to human endeavor. According to Benjamin, myths and rituals can no longer serve any function for consciousness and are simply archaic constructs that need to be replaced by rational critique.[28]

Yet Benjamin remains unhappy with this solution, not because he believes the intellect is inadequate to the task of replacing myth, but because he mourns the loss of any resistance to the human subject on the part of the object: "To perceive the aura of an object we look at means to invest it with the ability to look at us in return. This experience corresponds to the data of the *mémoire involontaire*."[29] The submission to the gaze of the object is a submission to one's own repressed, involuntary memories and consequently to those experiences that are fundamental to the construction of the psyche. Benjamin searches for a modern version of this experience of the object in Baudelaire's *correspondances* and Proust's *mémoire involontaire*. But in doing so, he must bring back into his theory that which he had been trying to ban from it all along: tragedy and mythic sacrifice. For the gaze of the object and the involuntary character of memories are nothing other than continuing reminders of the mythic violence that continues to limit and frustrate human aspirations, threatening the sovereign power of the human intellect. A recognition of this violence must lie at the basis of every attempt to recover the auratic gaze of the object, which by definition must be based in a realm that is beyond the control of the human intellect and is thus a potential source of danger.

To make a return to rituals and the gaze of the object possible without having to accept the necessity of mythic violence, Benjamin attempts to distinguish conceptually between the horror of nature in myth and the overcoming of this horror in the fairy tale. In this way, he is able to posit a secret harmonious bond between humankind and nature that overcomes the violence of myth: "The liberating magic which the fairy tale has at its disposal does not bring nature into play in a mythical way, but points to its complicity with liberated man."[30] Benjamin's attempt to separate the happiness of the fairy tale from the horror of myth is based on the assumption of nature's "complicity with liberated man." The belief in this harmony between humankind and nature betrays a naive faith in the power of technical means, not just to transform human life, but to completely subdue nature to the point that it no longer presents any resistance or danger to human endeavor. As Winfried Menninghaus writes in reference to Benjamin's distinction between myth and fairy tale, "the point of Benjamin's idiosyncratic definition of fairy tale (and partly also of epic) is the possibility of a liberation or redemption from the myth through a 'thwarting of the tragic,' and this means above all: without sacrifice and expiation."[31] Such a denial of the relevance of tragedy and sacrifice for the modern age is not based on any objective evidence but only on the belief that "one's chances increase as the mythical primitive times are left behind."[32] Benjamin's attempt to reconcile humankind with nature through visions of the happiness of fairy tales, profane illumination, or poetry as shock defense is based on his inability to accept the basic contradiction between humankind and nature that creates the necessity for myth and ritual. He denies this contradiction, first, as in the passage quoted earlier, by postulating a secret harmony between humankind and nature and, second, by arguing that the age of myth has been superseded in the modern era because of the advance of "productive forces."

Using this idea of the reconciliation between humankind and nature in the fairy tale, Benjamin seeks to find such harmonious forms of ritual in the work of Baudelaire and Proust. Specifically, he reads Proust's work as an effort "to restore the figure of the storyteller to the present generation."[33] But in his discussion of storytelling Benjamin notes an important difference between these modern ritual elements in the novel and traditional storytelling. In contrast to the collective context of the storyteller, "The novelist has isolated himself. The birthplace of the novel is the solitary individual, who is no longer able to express himself by giving examples of his most important concerns, is himself, uncounseled, and cannot counsel others."[34] Rather than submitting in the story to the collective experience embedded in the ritual, the individual in the novel submits to the force of associations derived from private memories. Benjamin's focus on the Proustian *mémoire involontaire*, though it is framed as an attempt to retrieve ritual, only demonstrates the novelist's inability to provide a collective, cultic experience of the object.[35] For the taste of the madeleine bringing back the involuntary memory of Combray for Proust can only reproduce on an individual level the collective remembrance embedded in the Passover bread or the Catholic communion. But since the primary function of ritual is to integrate individual experience into a collective totality, the *mé-*

moire involontaire cannot be a blueprint for a modern form of "profane illumination" as Benjamin contends. It can instead only be a symptom of the decline of collective experience in storytelling and of the institutionalization of social atomization in the novel. This shift from traditional to modern experience is not a form of technological progress nor a sign of the obsolescence of rituals. Rather, it is a result of a conscious turning away from collective rituals that, according to Einstein, has led, not to a new rationalized form of experience, but only to the proliferation of private neuroses.

In contrast to Benjamin's progressive stance, Einstein's primitivist refusal to accept the validity of an evolutionary understanding of the distinction between tradition and modernity leads him to view these two terms as opposite poles of a constant conflict within human society. Where Benjamin searches for reconciliation, Einstein maintains the irresolvability of contradiction. Einstein's conception of a modern primitivization does not differentiate between myth and fairy tale and does not offer any idea of a "complicity" between humankind and nature. Consequently, there is no possible return to a harmonious state but only to a primitive state of conflict in humankind's relation to nature. This perspective is founded on the assumption that the situation of the modern with respect to the outside world is fundamentally no different than that of the primitive.

In "The Storyteller" Benjamin describes the incommensurability between the individual and the outside world as a modern experience of alienation from a terrifying world. According to the primitivist viewpoint this incommensurability is nothing new, but rather the basic presupposition of every mythic system. Einstein writes: "But now, what is the relation of the artistic man to the world? Precisely that of the primitive man, he is fearful of it, he is inhibited by the multiplicity of impressions of civilization, he fears reality, which constantly wants to shock him and tear him out of himself."[36] Einstein interprets the "modern" alienation of the individual from external reality as a return to a primitive attitude toward a hostile world. This attitude is a characteristic of the twentieth-century "artistic man" who does not approach reality with the critical and conceptual attitude of the nineteenth-century positivist. Instead, he relates to the world with an aesthetic sensibility that recognizes both the power of outside forces and the corresponding inadequacy of rational constructs to organize human consciousness.

While Benjamin characterizes the irreversible decline of storytelling as "a concomitant symptom of the secular productive forces of history," for Einstein the modern decline of communal experience is the result of an abandonment of mythic structures that mediate between the individual and the outside world.[37] Like Benjamin, Einstein characterizes the modern situation as an alienation of the individual from the outside world, but instead of providing a technical and materialist explanation for this alienation he suggests a spiritual one. From his viewpoint, technological advances in themselves do not produce a cultural situation of modernity. Rather, modernity stems from the attempt to replace mythic structures of experience with scientific and rational ones that fail to recognize the unconscious forces of the psyche. In a lecture on twentieth-century art given in 1931, Einstein remarks: "The mechanization and intellectualization of life was so excessive that a mass of repressions was stored up of forces that could not be utilized within a rational system."[38] The alienation of the individual is a result of an application of scientific reasoning in a spiritual area in which it does not belong, leading to a buildup of repressed forces. Early-twentieth-century primitivist art, however, presents a return to mythic tendencies, which have hitherto been suppressed but are still necessary in the modern world: "thus something returns, the romantic valorization, the turn to the fairy tale, exactly like the primitive man. Now all of these mythic forces regain their rightful place and man no longer agrees to submit to the inhibitions of a selective rationality."[39] Because the structures of reason are incapable of organizing individual experience, the return of mythic forces in the fairy tale is not a regression but rather the return of a repressed dimension in human experience to its rightful place.

Because Einstein rejects the notion of progress, he also does not treat the return to a primitive attitude as a regression to an earlier stage of a supposed human evolution toward modernity. His primitivism does not advocate a rejection of modern technology, nor a "return to nature," nor a simple reestablishment of the myths of another era. Rather, he attempts to show that mythic thought addresses psychological and spiritual issues that remain relevant even in an age of technological modernization. Twentieth-century art is consequently bound by the same parameters that have governed the construction of myth up to the present day.

The consequences for Benjamin's and Einstein's aesthetics of their disagreement about tradition become most evident when we consider their readings of fascist cult rituals. While Benjamin has been described as the quintessential opponent of fascism, Einstein's defense of myth has been read as a sign of an ambiguous complicity with a fascist "neo-primitivism."[40] His differentiation between conceptual and aesthetic forms leads him to support an aestheticization of experience, bringing him very close to what Benjamin condemns as a characteristic of fascism in this passage from "The Work of Art in the Age of Mechanical Reproduction": "The logical result of Fascism is the introduction of aesthetics into political life. The violation of the masses, whom Fascism, with its *Führer* cult, forces to their knees, has its counterpart in the violation of an apparatus which is pressed into the production of ritual values."[41] The key issue for Benjamin in the aestheticization of political life is the production of ritual values in the cult. While Einstein sees them as essential for the collective integration of experience, for Benjamin cult and ritual have become as obsolete as the horsedrawn streetcar. For Benjamin, this obsolescence of ritual elements determines their reactionary character in the hands of the fascists.[42] Einstein, by contrast, insists on the continuing relevance of the experience of cultic submission as the only means for a collective appropriation of history.[43] For him, the cultic experience of submission is necessary for mediating between the outer world and the human psyche, and this mediation is essential for the primitive whether in the jungles of the Amazon or of the modern European city.

Yet Einstein's understanding of the cult ritual can still be clearly differentiated from the fascist one. For while the spectator submits to the leader in the fascist Führer cult and, according to Benjamin, the story similarly "bears the marks of the storyteller much as the earthen vessel bears the marks of the potter's hand,"[44] in Einstein's description of African sculpture the creator is not sovereign. Both artist and spectator submit to the power of the cult object and the forces that it invokes: "The effort [of the artist] is a distanced adoration and the work of art is therefore *a priori* something independent, more powerful than the creator; particularly since this creator invests his entire energy into the work and therefore sacrifices himself as the weaker one in favor of the work of art."[45] The power of the cult object derives from the psychic energy invested in the object by both the creator and the spectator, and both stand in an attitude of submission before the gaze of the object. This gaze, comparable to the gaze of the sirens, presents in plastic form neither a fascist nor a foreign Other. Rather, it presents the forces that limit human endeavor and thereby determine the structure of human experience in a particular cultural context. From Einstein's perspective, the fascist Führer cult is not an example of a functioning ritual whose role is to create a mimesis of the antinomies of experience for a collective. Instead, it is an attempt to manipulate ritual forms to serve the specific political goals of the creator. While Benjamin, in spite of his condemnation, essentially accepts the fascist reading of art as a form of manipulation, Einstein understands art as mimesis.

In its reaction to industrialization, the primitivist perspective was not a revolt against the particular technological products of natural science such as the railroad, the telegraph, or the cinema, for which primitivists often expressed a deep admiration. Rather, this revolt was directed against the modern worldview that accompanied these technical advances. The success of new technologies infused this worldview with the notion of the obsolescence of the old, borrowed from the history of natural science, in which older scientific models and technologies are superseded by newer ones and rendered irrelevant for later generations. By transferring this idea into the realm of culture, Enlightenment thinkers from the eighteenth and nineteenth centuries created more than just a particular revolt against a preceding tradition but a revolt against the idea of tradition itself. Hence, the term *modern* brings with it the implication that culture has advanced to a new dimension, undergoing a kind of Copernican revolution in which not only old ideas but an entire relationship to the past is overthrown. In contrast to the belief in progress expressed by this Enlightenment attitude, the reaction of early-twentieth-century artists to modernization was a primitivist one grounded in a critique of science rather than an emulation of it. Because nineteenth-century scientific objectivism was both antitraditional and antiprimitive, the twentieth-century critique of science paved the way for a reappraisal of the ideas of tradition and of the primitive.

The primary cultural component of this reappraisal consisted of a reevaluation of the status of art in modern society. Primitivists reacted against the ornamental, accompanying function to which they felt art had been relegated in a society that depends upon technological achievements and therefore attempts to regulate all social functions by means of rational systems. For the primitivists art was to fulfill essential social functions such as the creation of group identity and a common language, the establishment of law, and the regulation of generational processes of birth, marriage, and death. All these were functions that, so the primitivists thought, had simply been neglected by a technological worldview incapable of supplanting traditional forms. This primitivist reappraisal of the role of art in society goes beyond Peter Bürger's understanding of a merging of art and life that simply means a destruction of the institution of art and the treatment of art as a commodity.[46] The expressionist revolt must be understood primarily as a primitivist one that attempts to preserve the particularity of aesthetic experience but wishes also to make aesthetic experience into something more than entertainment or ornament.[47] Art for the primitivists provides the mytho-aesthetic template for the forms of everyday experience.

PRIMITIVISM IN PHILOSOPHY, ART, AND LITERATURE

The origins of twentieth-century primitivism lie in the work of Friedrich Nietzsche, whose defining influence on expressionism has been generally recognized, but whose primitivism has been obscured by the circumstances of his reception by critics.[48] This reception has wavered between two poles in which his work is defined as a philosophy of fascist totalization on the one hand and a philosophy of radical perspectivism and relativism on the other. He has been criticized both for his insistence on metaphysical truth and for his excessive aestheticization of reality. These contradictory characterizations of his work stem from the failure to recognize the primitivist nature of his philosophy.

Nietzsche first formulated the distinction between primitive and modern that is elaborated in expressionism by differentiating a Dionysian from a Socratic impulse in ancient Greek culture. This distinction, which affirms the validity of an intuitive, aesthetic mode of relating to the world as opposed to a logical, scientific one, sets up the philosophical foundations for the rise of primitivism in the twentieth century. Nietzsche argues that there has been a constant conflict between opposing forces or godheads rather than an evolutionary progress toward modernity. While the Socratic impulse maintains a scientific attitude that, according to Immanuel Kant, can never penetrate the thing-in-itself, the task of the Dionysian is to mediate between humankind and this metaphysical dimension. But this dimension, which Nietzsche calls the "primal unity" (*das Ur-eine*), is not a temporal origin of Greek culture so much as an experiential one. The Dionysian expression of the "primal unity" is indispensable to the construction of the experience of every individual in a culture and thus to the renewal of a culture's values within each member.

Nietzsche establishes a distinction between the rationalist attempt to repress and demonize "irrational" forces and the mythic attempt to aesthetically accommodate and thus interact with these forces on a day-to-day basis. According to Nietzsche, because of its antagonism to the irrational and the traditional, Socratic rationalism cannot sustain itself. Its naive faith in the power of rational thought leads it "again and again to its limits at which it must turn into art."[49] As Einstein would also argue, the rationalist approach to culture eventually reaches certain limits, after which the only viable alternative is a turn to art as an organizer of experience. Without the turn toward Dionysian art and the primitive, a consistent and thorough rationalization will continue to repress irrational forces until the culture collapses into barbarism—which is neither the primitive forerunner of civilization nor the end result of primitivization, but a product of a modern perspective that seeks to supplant traditions, either in classical Greek or twentieth-century European culture. By contrast, primitive traditions dependent upon mythic and aesthetic structures create a continual relation to those forces repressed by a rationalist culture. By recognizing a constant conflict, a primitive, Dionysian attitude makes the repeated sacrifices that avoid the rationalist descent into barbarism.

If Nietzsche can be considered the prophet of the primitive, pointing to the primal forces that continue to structure the modern psyche, the expressionists are amongst his most ardent disciples. In contrast to a rationalist culture that confines the spiritual dimension to an empty thing-in-itself, these writers and artists saw their art as a Dionysian expression of a deeper, spiritual reality. This idea that art must contain a metaphysical aspect led Wassily Kandinsky to conceive of art as a creator of ideal forms that, in liberating themselves from the restraints imposed by the material world, are free to mediate a spiritual reality. His key contribution to the development of primitivism lay in his recognition that the essence of primitive art does not reside in its dissolution or regression to an undifferentiated primal state but in its strict adherence to the formal aesthetic principles that make abstract art possible. In contrast to those expressionists such as Pechstein or Nolde whose exoticist approach sought to *represent* primitive life by painting scenes from life in the South Seas, for example, Kandinsky's move toward the primitive coincided with the development of his art away from representation and toward abstraction.

But by concentrating on a hermetic world of inner forms, Kandinsky runs the risk of breaking the relation between art and nature that is crucial to art's spiritual function as a creator of forms for experience. For this reason, it is useful to read Kandinsky alongside Sigmund Freud's theory of primitive culture in *Totem and Taboo*. This text fills in a gap in Nietzsche's and Kandinsky's theories by explaining the psychic significance of various myths and rituals. Art for Freud does not relate to nature simply by representing empirical reality but by mediating between psychic forces and external ones.

In Freud's reading, myths are not simply delusions but manifestations of psychic forces active in an individual (in which case the myth is considered pathological) or in a collective (in which case the myth must be taken as an integral part of the social fabric). In both cases, the psychic forces are not simply arbitrary mental or emotional impulses but arise out of an interaction between subjective desires and the outside forces that frustrate and channel these desires. Myth is the result of a crystallization of the competing forces of desire and necessity into a particular compromise formation. Freud's discussion of myth and ritual does not demonstrate the fallacies of myth and the uselessness of ritual, nor does he accept myths and ritual practices at face value. Instead, he interprets myths and rituals in order to divine the forces that have created their formal organization.[50]

In developing his reading of primitive culture, Freud proposes a structure of myth that resembles very closely Nietzsche's vision of a Dionysian art. In both cases, art or myth produces a mimesis of the forces of nature by enacting the conflicts that these forces create for human experience.[51] This similarity in the functioning of art and of myth, which Nietzsche explicitly affirms and Freud tentatively suggests, forms the theoretical basis for the primitivism of the German expressionists, who see in art the form for a "new" spiritual mode of truth that challenges the materialistic truths of science and technology.

The expressionist construction of truth does not translate concretely into either an arbitrary act of force imposed by a powerful authority nor a dissolution of truth into a series of arbitrary, self-referential constructions. Rather, this mytho-aesthetic truth is constructed out of a mimesis of the forces that comprise reality for human consciousness. Since these forces cannot be apprehended scientifically or philosophically, the aesthetic construction of truth does not replace scientific cognition, but rather occupies a different terrain.

Einstein's primitivism attempts to define the particularity of this terrain and specify its role in human experience. In his conception, primitive art, whether in the guise of African sculpture or expressionist or cubist painting, is more than a merely aesthetic experience. It is also an attempt to redefine the link between the individual and the outside world. Art recreates the parameters within which experience might exist. This goal leads to a nonrepresentational art that does not attempt to reproduce an outside reality but to mediate between the outside world and inner forces: "The test was before whether something is true, whereas today it is understood that the intellect, which was so tremendously overestimated, is merely a thin outer layer through which new mythic forces are constantly penetrating."[52] Instead of creating representations of objects, art for Einstein must provide a conduit for psychic, that is, mythic, forces.

Einstein's art historical works, *Negro Sculpture* (*Negerplastik*) (1915) and *Twentieth-Century Art* (*Die Kunst des 20. Jahrhunderts*) (1926) link aesthetic forms to the inner and outer forces governing the mental life of the individual. By creating an aesthetic organization of these forces, the work of art forges a concrete totality of experience that is indispensable for normal perception. Because such a psychic totality depends upon the forces of desire and external necessity that are active in consciousness, totality for Einstein is not an objective, rational construct, but depends upon the forces active in latent memories. By creating the parameters for the totality, aesthetic form determines ways of seeing for the individual. Yet because art is an objectified presentation of a way of seeing, its existence determines the perceptions of the entire group of individuals who are affected by it. In creating an artistic totality, the work of art also creates a community totality within which human experience can be properly assimilated and understood.

Primitive art functions like myth in order to construct collective social forms. On the one hand, these forms mediate to the individual an experience of the external forces that determine a community's survival and development. On the other hand, the shared reception of the work of art defines group identity. In this theory of the primitive, aesthetic form creates the parameters of psychic experience for all cultures, even modern, rationalist ones, and the primitive is more than just a particular type of society. It is a specific dimension of every society. Einstein is not so much interested in certain "tribal" cultures of Africa or the South Seas, but in the extent to which everyday life is experienced in every culture as a corollary to aesthetic experience.[53] For Einstein, art has an organizing function for the community, defining the community's relationship to the outside world. This view of art brings it into proximity with primitive religion, and Einstein's theory of art seeks to explain both the religious, metaphysical qualities of art and the aesthetic, formal characteristics of myth.[54]

The specific characteristics of a primitive art depend upon the genre involved. In the visual arts, primitive art attempts to make visible the fundamental structures upon which all vision is based. Both primitive African and primitivist European artists rely on abstraction to accomplish this goal. In both cases, the work of art controls the vision of the viewer in such a way that the final visual image is determined by the work of art's mode of perceiving reality. The assumption is that an "objective" visual reality does not exist. All seeing is determined by a particular perspective on the world. This perspective arises out of the interaction of forces that form the consciousness of individuals in a particular community. Through its mimesis of the forces active in the psyche, the work of art enforces a specific view of the world that is to be shared by the entire community of viewers. The extent to which this view is indeed shared by, and not alien to, that of the viewers will determine the power of the artistic image.

Though Einstein bases his argument on an analysis of painting (he refers specifically to artists such as Pablo Picasso, Joan Miró, and Paul Klee), a similar desire for such a mediation was evident in expressionist literature. In their construction of an idiosyncratic synthesis of psyche and outside world, expressionist poems—as well as the paintings that Einstein compares to poems—create a vision of a future mode of seeing the world. As Einstein comments: "and in the same way as these missionaries prophesied the visionary, in such poems—that is almost how I would like to refer to these paintings—the future intuition of the people is set forth as prophecy."[55] Myth is implicitly defined here as a construction of exemplary images and narratives that provide collective structures for the unfolding of experience. As a creator of visions that organize human experience, poetry, even in the modern world, begins to take on this mythic function.

Einstein was not alone in conceiving this metaphysical function for expressionist literature. In the 1919 preface to his famous collection of expressionist poetry, *Dawn of Humanity* (*Menschheitsdäm-merung*), Kurt Pinthus describes this poetry as an attempt to create a humanized landscape: "Because the human being is so totally starting point, central point, aiming point of this poetry, there is little room in it for landscape. The landscape is never painted, depicted, celebrated; instead it is completely humanized: it is horror, melancholy, confusion of chaos, it is the shimmering labyrinth from which Ahasuerus longingly seeks to extricate himself; and forest and trees are either places of the dead or hands that are groping toward God, toward infinity."[56] Just as Einstein describes primitivist painting as poetry, Pinthus describes expressionist poetry as paintings in which the boundary between subjective impressions and an outside reality has been dissolved. This dissolution functions neither as an expansion nor as a reification of the subject. It functions as a disappearance of a distinction between subject and object, creating the psychic occupation of the outside world as a totality necessary for the integration of an individual into a particular environment.

In dissolving the distinction between subject and object, the expressionists attempt to reverse the Enlightenment destruction of the particularity of objects documented by Horkheimer and Adorno in their pronouncement: "Myth turns into enlightenment, and nature into mere objectivity."[57] Like Einstein, Horkheimer and Adorno bemoan the advance of a scientific mode of cognition that reduces nature to the status of object and thereby destroys a primitive totality and with it the differentiation of qualities in experience inherent to a mythic consciousness.

Horkheimer and Adorno discern a regressive development from animistic magic, which pursues its goals through mimesis rather than an increasing distance to the object, to modern science, in which reality is gradually reduced to "universal interchangeability."[58] In contrast, Einstein does not perceive an inexorable progression (or regression) from the mythic to the rational. Instead, he reads the opposition between scientific cognition and aesthetic mimesis as a constant conflict in history. On the one hand, modern manipulation of nature is based on a subject/object distinction. On the other hand, the primitive recognition of the incommensurability of nature leads to the qualitative distinction between the divine and the human. This initial differentiation of qualities creates a totality as a system of distinct qualities within which human experience unfolds.

In prose, such a totality takes the form of stories that organize experience according to certain patterns of action and consequence. These stories function as parables in which the narrative patterns imitate the patterns of fate that result from the forces acting upon everyday life. Because prose depends upon the inevitability of a plot sequence in order to attain a closed form, Einstein's models for prose are religious parables that recapitulate experience for the audience in such a way that it becomes fateful. As with Nietzsche, a tragic fate becomes the basis for a mythic prose.

The primary goal for the character Bebuquin in Einstein's *Bebuquin or The Dilettantes of Wonder* (1912) is consequently the creation of a "corporeal miracle" in which fate and fantasy are merged into a single experience. By insisting on the "corporality" of the miracle, Einstein attempts to dissolve the distinction between fantasy and reality so as to reestablish a more important differentiation between mundane and sacred experience. After a series of failed attempts, the novel finally affirms sacrifice as the narrative form that creates the metaphysical, not as a positive replacement of the physical, but as a negative projection from out of the structure of mundane experience.

Though primitive culture is based on ritual and sacrifice, this does not entail a concentration on indigenous culture nor an objectification of foreign ones. Rather, the primitive element in prose fosters cultural exchange, not by breaking down rituals but by building up new ones that can regulate cross-cultural interaction. Einstein's translation of African legends into German demonstrates a link between an expressionist vision of prose and a primitive one by integrating these legends into a European context, not as artifacts, but as models.

The similarity of his translation of "The Wanderer of the Plain," a legend from the Thonga people of southeast Africa, to the story of Oedipus allows a reinterpretation of the Western tradition from a primitivist perspective. In this African legend, marriage is both the nexus of cultural exchange and the potential site of cultural conflict. In the story, the young couple dismisses the importance of kinship relations and consequently dispenses with the marriage rituals that could create an understanding between the disparate cultures of the two kinship networks being brought together. The two cultures never have the opportunity to create a common vocabulary to regulate their relations with one another. The result is a set of misunderstandings leading to the destruction of the bride's culture and the consequent death of the entire family. In translating the story into German, Einstein attempts to create the mediation between African and German culture that fails in the context of the story itself. On the one hand, the African legend becomes a variant of the Oedipal story familiar in the West. On the other hand, the Western reception of Oedipus is transformed by the example of the African legend. Seen from the perspective of "The Wanderer of the Plain," the Oedipal myth becomes the story of an undervaluation of kinship bonds leading to a disintegration of the ritual foundations of culture.

The primitive perspective linking the works discussed in this book is founded upon the idea that while science grasps reality with conceptual categories that eradicate particularity, myth is grounded upon an aesthetic intuition of reality that enables both the differentiation of qualities and the particularity of experiences. According to this argument, mythic structures are necessary for human experience, and a suppression of myth will lead to an alienation of the individual from the outside world and eventually to a cultural crisis. But because myth functions according to aesthetic rules, art and myth become inseparable, both embodying the organizing structures that govern everyday perception and behavior.

Because the turn to myth has, since World War II, been linked to fascism, a proper understanding of primitivism and particularly of Einstein's work on the subject has never been allowed to develop. His theoretical presentation of a primitivist aesthetic was not only obscured by the same historical circumstances that had suppressed Benjamin's work, but Einstein's work was coupled with a vehement attack on liberalism that he never ceased to reformulate throughout his career but which rendered his work unassimilable by a Cold War liberal consensus.[59] A serious consideration of primitivism and an accompanying appreciation of Einstein's ideas can only take place once it becomes clear that they in fact presented an alternative to both the fascist and the liberal readings of the relation between myth and experience.

1. Primitivist Aesthetics

1

THE PRIMITIVE
AND THE CIVILIZED IN
FRIEDRICH NIETZSCHE'S
BIRTH OF TRAGEDY

GENEALOGY OF THE PRIMITIVE

The first three decades of the twentieth century saw an intense interest in African and Oceanic art on the part of a number of artists. This interest arose during a period in which ethnologists were virtually unanimous in rejecting the objects arriving from Africa and the South Pacific as being art at all.[1] What characteristics of African and Oceanic art attracted the interest of early-twentieth-century artists and writers? The issue here is not so much the ability of Europeans to recognize the validity of the art of a foreign culture; a consciousness of the qualities of the art of the Near and Far East had already existed for centuries.[2] Rather than simply the encounter with the "Other," the issue here is the fascination with the "primitive."

Problems arise as soon as the word *primitive* appears. Like other art historical terms such as *gothic* or *baroque*, *primitive* began as a term of denigration. It was used not just to denigrate an artistic style but to justify the colonization and extermination of whole peoples. This raising of the stakes makes any attempt at a rehabilitation of the term *primitive* nearly unthinkable, yet at the same time all the more crucial. As destructive as the derogatory use has been, the fascination with the primitive has been just as essential to the term's history—to the point that the word *primitivism* is used exclusively to designate an imitation of the primitive rather than a contempt for it. Coupled with these contradictory uses is the ambiguous evaluation of the primal and the fundamental embedded in the term. The primitive has been defined both as the first step in an evolution in which the European is the most distant from the primal and as the primary and thus the fundamental core of every culture. The varying definitions lead to the conclusion that the primitive is not so much a fixed term with a particular political valence as a contested terrain whose particular occupation determines its uses.

Twentieth-century primitivism did not begin merely as a fascination with the primitive but as a transformation of the European understanding of the word *primitive* away from Enlightenment usages. For it was only in the eighteenth century that the term took on its negative connotations. In French and English, the early, pre-eighteenth-century usages signified "earliest, original" or the "original as opposed to the derivative," and *primitive* was used primarily to describe "the Christian Church in its earliest and (by implication) purest times."[3] Up until the eighteenth century the documented usages are either value neutral or positive, as in 1540, "which good primitive successe purchased him muche quietnes," or in 1628, "God is the primitive, he is the originall, he is the first, the universal cause."[4] In both French and English the positive usages of the word *primitive* were connected to the church and extended into the eighteenth century where in 1704, for instance, the question is posed "whether this Primitive Church of his was primitively pure, or originally Profane."[5] Here, the word *primitive* is the positive counterpart to *original*, and an opposition between positive and negative value judgments about origins begins to take shape.

The value opposition begins the shift toward the Enlightenment usage of *primitive* as a designation for humans in an early state of development. Though he praises the primitive, Rousseau's idea that "the progress of the human species continually moves it farther away from its primitive state" connects the primitive to the simple and establishes the terms for the eighteenth- and nineteenth-century denigration of the primitive.[6] By placing the primitive condition at the beginning of a civilizational development toward knowledge, Rousseau's critique of civilization depends upon a romantic idealization of the primitive that confines it to a state of simplicity and underdevelopment.

During the course of the eighteenth century, *primitive* begins to connote "simple, rude, or rough like that of early times; old-fashioned. (With implication of either commendation or the reverse.)"[7] Whether primitive simplicity is praised or condemned, the connection between origins and simplicity established in Rousseau's time becomes the basis for a separation between civilized peoples and primitive ones in an evolutionary framework. This is evident, for example, in descriptions of the native peoples of non-European lands as "primitives."[8] The usage of *primitive* to designate specific cultures as either simple and good or simple and backward lasts into the twentieth century, but with the beginnings of primitivism a new attitude toward the primitive begins to compete with the Enlightenment understanding.

Friedrich Nietzsche (1844–1900) prepares the way for this new understanding of the primitive in *The Birth of Tragedy* (1872), but his interest in the primitive has been obscured partly by his terminology. He never speaks of *das Primitive* or *Primitivismus* because these German terms do not have the same history as do their counterparts in English and French, where the meaning of *primitive* was transformed during the Enlightenment. The German adjective *primitiv* was borrowed from the French in the eighteenth century at a time when the French word had already begun to take on negative connotations. Thus, the word in German is not to be found in the *Grimm Deutsches Wörterbuch* but rather in the *Deutsches Fremdwörterbuch*, a dictionary of foreign words.[9] *Primitiv* began as a negative term to be contrasted with the alternative term *ursprünglich* (original). With the introduction of *primitiv* in the eighteenth century, the term *ursprünglich* becomes a more and more positive term, connected to purity and excellence. The *Grimm Deutsches Wörterbuch* notes that the prefix *ur-* does not acquire the connotation of purity and unspoiled excellence until the second half of the eighteenth century: "The transformation of the meaning occurs almost unnoticeably, partly due to the influence of foreign words."[10] In the section dealing with the similar shift in the term *Ursprung*, *Grimm* also notes that it means "where the original epoch [*urzeit*] of society lies, the land of origins and the youth of humanity."[11] The opposition between *primitiv* and *ursprünglich* in German illustrates the good-versus-evil polarity into which the idea of origins was pulled during the Enlightenment. While *primitiv* means rude and undeveloped, *ursprünglich* begins to connote pure and untrammeled.

Nietzsche's primitivism is marked by his use of the word *ursprünglich* rather than *primitiv*. Yet his use of *ursprünglich* tries to break out of the Enlightenment polarization by considering origins, not as a temporal state of beginnings to be praised or condemned, but as a particular cultural formation that can arise in any society. Nietzsche introduces the word *ursprünglich* in the first section of *The Birth of Tragedy* to describe the Dionysian as the terrifying yet blissful dissolution of subjectivity: "Either under the influence of the narcotic draught, of which the songs of all primitive (*ursprünglichen*) men and peoples speak, or with the potent coming of spring that penetrates all nature with joy, these Dionysian emotions awake, and as they grow in intensity everything subjective vanishes into complete self-forgetfulness."[12] Rather than designating the worshippers of the Dionysian as *primitiv*, Nietzsche chooses *ursprünglich*. The ritual dances and ceremonies that he then goes on to describe are the European forms of primitive festivals also to be found in other parts of the world. Rather than distinguishing between the primitive and the European, Nietzsche emphasizes the continuity between the German medieval festivals of St. John, the Bacchic choruses of Greece, and similar gatherings in Asia Minor and Babylon: "In the German Middle Ages, too, singing and dancing crowds, ever increasing in number, whirled themselves from place to place under this same Dionysian impulse. In these dancers of St. John and St. Vitus, we rediscover the Bacchic choruses of the Greeks, with their prehistory in Asia Minor, as far back as Babylon and the orgiastic Sacaea" (BT 36, GT 29). The Dionysian exists as an aspect common to many cultures, and neither prehistoric nor non-European cultures are the specific site of the primitive.

In fact, in Nietzsche's understanding there is no site of the primitive at all because it cannot be objectified into a temporal or spatial state. This conceptual rather than temporal understanding of the primitive distinguishes Nietzsche's primitivism from both Rousseau's idealization of the "noble savage" and the early-twentieth-century exoticist visions of the primitive often described by critics as primitivist.[13] The primitive for Nietzsche is neither a temporally original state nor a spatially exotic location but a specific cultural strategy for confronting nature that exists as a constant alternative in every society.

He thus depicts the opposition between primitive and civilized as a continuing conflict within Western culture, not one that is fought between Western and non-Western cultures. Nietzsche also makes a distinction between a primitive and a civilized attitude in which both can exist simultaneously within one culture. He places the scene of the conflict between the primitive Dionysian and the civilized Socratic within Western culture. The thematic starting point for Nietzsche's analysis is a primitivist reinterpretation of ancient Greek tragedy, and the cultural example that Nietzsche uses to illustrate his image of Dionysian intoxication is Beethoven's Ninth Symphony (BT 37–38, GT 29–30). He uses this differentiation in order to denigrate, not the primitive, but the civilized attitude toward culture: "There are some who, from obtuseness or lack of experience, turn away from such phenomena as from 'folk-diseases,' with contempt or pity born of the consciousness of their own 'healthy-mindedness.' But of course such poor wretches have no idea how corpselike and ghostly their so-called 'healthy-mindedness' looks when the glowing life of the Dionysian revelers roars past them" (BT 36–7, GT 29). Nietzsche does not oppose a European "civilized man" to a non-European primitive "other." Rather, the civilized critics of the people are to be differentiated from the expressions of a primitive spirit that appears in modern Europe as well.

To arrive at a primitivist understanding of Nietzsche's work, it will be necessary to demonstrate that the Dionysian is not the "real" for Nietzsche but an aesthetic strategy. The primitive must be recognized as a cultural strategy in its own right and not as an unarticulable emptiness to be colonized by a conceptual framework.

Unfortunately, virtually all recent interpretations of *The Birth of Tragedy* follow the latter schema in their readings of Dionysus. Whether they refer to the Dionysian as a pure and original reality, an undifferentiated chaos, or a repressed Freudian unconscious that threatens to break loose from the civilizing forces of order, commentators such as Paul de Man, Manfred Frank, and Peter Sloterdijk reduce the Dionysian to an undifferentiated void. They read the distinction between Apollo and Dionysus as one between the aesthetic and the "real" (as if the Dionysian belonged to a pre-aesthetic dimension) and criticize Nietzsche for postulating a direct, metaphysical link to this Dionysian "real" instead of maintaining an Apollinian, aesthetic stance.[14] They consequently seek to maintain an Apollinian ascendancy over the threat of Dionysian violence. Others, such as Walter Kaufmann and Arthur Danto, have attempted to pose the Socratic against the Dionysian as a philosophical antidote to a mythic barbarism. In all of these cases, the anti-primitivism of the interpreters expresses itself as an understanding of the Dionysian as an undifferentiated primal force that, if set loose, would plunge society into chaos and barbarism. This anti-primitive attitude, closely allied to an exoticist perspective, attempts to objectify rather than reenact primitive culture. But for primitive culture to become a model, it must be considered as a particular mode of organizing social and aesthetic life. By contrast, if one understands the primitive to be an undifferentiated state or a result of a repression, it will never be recognized as having an existence that is independent of conceptual, formalized culture, and the primitive will always be considered the opposite of and thus dependent upon the conceptual and civilized.[15] This conflict between primitivist artists and antiprimitive commentators has not only determined twentieth-century attitudes toward the primitive and the thought of Nietzsche, it is the primary subject of Nietzsche's reflections in *The Birth of Tragedy*.

SCIENCE FROM AN ARTIST'S PERSPECTIVE

For Nietzsche, the primary criterion for distinguishing the primitive from the civilized perspective in a culture is the relation each establishes with nature. While the primitive uses an aesthetic attitude in the confrontation with nature, the civilized uses a scientific one. The opposition between the Dionysian and the Socratic in *The Birth of Tragedy* describes this fundamental cultural conflict between art and science in both ancient Greece and modern Germany.

In discussing this conflict, Nietzsche's work takes as its point of departure Immanuel Kant's discernment of the limitations of scientific rationality. In Nietzsche's account, Kant defines the boundaries of reason's authority by distinguishing between appearances, about which science can give us knowledge, and the thing-in-itself, which is the place of the true essence of nature and is totally inaccessible to scientific methods. "After all," Nietzsche asks, "what is a law of nature as such for us? We are not acquainted with it in itself, but only with its effects, which means in its relation to other laws of nature—which, in turn, are known to us only as sums of relations. Therefore all these relations always refer again to others and are thoroughly incomprehensible to us in their essence."[16] Though Nietzsche's limiting of scientific reason to relations amongst human constructions may seem like a detail to the natural scientist, it in fact disqualifies science from joining any discussion of the metaphysical foundations that give structure to all human existence. Defenders of science are wont to interpret this limitation as a confirmation that such metaphysical foundations do not exist, that the thing-in-itself is actually a void or an abyss that can essentially be ignored.

In contrast to this interpretation, Nietzsche reads this limitation on science as a justification for proposing art, especially in the form of myth, as the sole mediator of such foundations. In his 1886 preface Nietzsche describes *The Birth of Tragedy* as an attempt *"to look at science in the perspective of the artist, but at art in that of life"* (BT 19, GT 14). In Nietzsche's book, this artistic perspective, "that sought to exclude right from the beginning the *profanum vulgus* of 'the educated' even more than 'the mass' or 'folk' " (BT 19, GT 14), supports traditional society and turns against the scientist by demonstrating how science will eventually reach its limits and be thrown back upon mythic structures.

Nietzsche's critique of science and his turn to a metaphysics of art has often led readers to dismiss his ideas as hopelessly irrational and completely untenable given the achievements of natural science and Enlightenment rationality. Jürgen Habermas, for instance, condemns the recourse to myth as a repudiation of all truth and morality and a reduction of reality to power relations. For him, Nietzsche's transformation of ultimate value judgments into "judgments of taste" paves the way for "his complete assimilation of reason to power."[17] Insofar as he delegitimates reason and affirms myth and art as the foundation of social relations, Nietzsche nihilistically destroys all truth and replaces it with power as the ultimate decider of all practical questions. According to Habermas, "Nietzsche seeks refuge in a theory of power, which is consistent, since the fusion of reason and power revealed by critique abandons the world to the irreconcilable struggle between powers, as if it *were* the mythic world."[18] By casting Nietzsche's critique of science as a submission to the reign of pure power, Habermas denies Nietzsche's claim that art might contain an independent objectivity that could be the basis of a critique of science and rationality.

Alternatively, Arthur Danto has defended Nietzsche's ideas, but only by denying that Nietzsche affirmed myth over science. In this reading, Nietzsche was a defender of science for whom both art and science are simply two stages in the same process of illusion-making. In considering science from the viewpoint of art, Nietzsche is merely categorizing science as a form of art and thus placing them on an equal level: "Art consists in fresh illusions, while 'truth,' which we contrast with it (as we contrast art with nature, fiction with fact), consists in stale illusions, illusions so worn with use that they have come, with time, to be accepted as expressing the rock-bottom facts of the universe. The difference between (so-called) fact and (so-called) fiction is virtually quantitative, that being taken as fact which has been repeated a sufficient number of times."[19] Since the ultimate truth of nature cannot be known, all truths that are accepted as scientific fact began as aesthetic intuition considered as metaphor. Science and art are simply two phases of the same process of illusion-making. Moreover, because there can be no qualitative distinction between the two, Danto argues that Nietzsche could not have been attacking science but in *The Birth of Tragedy* regards science and art as complementary forces that depend upon each other to form a cultural totality: "neither here nor in any later work was Nietzsche ever hostile to rationality or to science, and he never regarded either of them as inimical to 'life.' "[20] Danto points out that Nietzsche's categorization of science as a form of art is ultimately meaningless as an attack on science because if everything is art, then nothing can be criticized for being art.[21]

The basic premise of Danto's argument, which continues to shape contemporary scholarship, is that Nietzsche, rather than opposing art to science, was at root a "nihilist," for whom nature is "a blank tablet upon which *we* make imprints."[22] In such a world, the primary opposition will be between the formative power of human invention (in both art and science) and the formless chaos of nature: "It [science], no more and no less than religion, morality, and art, was an instance of what he [Nietzsche] termed Will-to-Power, an impulse and a drive to impose upon an essentially chaotic reality a form and structure, to shape it into a world congenial to human understanding while habitable by human intelligence."[23] The incomprehensibility of the thing-in-itself leads for Danto to the conclusion that all human attempts to relate to it must take the structure of science and philosophy, which makes the world philosophically comprehensible. As Danto argues, those irrational aspects that cannot be integrated into human understanding do not subvert science, but are simply left out of the field of human experience. Though Danto defends Nietzsche's ideas and Habermas attacks them, they agree to the extent that the only options they present are rational science and chaotic nature. While Habermas categorizes art as a form of chaos, Danto relates it to the structures of science. Neither can accept Nietzsche's notion that art and myth can establish their own separate forms of legitimacy independent of both science and nature. Though they come to different conclusions about Nietzsche's attitude toward myth, they both themselves reject myth as a possible foundation for social order.

Though poststructuralist readings of Nietzsche have recognized and praised the antiscientific and aestheticist impulses in his work, they share with Danto the view that nature for Nietzsche is a chaotic void that needs human constructions to gain form. As Stanley Corngold has pointed out, deconstructionist readings of Nietzsche are very similar to Danto's in their basic assumptions, though they replace his idea of science with their idea of the text.[24] Paul de Man, for instance, uses the opposition between the aesthetic forms of humans and the nonaesthetic formlessness of nature to reestablish the primacy of the text against possible "genetic totalizations" that would reduce the text to an emanation of the thing-in-itself. In order to consider human constructions as the sole source of form in Nietzsche's thought, de Man interprets Nietzsche's statements about the primal unity and the Dionysian, which contradict this view, as aberrations. De Man notes for instance that "Dionysos, as music or as language, must now belong either to the teleological domain of the text and then he is mere error and mystification, or he belongs to 'nature' and then he is forever and radically separated from any form of art, since no bridge, as metaphor or as representation, can ever connect the natural realm of essences with the textual realm of forms and values."[25] For de Man, the realm of the thing-in-itself can only be conceived as "error and mystification" in a text or a nature that is "radically separated from any form of art." He recognizes, however, that, contrary to this view of the radical alterity of the thing-in-itself, "*The Birth of Tragedy* dramatizes a variety of manners by means of which the distinction between essence and appearance can be bridged."[26] Such a bridge is impossible in de Man's view, and he relativizes Nietzsche's attempts at creating such a relation to the thing-in-itself by arguing that "[t]he unpublished fragments, contemporaneous with the main text, deny this very possibility and thus reduce the entire *Birth of Tragedy* to being an extended rhetorical fiction devoid of authority."[27] Though he recognizes Nietzsche's attempt to understand how humans relate to the essence of nature, de Man uses both unpublished fragments and a rhetorical analysis of *The Birth of Tragedy* to dismiss the explicit claims that Nietzsche makes in the main text concerning such a possibility.

As de Man and Allan Megill have demonstrated, in *The Birth of Tragedy* Nietzsche launches an attack on science and reason that continues to permeate his work throughout his career: "The problem, then, is to recover myth, and thus to restore the lost vitality of culture. This problem is central for both the 'early' and the 'mature' Nietzsche—the focus of his entire enterprise."[28] But if one takes Nietzsche's statements regarding the primal unity and the Dionysian seriously, it becomes clear that his recovery of myth is not an attempt to establish a radical relativism or the primacy of the text in the place of scientific objectivity, as poststructuralist interpretations go on to argue. (Megill claims, for instance, that "Nietzsche envisages not the destruction of the conceptual world but rather (to borrow Derrida's terminology) its deconstruction—that is, its transformation into a realm of aesthetic illusion and play."[29] Nor does Nietzsche seek to vindicate brute force against truth claims, as Jürgen Habermas has argued. Rather, Nietzsche attempts to overturn science and reason by demonstrating how their age-old enemies, myth and tradition, can function as an alternative means of relating to nature that avoids representation but at the same time is not pure and arbitrary creation. He plots out a direction for myth that breaks out of the conceptual opposition between the dream of an objective mapping of reality by science and the "total self-containedness" of art.[30] Demonstrating that both of these alternatives are variations of an Apollinian aesthetics of representation, Nietzsche envisions an alternative Dionysian aesthetics of mimesis.

In the remainder of this chapter, I will argue that it is possible to differentiate between conceptual and aesthetic modes of relating to nature along the same lines that Nietzsche develops in *The Birth of Tragedy*. To make this argument, I will first refute alternative views of Nietzsche's intentions: Danto's claim that Nietzsche does not oppose science to art and de Man's idea that Nietzsche did not seek a bridge between essences and appearances. Both of these readings set art against nature and claim that Nietzsche's description of the world as an aesthetic phenomenon casts nature as a void that only gains form through the constructive activity of human consciousness. Against this claim, I will show that nature for Nietzsche is not an abyss but itself an aesthetic phenomenon that our works of art must imitate. This vision of nature as aesthetically organized leads Nietzsche to argue that Dionysian art rather than science (which has the structure of Apollinian semblance) is the form of human activity that can best mediate the essence of nature to humans. As Nietzsche notes in the passage from his 1886 preface quoted earlier, the aesthetic critique of science is one of the main goals of *The Birth of Tragedy*, and it is a goal that can only be achieved by demonstrating the representational and thus illusory character of science in contrast to the mimetic power of myth. This differentiation pro-

vides an escape from the confinement within the structure of representation that both poststructuralist and analytic interpretations of
Nietzsche share.

While Habermas's appeal to reason, Danto's defense of science, and
de Man's plea for self-referentiality all stem from the idea that nature is formless, Nietzsche's defense of myth and metaphysics is
based on his view that nature in its essence is aesthetically structured. Rather than suggesting that humans are the only source of
form, Nietzsche sees nature as itself composed of aesthetic forces.
He notes for instance that the Dionysian and Apollinian art forces
must first be considered forces in nature before they can be recognized as forces in art. Moreover, his initial description of Apollo
and Dionysus presents them as the fundamental art forces of nature
that exist prior to the intervention of a human artist. At the beginning of section two of *The Birth of Tragedy*, he writes:

> Thus far we have considered the Apollinian and its opposite,
> the Dionysian, as artistic energies which burst forth from na-
> ture herself, *without the mediation of the human artist*—ener-
> gies in which nature's art impulses are satisfied in the most im-
> mediate and direct way—first in the image world of dreams,
> whose completeness is not dependent upon the intellectual at-
> titude or the artistic culture of any single being; and then as in-
> toxicated reality, which likewise does not heed the single unit,
> but even seeks to destroy the individual and redeem him by a
> mystic feeling of oneness. With reference to these immediate
> art-states of nature, every artist is an "imitator." (BT 38, GT 30)

Apollo and Dionysus in nature precede the human artist and enact
a conflict within nature itself between the forces of individuation
and the forces of dissolution. In this passage, Nietzsche employs the
terms art forces (*Kunsttriebe*) and art states (*Kunstzustände*) in the
plural, thus depicting a constant conflict within nature itself between competing forces. Moreover, he uses the terms *forces* and
states interchangeably, and this vacillation between a fluid and static

term itself imitates the conflict within nature between Dionysian dissolution and Apollinian individuation in which neither ever gains the upper hand. Yet Nietzsche does not understand the art forces and states of nature as existing in a realm of the thing-in-itself totally separate from human experience. Rather, he defines them as a part of the human experiences of dream and intoxication. The conflict of forces in nature manifests itself aesthetically for humans in the fixation of images as dreams and then the dissolution of images into an intoxicated reality (BT 33–37, GT 25–30).

Nietzsche's view of nature as aesthetically organized is the key point where he diverges from the perspective of his critics. By conceiving the world as an opposition between the formlessness of nature and the human construction of forms, Danto and de Man adhere to the Kantian analysis in which the thing-in-itself has nothing to do with the appearances. However, they use this insight, not as a critique of reason and its self-referential models, but as a critique of nature that consigns it to a chaotic abyss. Nature in its essence can be safely ignored in their view because its formlessness remains outside the realm of appearances. As a result, all human activity takes on the structure of science and knowledge, and art itself becomes a form of science — a means of shaping a formless nature "into a world congenial to human understanding while habitable by human intelligence." The difference between knowledge and illusion shrinks in Danto's account to the point where they are virtually interchangeable terms. This accords with Nietzsche's view that all science is a form of illusion, but it also indicates that Nietzsche's attack on science implies a devaluation of Apollinian art, which shares science's representational structure.

Deconstructionist critics recognize that their view of nature as inaccessible contradicts statements by Nietzsche that support a Schopenhauerian perspective in which the world is conceived as an aesthetic emanation of the will.[31] They attempt to marginalize such statements by invoking fragments from Nietzsche's unpublished manuscripts in which he criticizes the "thing-in-itself" and the "will" for being inadequate expressions for the core of nature. John Sallis cites a passage from the manuscripts from the 1867–1871 period immediately before the publication of *The Birth of Tragedy* where Nietzsche criticizes Schopenhauer's equation of the will with the thing-in-itself: "The will already a form of appearance."[32] Sallis draws the conclusion that "the very distinction between thing-in-itself and appearance is threatened."[33] Similarly, de Man quotes another passage from these same notes that states: "In the realm of nature and of necessity, all teleological hypotheses are absurd. Necessity means that there can only be one possibility. Why then do we have to assume the presence of an intellect in the realm of things?—And if the will cannot be conceived without implying its representation, the 'will' is not an adequate expression for the core of nature either."[34] De Man comments on this passage that "[t]he radical separation of origin from purpose (*Ursprung* from *Zweck*) that is established here eliminates all possible claim at genetic totalization."[35] Both Sallis and de Man attempt to demonstrate that Nietzsche disputed the idea that the will or the thing-in-itself could have any direct impact on the world of appearances. Such a "genetic totalization" would undermine their idea that the pure representation cannot be indebted to anything outside of itself for its meaning. In order to protect the self-referentiality of the text, they must eliminate anything such as a will or a thing-in-itself that might exist outside of the text.

But in citing these passages where Nietzsche critiques the will and the thing-in-itself, Sallis and de Man mistake his rejection of these terms for a rejection of the entire idea of "a core of nature." Nietzsche rejects the terms *will* and *thing-in-itself*, not to validate the self-referentiality of appearances, but to preserve "the core of nature" as an independent entity, irreducible to the laws of cognition but still a part of human experience. Whereas the thing-in-itself presents nature as inert and the will presents nature as conforming to a human notion of intention, Nietzsche understands nature as an active and unpredictable force that is chaotic but not completely random. While continuing to depend on Kant's insight into the unknowability of the essence of nature, Nietzsche rejects Kant's and Schopenhauer's terms in order to reinterpret the thing-in-itself and the will as the primal unity (*das Ur-Eine*). Whereas for Kant nature understood as the thing-in-itself always lies behind the appearances (the human reconstruction of nature), Nietzsche criticizes the appellations *thing-in-itself* and *will* because they place artificial human limits on nature. He emphasizes that nature in its essence is foreign to all things, even a "thing-in-itself," and must be understood as a primal unity in which everything exists in a state of nonobjectification.[36] Thus, in *The Will to Power*, Nietzsche rejects the validity of the distinction between thing-in-itself and appearance because it reinforces the tendency to conceive of the thing-in-itself in cognitive categories of constancy and permanency: "The 'thing-in-itself' nonsensical. If I remove all the relationships, all the 'properties,' all the 'activities' of a thing, the thing does not remain over; because thingness has only been invented by us owing to the requirements of logic, thus with the aim of defining, communication (to bind together the multiplicity of relationships, properties, activities)."[37] Because the very concept of a thing is already a reification of a dynamic process into a cognitive category, the idea of a thing-in-itself already presupposes that which it must exclude. The tendency is to speak of nature in terms of a fixed entity rather than an unpredictable flux. As a consequence, the idea of a thing-in-itself on the one hand renders nature harmless by relegating it to a separate realm that can be excluded from human calculations. On the other hand, it reduces appearances—the properties and activities of an object—to a set of conceptually determined attributes rather than seeing them as a part of the unpredictable play of the forces of nature.[38] Similarly, because the idea of nature as will implies that nature might have specific purposes and intentions just as an intellect would, Nietzsche also rejects this formulation for the essence of nature, which for him is not organized teleologically. Rather than discarding the whole idea of nature, however, Nietzsche replaces the terms *thing-in-itself* and *will* with the *primal unity* (*das Ur-Eine*). In doing so, he is able to conceive of nature both as a state of nonobjectification, which does not precede the world but is coexistent with it, and as an unpredictable but defining force for human existence. The primal unity does not exist prior to appearances but rather as a dimension of unpredictable forces that govern the way in which the world gains sensuous form.

The primary characteristic of these forces is not that they are logical and consistent but that they are contradictory: in the "heart of the primal unity" lies a "primordial contradiction and primordial pain" ("Urwiderspruch und Urschmerz im Herzen des Ur-Einen," BT 55, GT 51). The insistence on contradiction as an attribute of nature implies that it must be understood as a conflict of forces rather than as a set of laws or as a chaotic formlessness. Rather than being the key that assures victory over nature, natural laws are generated by the human will as a tool that acts as a single force within this continuing conflict with other forces in nature. Though humans can have an impact on the interaction of forces that determine the appearance and dissolution of individual objects, they cannot control or escape this process:

> For to our humiliation *and* exaltation, one thing above all must be clear to us. The entire comedy of art is neither performed for our betterment or education nor are we the true authors of this art world. On the contrary, we may assume that we are merely images and artistic projections for the true author, and that we have our highest dignity in our significance as works of art—for it is only as an *aesthetic phenomenon* that existence and the world are eternally *justified*—while of course our consciousness of our own significance hardly differs from that which the soldiers painted on canvas have of the battle represented on it. (BT 52, GT 47)

In this well-known passage, Nietzsche designates the world as an aesthetic phenomenon because its objects are the unpredictable result of contradictory forces. The pattern of clouds in the sky, the appearance and extinction of species on the planet, and the rise and fall of human civilizations are all determined by nature understood as a situation of unpredictable and conflicting forces. Rather than objects of natural science, the world is made up of phenomena that are constantly transforming themselves according to an ensemble of forces whose patterns Nietzsche designates as aesthetic rather than rational. The impact of the individual human will on these processes is unpredictable because, though they may exhibit patterns of development, they do not follow fixed scientific or philosophical rules. Though Nietzsche counts science as one of the tools with which humans engage in the aesthetic play of forces, he believes it is impossible to approach the totality of nature through scientific means based on critique that seeks to grasp nature as a set of laws. Rather, nature's totality can only be approached through aesthetic means grounded in the intuition of the artist, whose visions depend upon the ability to identify "with the primal unity, its pain and contradiction" (BT 49, GT 43–44). It is for this reason that Nietzsche can say that within this world of aesthetic constructs the role of our own works of art is to imitate the world as work of art: "With reference to these immediate art-states of nature, every artist is an 'imitator' " (BT 38, GT 30). Aesthetic imitation is not merely an imitation of a static set of objects or laws but an imitation of the play of forces through which the world itself is aesthetically created as a constant creation and dissolution of objects.

By insisting on the aesthetic quality of nature, Nietzsche argues against both a rationalistic understanding of the world as a set of mechanistic laws and a nihilistic understanding of the world in which events take place in a state of completely random chaos. Since he considers nature to be neither strictly predictable nor totally random, Nietzsche uses the term *aesthetic* to designate the peculiar quality of nature whereby patterns exist but cannot be accurately predicted.

Because reason is limited to the realm of appearances, alternative, nonrational strategies can and must be used to approach this aesthetic essence of nature: "For between two absolutely different spheres such as between subject and object there can be no causality, no correctness, no expression, but rather at the most an *aesthetic* attitude, by which I mean an indicative transcription, a stammering translation into a totally foreign language."[39] Because the natural scientist never has pure objects before him or her but only a mental model that is set up in place of truth, science is incapable of forging a link to nature. But for Nietzsche this limitation of science does not imply that a bridge to nature is an impossibility. Though humankind's relation to the primal unity cannot be based on knowledge and cognition, Nietzsche argues that this relation can be established as an aesthetic experience in which natural forces are translated into human terms.

By conceiving of the core of nature in terms of a "primordial pain," Nietzsche rejects reason and proposes *pain* as the faculty that provides the bridge between the essence of nature and human experience. Though humans can never attain a true knowledge of nature's essence, they can nevertheless experience it through pain and suffering. Pain provides the measure for gauging nature's impact on human life, not only quantifying its influence but also providing indications of the patterns of nature's effects on humans. Though pain in human life is to a certain extent arbitrary, it is not entirely so, and the human rules that have been developed to minimize pain are created out of the human mimesis of nature—an aesthetic intuition of the patterns of pain. As a consequence, Nietzsche conceives human existence, not as a triumph of knowledge's ability to understand nature's laws, but as a constant tragic struggle with the forces of nature. Art forms such as tragedy, which focus on pain and suffering, thus become central for constructing the total understanding of the world that humans must have to structure their existence. Just as nature is neither strictly rational nor totally arbitrary, the world cannot be justified rationally, nor through the arbitrary reference to past traditions. Instead, it must be constructed according to aesthetic rules that reflect the constraints that nature sets upon human existence at any given moment.[40] For Nietzsche, the only possible approach to the essence of nature is not through scientific cognition, which only creates illusions, but through tragic myth, which aesthetically translates between the realm of nature and the realm of humankind.

SCIENCE'S TURN TO MYTH

In contrast to the reality of pain that Nietzsche finds in mythic tragedy, science is based on a "profound *illusion*," which is summed up in "the unshakable faith that thought, using the thread of causality, can penetrate the deepest abysses of being, and that thought is capable not only of knowing being but even of *correcting* it. This sublime metaphysical illusion accompanies science as an instinct and leads science again and again to its limits at which it must turn into *art—which is really the aim of this mechanism*" (BT 95–96, GT 99). Danto uses this argument about the aesthetic quality of science to support his view that Nietzsche does not champion art or myth against science. And indeed Danto is correct in stating that for Nietzsche science can become valuable to the extent that it also functions as art in that it uses an optimistic view of the "lawfulness of an entire solar system" to channel human energy into the pursuit of knowledge. Were it not for this pursuit, human energy would be channeled into "the practical, i.e., egoistic aims of individuals and peoples," which would eventually lead to "universal wars of annihilation" and mass suicide (BT 96, GT 100). For Danto, not only science but all forms of art and religion as well function by diverting attention from the horror of nature and toward ideals that allow people to endure life.[41]

Danto errs, however, in assuming that science is indistinguishable from myth in this creation of illusions. Though it is true that Nietzsche considered science as a form of art, Danto ignores the distinction between Apollinian and Dionysian art that distinguishes science from myth. Dionysian art is not based on illusion but on the tragic insight that nature expresses itself to humans as pain. Only Apollinian art is based on illusions that divert attention from this pain (BT 44–47, GT 38–42). To the extent that the models of science also create an illusion of lawfulness that substitutes for the experience of nature as pain, science also functions according to an Apollinian aesthetic. According to Nietzsche, the scientist will ultimately have to confront the incommensurability of nature and the consequent inevitability of human suffering. At this point, when science realizes its limits and understands itself as delusion, it must reject its own foundations in knowledge and illusion, transforming itself into a Dionysian myth:

> But science, spurred by its powerful illusion, speeds irresistibly toward its limits where its optimism, concealed in the essence of logic, suffers shipwreck. For the periphery of the circle of science has an infinite number of points; and while there is no telling how this circle could ever be surveyed completely, noble and gifted men nevertheless reach, e'er half their time and inevitably, such boundary points on the periphery from which one gazes into what defies illumination. When they see

to their horror how logic coils up at these boundaries and finally bites its own tail—suddenly the new form of insight
breaks through, *tragic insight* which, merely to be endured,
needs art as a protection and remedy. (BT 97–98, GT 101)

Nietzsche allows that the advances of natural science have been able
to integrate increasing sectors of the world of nature into the lawfulness and predictability of the world of humankind. These advances, however, do not conquer nature itself but merely shift the
boundary points on the "periphery of the circle of science." Science
cannot overcome the opposition between human models, which
create laws, and the flux of nature, which is the fundamental origi-
nator of all objects.

Because science must again and again perceive the limits of
thought, it will eventually return to the Dionysian aesthetic principles that permeate a religion where sacrifice replaces knowledge as
the dominant theme. Nietzsche discovers this transformation of
knowledge into sacrifice in the story of Socrates:

he appears to us as the first who could not only live, guided by
this instinct of science, but also—and this is far more—die that
way. Hence the image of the *dying Socrates*, as the human being
whom knowledge and reasons have liberated from the fear of
death, is the emblem that, above the entrance gate of science,
reminds all of its mission—namely, to make existence appear
comprehensible and thus justified; and if reasons do not
suffice, *myth* has to come to their aid in the end—myth which I
have just called the necessary consequence, indeed the purpose, of science. (BT 96, GT 99)

The archetypal story of the triumph of reason over myth itself functions according to a mythic structure. Whereas Socrates spent his
life defending knowledge as the justifier of existence, the story of
Socrates' death is not a story of the triumph of knowledge but of
sacrifice.[42] By sacrificing physical existence for the sake of an ideal,
he demonstrates that any ideal—reason included—ultimately depends upon a mythic sacrifice for its justification. This mythic plot
structure immortalizes Socrates and transforms science into a reli-

gion in the same way that the story of Christ's crucifixion founds Christianity.[43] The justifying act for science considered as a religion (that is, as an organizing structure for human behavior) is not an Apollinian aesthetic construct based on illusion but a mythic story of sacrifice.

By demonstrating the mythic structure of the social ideals embedded in the scientific perspective, Nietzsche delegitimates reason and the scientific method as creators of ultimate truths for a society. To the extent that scientific culture exhibits ideals, it must also be permeated by myth and thus coexist with primitive culture. At the same time, Nietzsche understands myth as a human construction that obeys aesthetic rules. For the enduring significance of the story of Socrates derives neither from its cognitive value nor its direct tie to a supernatural dimension but from its plot structure.

Nietzsche thus distinguishes within every culture two separate and opposed aesthetic modes of relating to nature, each with its own consequences for human activity and destiny. He refers to these two modes as the Dionysian and the Apollinian. While the Dionysian maintains an intuitive, mimetic attitude to nature, the Apollinian attempts to replace nature with an aesthetic illusion. Nietzsche sees both strategies as aesthetic because both are constructions that structure the human relation to nature rather than sources of a true knowledge of nature. Within this framework, the scientific construction of natural laws adheres to an Apollinian aesthetic because it hides nature by replacing it with a set of concepts. The tragic myth is Dionysian to the extent that it translates natural forces into human terms through an aesthetic imitation. In comparing these two aesthetic modes, Nietzsche does not use truth or falsehood as the indicator of their value. Indeed, the very terms *truth* and *falsehood* only have meaning within an Apollinian representational aesthetic that seeks to create a model of reality. The rejection of truth and falsehood as valid criteria for judgment does not relegate nature to a random abyss, cut off from all human calculations. Instead, Nietzsche's form of aestheticism considers science and art, not in terms of their supposed truth content, but in terms of their consequences for human society. While truth is no longer the measure of value, this does not lead, as Megill argues, to the abandonment of "the natural and social needs of humankind for the unconstrained freedom of the artist."[44] Because pain rather than truth becomes the determining measure of value in Nietzsche's framework, the aesthetic mimesis of pain (that is, of natural and social needs) constrains the freedom of both artist and audience.

2

THE DIONYSIAN
AESTHETICS OF MYTH

THE AESTHETIC STRUCTURE OF MYTH

The crucial insight that defines Nietzsche's primitivism is the idea that art and myth share a common aesthetic structure. Referring to art as "the highest task and the truly metaphysical activity of this life" (BT 31–32, GT 24), Nietzsche argues that aesthetic intuition is more important than philosophical insight for the formation and stability of a culture. Art and myth for Nietzsche are not simply play, error, or childish fantasy but rather aesthetic manifestations of the truth of nature.

To establish the plausibility of Nietzsche's ideas, they must be defended against two opposing views of myth. Though these views come from different theoretical perspectives, they share the conviction that art and myth must be clearly differentiated from each other because art is the semblance while myth is the truth. The first of these views is exemplified in the ideas of the Nazi philosopher, Alfred Baeumler. In his 1926 introduction to Johann Bachofen's *Der Mythos vom Orient und Okzident*, Baeumler rejects the idea that the Dionysian myth is merely an aesthetic construction rather than something real and cites Nietzsche's aesthetic explanation in support:[1]

"The myth wants to be experienced vividly as a unique example of a universality and truth that gaze into the infinite" (Nietzsche, *Birth of Tragedy*, 107). Example! A "sublime parable"— the myth! (*Birth of Tragedy*, 126) The "concentrated image of the world," a "condensation of phenomena" (*Birth of Tragedy*, 135). If ever the symbol was confused with the metaphor, the original with the derivative, then it has happened here! An *aesthetic* experience has invaded the world of the myth and its greatest manifestation, the ancient tragedy; that which should have a religious power and meaning has become play and illusion, the venerable symbol has become a fleeting parable—this is truly a profanation![2]

Baeumler accurately describes Nietzsche's view of myth as one that emphasizes its aesthetic status. But then Baeumler rejects this definition of myth as example and parable in order to use Bachofen's ideas to interpret myth as a religious symbol whose force derives from the symbolic connection to a primordial reality. In criticizing Nietzsche's aestheticization, he pursues a reading of Dionysian myth in which it is read as a force in reality that a leader imposes upon a people.[3] The determining factor in Baeumler's condemnation of the idea of myth as a form of art is his equation of all art with "play and illusion." Because for Baeumler all art is illusion, any attempt to attain truth must be nonaesthetic and thus "real."

Paul de Man also reduces art to its semblance character.[4] But unlike Baeumler, he praises this aspect of Nietzsche's argument, in which art, rather than referring to an outside reality, functions nonrepresentationally as an autonomous illusion: "Representation (mostly referred to, in this text, as *Vorstellung* or *Abbild*) functions throughout with a negative value-emphasis. From a purely historical point of view, *The Birth of Tragedy* could be ordered among the pre-expressionist critical documents in which a nonrepresentational art is being prepared; this may well be the text's main function in the history of criticism."[5] Because for de Man art should be self-referential, it should also be beyond the question of truth and falsehood.[6] Therefore, de Man criticizes Nietzsche for linking myth to art because doing so reestablishes a connection between reality and art in the description of the Dionysian as the only "access to a substantial truth."[7] Yet unlike Baeumler, who decries Nietzsche's abasement of the religious seriousness of truth with the illusion of art, de Man defends artistic illusion against the intrusion of a metaphysical reality that would subordinate the autonomous figures of art to a representational function.

While de Man clearly opposes Baeumler to the extent that he rejects the possibility of a direct access to the real, the structure of their arguments is very similar. De Man defends art as semblance against myth, criticizing Nietzsche for debasing the play of art with references to an outside reality. Baeumler by contrast defends myth against art as semblance, berating Nietzsche for his abandonment of the real in favor of aesthetic constructions. But for both, Nietzsche's chief crime is that he has mixed art with religion, aesthetic experience with the claim to truth. Because they are primarily concerned with maintaining a strict separation of art from reality, neither Baeumler nor de Man can accept a situation in which art could be anything other than play and illusion.

Rather than strictly differentiating the aesthetic from the real, Nietzsche demonstrates that the reality of nature is itself aesthetically organized. The relation between art and nature does not derive from the opposition between Apollo and Dionysus, as de Man suggests. Rather, as we saw in chapter 1, it stems from the relation between the conflict between Apollo and Dionysus in nature and the reenactment of this conflict within the work of art.

Because art and reality are governed by the same forces and conflicts, they relate to each other as two examples of the same mechanisms. For Nietzsche, art can be as much an expression of the primal unity as reality is. Consequently, art is not limited to its semblance character, its status as play and illusion, as Baeumler and de Man suggest. Rather, art also has an expressive dimension that transcends its illusory character.

The dichotomy of Apollo and Dionysus does not differentiate between an aesthetic force and a force in reality but between two aspects of the aesthetic that combine to create both reality and the work of art.[8] Rather than equating all art with semblance and illusion, Nietzsche designates semblance as the Apollinian aspect and opposes it to a mimetic and expressive aspect called the Dionysian. All art contains both aspects, but while the Apollinian aspect replaces nature with an illusion, creating the semblance character of art, the Dionysian aspect imitates nature as a dissolution of objects into a flux of forces, creating expression in art. In contrast to an Apollinian aesthetic that creates either a copy of or a replacement for nature, a Dionysian aesthetic creates a mimetic enactment of nature.

53

The elaboration of the Dionysian aspect in art allows Nietzsche to make the argument that myth is aesthetically organized. At the same time that the myth is an aesthetic illusion adhering to an Apollinian structure, the Dionysian aspect lends it a metaphysical significance that goes beyond its Apollinian status as aesthetic play. The Dionysian aspect of art creates an imitation, not of an outside reality, but of the interaction of forces that leads to creation in both art and reality. In Nietzsche's words, the Dionysian aspect arises out of art's attempt to imitate in its form "the primordial contradiction and primordial pain in the heart of the primal unity" (BT 55, GT 51).

This primal unity does not precede reality temporally; rather, it is reality's most essential and fundamental aspect in that it exists prior to human categories. Because this primal unity does not exist as a thing in the world, an imitation of it cannot consist of a direct representation of empirical reality. The tragedy, however, is not just an imitation of empirical reality. Such a representation of reality is an example of the Apollinian aspect of art, which, in creating an image of an object, maintains art as a representation of the real world and not as a part of the real world. Rather than representing nature, the Dionysian in art creates a mimesis of nature. Both art and reality become two manifestations of the same primal unity, the conflict of forces that determines the creation of objects both within and outside the work of art. The tragedy attains its mythic status by directly enacting in its Dionysian aspect this play of forces.

THE LYRIC POET

The Dionysian mimesis of nature consists of an enactment of a conflict between forces rather than a representation of objects. As a result, the Dionysian aspect of art, in its attempt to transcend the immanent character of the work of art, functions as an imitation, not of the external world, but of an inner, subjective world. In his description of the lyric poet, Nietzsche argues that the artist arrives at the essence of nature by investigating the development and contradictions of subjectivity. The poet cannot directly grasp the primal unity of nature itself. Instead, by focusing on subjectivity, the poet gains access to the forces of nature through a passive, mimetic attitude that registers the forces governing human subjectivity in a particular context. Nietzsche's description of the Dionysian consequently focuses on the individual artist as the vessel through which the primal unity of nature manifests itself in a way that is relevant to the life of a particular community.

But though individual artists become the mediators of the metaphysical, they can only do so by abandoning their individuality to experience a communion with the primal unity in an ecstatic experience of self-dissolution: "The 'I' of the lyrist therefore sounds from the depth of being [*aus dem Abgrunde des Seins*]: its 'subjectivity,' in the sense of modern aestheticians is a fiction" (BT 49, GT 43–44).[9] Though subjectivity provides the starting point for the Dionysian transcendence of aesthetic illusion, the artist's inner, subjective experience must dissolve in order to create a more general mediation between humans and nature. The Dionysian artist's loss of individuality is the crucial step in the process leading to the work of art: "In the first place, as a Dionysian artist he [the lyricist] has identified himself with the primal unity, its pain and contradiction. Assuming that music has been correctly termed a repetition and a recast of the world, we may say that he produces the copy of this primal unity as music" (BT 49, GT 43–44). The lyricist begins as a Dionysian artist in communion with the primal unity, in which the artist's subjective pain merges with the pain and contradiction of nature. That is, the artist's pain is only a specific manifestation of a recurring contradiction. The poet's expression of this pain through music can only become art to the extent that the music is recognized by others as another manifestation of a contradiction that they also experience subjectively. The achievement of the artist is to transform his or her subjective pain into a communal event in music. The musicality of poetry consequently consists of its presentation of the primal unity through a Dionysian enactment rather than through an Apollinian representation.

Because the Apollinian impulse only creates copies of things, it cannot create a mimesis of pain. Rather, pain in the work of art is expressed by its Dionysian aspect, which manifests pain through "musical dissonance" (BT 141, GT 152). Dissonance is Nietzsche's example of a form of expression that does not depend upon the communication of a particular contents, but rather upon the relationship between two elements within a composition. Because music has no empirical original, it provides the model for a purity of form whose dissonance imports into the work of art that which cannot be directly represented—in this case, the primal contradiction that does not exist as an empirical object in reality. Though dissonance consists of an immanent relation within a composition, this inner relation attains its power by enacting forces that also exist outside the composition. Because it enacts a conflict of forces, dissonance in music does not create a representation of an empirical reality but a manifestation of the primal contradiction of forces. Music is as real as the world of things. Like the objects of empirical reality, it comes into existence as a momentary compromise formation of the forces of nature (human will is considered here as another one of these forces). The task of the artist is to make sure that dissonance within the work relates analogically to the conflict of forces that govern reality outside the work of art.

But since poetry consists of images as well as musical rhythm, the lyricist must translate the imageless and nonconceptual presentation of primal pain in music into a language of images.

> Now, however, under the Apollinian dream inspiration, this music reveals itself to him again as a *symbolic* [gleichnissartigen] *dream image*. The inchoate, intangible [*bild- und begrifflose*] reflection of the primordial pain in music, with its redemption in mere appearance, now produces a second mirroring as a specific symbol or example. The artist has already surrendered his subjectivity in the Dionysian process. The image that now shows him his identity with the heart of the world is a dream scene that embodies the primordial contradiction and primordial pain, together with the primordial pleasure, of mere appearance. (BT 49, GT 43–44)

The subjectivity of the lyric poet functions as an example of the play of forces that "sounds from the depth of being" (BT 49, GT 43–44). Because the poet's Apollinian dream images are mobilized to present a Dionysian pain (and not to represent objects in empirical reality), these images are no longer arbitrary; rather, they become para-

bolic (*gleichnissartig*) and exemplary. Once the musical enactment
of suffering is translated into a language of images, the primal unity
expresses itself as a set of Apollinian images with a Dionysian organization upon which the exemplary character of the images is based.

Commentaries on *The Birth of Tragedy* have generally ignored
how this merging of Apollinian and Dionysian aesthetics guarantees the work of art's capacity for transcendence. Because they view
all art as either representation or autonomous illusion, interpreters
reduce art to its Apollinian aspect, in which it is understood exclusively as semblance. Consequently, they equate the Dionysian with
the real rather than recognizing its particular aesthetic structure.

Once the Dionysian is equated with the real, as in Manfred
Frank's reading, Nietzsche's description of the lyricist becomes incomprehensible. After quoting the passage in *The Birth of Tragedy*
concerning the lyricist cited earlier in this chapter, Frank notes:

> In this passage a great deal is obscure, and not simply because
> of the loading with metaphors, but conceptually. First it is in-
> comprehensible why Nietzsche designates the will itself as
> pain (pain must, after all, originate first with the principium
> individuationis); second it is incomprehensible, though he
> himself explains in this passage that the Dionysian intoxica-
> tion is only an image of being, how he can claim at the same
> time that the artist escapes from his subjectivity in the aes-
> thetic production and descends into the primal source of be-
> ing—which cannot be presented as such. (The music which
> the lyricist hears is itself merely a copy of the primal unity,
> therefore mediated by the Apollinian.)[10]

For Frank suffering is the result of individuation, and he does not
understand why Nietzsche seems to attribute suffering to the will
and the Dionysian. Against Nietzsche's location of pain and contradiction in nature and the primitive, Frank demonstrates a Rous-
seauist idealization of the primitive in which it is understood as being pure and simple while only the individuated can be painful and
contradictory. Moreover, Frank assumes that music, as imitation of
the primal unity, can only be aesthetic to the extent that it is Apollinian. By interpreting the Dionysian as real and the Apollinian as

57

aesthetic, he misses Nietzsche's explanation that the Dionysian is a specific aspect of aesthetic imitation through which both suffering and the primal unity are presented in music.

Similarly, in his reading of this passage de Man notes a contradiction between the idea of a dissolution of the poet's subjectivity and the link to a primal unity: "The narrative falls into two parts or, what amounts to the same thing, it acquires two incompatible narrators. The narrator who argues against the subjectivity of the lyric and against representational realism destroys the credibility of the other narrator, for whom Dionysian insight is the tragic perception of original truth."[11] Like Frank, de Man is unable to conceive of an art that is not representational yet also maintains a connection to a reality outside of the work of art. Frank and de Man both overlook the mechanism of Dionysian art and assume that all art must be either representation or illusion. In Nietzsche's view, however, the dissolution of subjectivity in Dionysian art allows an aesthetic truth to be discerned. While the dissolution of subjectivity does present a turn away from representational realism, this turn does not necessarily mean all claims to truth must be abandoned. Instead, a Dionysian, aesthetic truth arises from the work of art's enactment of the forces that determine the structures of subjective experience for an entire community.

DISSONANCE IN DRAMA

Nietzsche provides a more detailed description of the workings of this Dionysian aesthetic in his descriptions of Greek tragedy. As with lyric poetry, the tragedy merges the Apollinian and Dionysian aspects of art into a single form. The characters and scenes of tragedy are Apollinian and, however fantastic they might be, refer to an empirical original in reality that the drama imitates. But despite this undeniable Apollinian representational aspect, tragedy functions as a Dionysian experience as well. Nietzsche describes the Dionysian aspect of tragedy as a kind of dramatic dissonance in which "[t]he structure of the scenes [*das Gefüge der Scenen*] and the visual images reveal a deeper wisdom than the poet himself can put into words and concepts" (BT 105, GT 109–10). The Dionysian element lies in the inner structure of the drama and not in any directly presented character or concept.

The tragedy creates an imitation of empirical reality in its Apollinian mode by presenting the hero. At the same time, the tragedy also adheres to a plot structure in which the tragic conflict remains unresolvable and the hero must be annihilated. Thus, tragedy creates in its internal form the equivalent of Dionysian musical dissonance. "The metaphysical joy in the tragic," Nietzsche writes, "is a translation of the instinctive unconscious Dionysian wisdom into the language of images: the hero, the highest manifestation of the will, is negated for our pleasure, because he is only phenomenon, and because the eternal life of the will is not affected by his annihilation. 'We believe in eternal life,' exclaims tragedy; while music is the immediate idea of this life" (BT 104, GT 108). The tragic conflict expresses that which the drama cannot depict in its images: a structural contradiction between human aspiration and the limitations of nature.

The exemplary character of this contradiction is not a given for Nietzsche. Rather, he deduces it from the structure of the most successful tragedies. From this method, we may infer that the truth of myth cannot be demonstrated logically or conceptually; it can only be experienced aesthetically. The act of reception determines the basis of tragedy and the source of its Dionysian character. For the truth of a particular drama to be demonstrated, it must reveal itself in the consciousness of its spectators not just as a singular event but as an exemplary one, not just as a story but as a parable:

> Dionysian art therefore is wont to exercise two kinds of influences on the Apollinian art faculty: music incites to the *parabolic* [gleichnisartigen] *intuition* of Dionysian universality, and music allows the parabolic [*gleichnissartige*] image to emerge *in its highest significance*. From these facts, intelligible in themselves and not inaccessible to a more penetrating examination, I infer the capacity of music to give birth to *myth* (the most significant example), and particularly the *tragic* myth: the myth which expresses Dionysian knowledge in parables [*in Gleichnissen*]. (BT 103, GT 107)

The combination of musical dissonance and dramatic images results in a parabolic intuition of the Dionysian in nature. Dionysian truth is transmitted through an example, and the tragedy gains its mythic status through the exemplary, paradigmatic character of the story that it tells. "The most significant example," in the form of a parable, transmits the experience of the Dionysian in nature.

Nietzsche's readings of Greek tragedies explain how the stories of Oedipus and Prometheus attain this exemplary status. Nietzsche interprets both as stories of sacrilege against nature. In the case of Oedipus, the solving of the riddle of the Sphinx, a victory over nature, is connected to incest and patricide, crimes against nature. The plot of the tragedy connects Oedipus's solving of nature's riddles with his transgression against the natural order (BT 68–69, GT 66–67). The source of the Dionysian aspect of the tragedy is this relationship within the tragedy between Oedipus's actions and the natural forces that oppose him, not the realistic portrayal of Oedipus nor anything in particular that he says.

Likewise, in *Prometheus Bound* the Dionysian expresses itself according to Nietzsche as a dialectical contradiction between wisdom and suffering, between Prometheus's "superior wisdom" and the fact that he must atone for this wisdom "with eternal suffering" (BT 70, GT 68). The dissonance created by the simultaneity of higher wisdom and eternal suffering in Prometheus demonstrates a tension between wisdom and happiness and sets the drama in opposition to the rational, Socratic view that would harmonize the two. The Prometheus myth mediates nature, not as harmony, but as a fundamental contradiction between human aspiration and the limits set by the forces of nature.

Nietzsche's reading of *Prometheus Bound* demonstrates how, to be effective, Dionysian dissonance must resonate with the experience of the audience. For the link between wisdom and suffering expressed in the dissonant structure of *Prometheus Bound* has its origins in the philosophical problem that accompanies humankind's progress in subduing nature:

The presupposition of the Prometheus myth is to be found in the extravagant value which a naive humanity attached to *fire* as the true palladium of every ascending culture. But that man should freely dispose of fire without receiving it as a present from heaven, either as a lightning bolt or as the warming rays of the sun, struck these reflective primitive men as sacrilege, as a robbery of divine nature. Thus the very first philosophical problem immediately produces a painful and irresolvable contradiction between humankind and god and moves it before the gate of every culture, like a huge boulder. The best and highest possession mankind can acquire is obtained by sacrilege and must be paid for with consequences that involve the whole flood of sufferings and sorrows with which the offended divinities have to afflict the nobly aspiring race of men. (BT 71, GT 69)

The connection between wisdom and suffering in *Prometheus Bound* arises from the guilt and sense of sacrilege that followed the discovery of fire and that were then recapitulated in the Prometheus myth. The imperatives that determine the myth's plot express a necessary contradiction between human aspiration and the forces of nature. It does not make sense that wisdom and knowledge should lead to suffering. Yet the power of the tragedy depends upon the extent to which this plot structure recurs in Greek experience. The plot structure of the tragedy recapitulates the structure of experience, and the "primordial pain" (*Urschmerz*) expressed in the myth is a recapitulation of the ancient Greek (but also, in the case of Nietzsche, the nineteenth-century German) experience of nature.

In Nietzsche's readings of Greek tragedies he limits himself to uncovering the basic contradiction that is the source of a tragedy's effect. He does not attempt to resolve the contradictions; he seeks to show that the aesthetic success of a tragedy is based upon the irresolvability of the contradictions it embodies. In effect, the creation and survival of tragedy and Dionysian art in general are direct manifestations of the contradictions that govern human existence. The aesthetic effect of mythic tragedy demonstrates the continuing actuality of "the contradiction in the heart of the world" between human aspiration and natural forces (BT 71, GT 70).

Because the Dionysian is an art force whose exemplary character resonates with the experiences of a people, for Nietzsche the importance of myth and of the Dionysian lies in their aesthetic character. Moreover, the power of myth does not proceed from a supernatural reality or an attitude of passive subservience but rather from its aesthetic structure. By expressing the antagonism between human endeavors and the natural forces opposing them, myth creates a mimesis of experience.

Nietzsche's linking of myth and aesthetic reception creates at once an art that is connected to an outside reality and a myth that depends upon aesthetic experience. Because structure provides the point of entry in both music and myth for that which cannot be represented directly, musical dissonance is also the model for the structure of myth: "Music and tragic myth are equally expressions of the Dionysian capacity of a people, and they are inseparable" (BT 143, GT 154).

MYTH AND COMMUNITY

Despite the fact that Nietzsche links myth to aesthetic experience, his claim that he has developed a metaphysics of art should not lead one to place too much emphasis on the role of the individual artist in this metaphysics, even if Nietzsche himself was prone to do so at times. For if the key characteristic of the mythic tragedy is its exemplary character, it cannot be constructed by the individual artist but only by a community of spectators.

While the artist's task is to create a story that is imaginative and extraordinary, only the audience can determine whether a particular drama is exemplary. As a result, the "editing" process whereby particular stories are chosen by a community as paradigmatic for its experiences becomes integrated into the creative process. A myth cannot simply be created by an artistic genius. It can only be received from a tradition within which a particular story undergoes numerous revisions and is gradually elevated to the status of myth through its interaction with community experience. The Dionysian aesthetic truth of myth results from a communal and not an individual mimesis of nature. The work of art as the creation of an individual artist must consequently be differentiated from myth, which cannot be created but can only be "given" to a community by the processes of tradition.

When seen in this way, myth can be understood neither as a set of fixed and unchanging truths nor as a set of arbitrarily constructed artistic "creations." Myth in this view is an aesthetic field that is open to change and renewal of the particular forms that inhabit it. Since the significance of the myth is dependent upon the structure of forces active in a community's history, differences in the structure of a community's experience correspond to changes in the structure of that community's myths. Each objectification of the myth into a particular rendering of it is necessitated by the myth's Apollinian quality as dramatic image. Yet each rendering of the myth also presents a momentary image of its Dionysian aspect. Because its force depends upon its status as an example, the Dionysian aspect must continually transform the myth in order to reflect changes in the structure of human experience. The aesthetic truth that results is experienced not as a human construction but as a divine intervention, a miracle:

> Whoever wishes to test rigorously to what extent he himself is related to the true aesthetic listener or belongs to the community of the Socratic-critical persons needs only to examine sincerely the feeling with which he accepts miracles represented on the stage: whether he feels his historical sense, which insists on strict psychological causality, insulted by them, whether he makes a benevolent concession and admits the miracle as a phenomenon intelligible to childhood but alien to him, or whether he experiences anything else. For in this way he will be able to determine to what extent he is capable of understanding *myth* as a concentrated image of the world that, as a condensation of phenomena, cannot dispense with miracles.
> (BT 135, GT 145)

Nietzsche identifies the aesthetic experience of the tragedy with the religious experience of the miracle. The intuition of the miracle in the work of art, which occurs on the level of reception, is that which separates the aesthetic listener from the Socratic rational critic. The rational critic is incapable of participating in the experience of the miracle and calls it a childhood phenomenon from which he or she is alienated. This critical attitude in the reception is inappropriate for understanding the mythic quality of the tragedy. In contrast to this critical attitude, Nietzsche favors the aesthetic reception that connects the tragedy to myth through the experience of the miracle. This miracle cannot be created like a work of art; it can only be received like divine revelation. In berating the Socratic critics for the rationalistic perspective that prevents them from perceiving the miracle for what it is Nietzsche does not oppose the idea of critique to passivity, he opposes the critical faculty to the aesthetic one.

According to Nietzsche, to maintain a unified culture and a stable community, society must accept the miracle and the religious tradition supporting it. Neither scientific rationality nor artistic creation but myth and tradition become the essential pillars of society. Arguing that the decline of tragedy also meant a fading of religious experience, Nietzsche emphasizes the connection between mythic tragedy and social order:

> It had to appear to us that the demise of Greek tragedy was brought about through a remarkable and forcible dissociation of these two primordial artistic drives. To this process there corresponded a degeneration and transformation of the character of the Greek people, which calls for serious reflection on how necessary and close the fundamental connections are between art and the people, myth and custom, tragedy and the state. This demise of tragedy was at the same time the demise of myth. Until then the Greeks had felt involuntarily impelled to relate all their experiences immediately to their myths, indeed to understand them only in this relation. Thus even the immediate present had to appear to them right away *sub specie aeterni* and in a certain sense as timeless. (BT 137, GT 147)

The transcendental character of the tragedy lies not just in the piety of the recipients but in the tragedy's ability to plausibly link the eternal to individual experience. As Julian Young notes, "*The Birth of Tragedy* has religion as its fundamental concern."[12] Nietzsche's analysis clearly illuminates the religious function of tragedy as that which mediates the community's experience of the eternal. However, he also postulates an aesthetic structure for all religion insofar as religious rituals and narratives must conform to certain aesthetic rules to retain their legitimacy.

The legitimacy and power of the community for each individual in it depend on the extent to which its myths are constructed in such a way as to be able to impose "the stamp of the eternal" on all individual experience (BT 137, GT 148). The myth's creation of a connection between "the eternal" and individual experience links abstract ethical values to individual acts: "The images of the myth have to be the unnoticed omnipresent demonic guardians, under whose care the young soul grows to maturity and whose signs help the man to interpret his life and struggles. Even the state knows no more powerful unwritten laws than the mythical foundation that guarantees its connection with religion and its growth from mythical notions" (BT 135, GT 145). The authority for deriving ethical values from myth is an aesthetic one. That is, the justification for the myth does not derive from philosophical proofs nor from the mere fact of custom, but rather from the ability of the myth to create in its structures an exemplary parable that makes sense in terms of the specific experiences of the individuals in the community. Aesthetic experience cannot be separated from religious community, and the ethical strength of the community depends upon the success of the mythic tragedy.

3

THE PRIMITIVE AND
THE BARBARIC

PRIMITIVISM AND LAW

Walter Benjamin criticizes Nietzsche's aesthetic vision of the world as a regression to a mythic consciousness in which humans are at the mercy of unknown and uncontrollable forces. Dismissing as ludicrous Nietzsche's description of humans as, themselves, aesthetic phenomena rather than originators of art, Benjamin argues that Nietzsche's metaphysics of art subjects humans to an aestheticization of life in which humanity is sacrificed for the sake of metaphysical beauty: "Where art so firmly occupies the centre of existence as to make man one of its manifestations instead of recognizing him above all as its basis—not in the sense of being its creator, but in the sense that his existence is the eternal theme of its formations—then all sane reflection is at an end."[1] In opposing Nietzsche's aesthetics of myth, Benjamin first accepts his reading of Greek tragedy as constituting an episode in a continuing conflict between knowledge and sacrifice, human achievement and divine power. But he then historicizes this conflict by interpreting tragedy as a form that marks the transition from the mythic world of demons to the world of humankind: "for in tragedy the hold of demonic fate is broken."[2] Seeing in tragedy an historical contradiction between an old, mythic, religious system of morality and a new, humanistic one, Benjamin reads tragedy redemptively as a historical moment in an emancipatory development away from the inhumanity of myth.[3] Prefiguring Jürgen Habermas's approach, Benjamin transforms the opposition between science and myth into an alternative opposition between civilization and barbarism, thus demonizing the mythic conception of the world that Nietzsche seeks to vindicate.[4]

But Niezsche's critique of reason does not amount to an abandonment of truth for power and civilization for barbarism, as Benjamin and, later, Habermas suggest. Rather, the difference between Benjamin's and Nietzsche's positions rests in their belief or nonbelief in the ability of human reason to subjugate nature. Nietzsche does indeed turn against reason. This move is not insane, however. It depends upon his demonstration of the possibility that art, as established in myths and rituals, constitutes its own means of relating to nature. In contrast to Benjamin's optimistic belief in reason's ability to overcome nature and with it a mythic past, Nietzsche's view of nature as aesthetic phenomenon leads to a pessimism toward the capabilities of reason. He affirms myth and tradition over critique and reason as the best means for organizing social life so as to take nature's power into account.

From Nietzsche's perspective, Benjamin's belief in emancipation from demonic fate is based on a delusionary optimism concerning humankind's ability to understand and control nature by learning its laws. Since for Nietzsche the objects of nature cannot be considered as fixed entities that behave according to predictable laws, there can be no progress in subjugating natural forces and thus no point at which humans can escape "the hold of demonic fate." Consequently, no matter how far it progresses human knowledge is as incapable of delegitimating myth as of eradicating nature itself. The belief in its ability to do so is Nietzsche's primary target for critique in his vision of tragedy. In contrast to Benjamin's optimistic vision of tragedy as the document of a possible human emancipation from nature, Nietzsche sees in tragedy the depiction of an irresolvable conflict between humankind and nature in which nature and fate set fundamental limits on human aspiration. Science and knowledge alter the particular boundaries of these limits but can never eradicate them. The essential aspect of tragedy for Nietzsche is that it imitates the primal contradiction (*Urwiderspruch*) of nature rather than replacing it with an illusion of harmony.

This tragic vision is not the source of barbarism, as Benjamin argues, but rather the basis for human law and morality. In *Human, All Too Human*, the opposition between the Socratic and the Dionysian reappears as a distinction between a modern and a primitive perspective on nature. Here, Nietzsche argues that human laws and discipline derive from a primitive, mythic vision of nature as violent and contradictory rather than a civilized, "emancipatory" view of nature as a place of peace and harmony.

Like the nineteenth-century natural science that ignores the real horror of nature as an unpredictable force, the modern, civilized experience of nature as a place of calm is not an encounter with nature but an escape from the flux of nature into oneself. This inward escape leads to a state of self-enjoyment, solipsism, and alienation not only from nature but also from other humans.[5] Because nature as repose is actually the solipsism of the human, such a vision only creates an ideal image of nature as law and predictability, which is in fact a delusion.[6] The primary effect of this delusion is to convince the civilized person that nature is no longer an opponent of human desires but the means to their fulfillment.

In contrast, the basic premise of primitive cultures is that nature is unpredictable. The absence of laws in nature means that humans must impose laws on nature.[7] Like the natural scientist, the primitive wants to control nature with laws and conceives them as a reaction to the unpredictability of nature. But whereas the civilized mind claims to find lawfulness already in nature, the primitive imposes lawfulness on nature: "The meaning of the religious cult is to determine and constrain nature for the benefit of mankind, that is to say *to impress upon it a regularity and rule of law which it does not at first possess*; while in the present age one seeks to *understand* the laws of nature so as to accommodate oneself to them [*um sich in sie zu schicken*]."[8] In contrast to a scientific optimism regarding the human domination of nature, the primitive understands nature as lawless and is therefore forced to construct laws that, in attempting to limit the danger of nature, apply primarily to humans themselves. These laws thus make primitives at once more natural and more disciplined than the civilized.[9]

The primitive understanding of nature as lawlessness connects nature to the sacred, and magic, though directed at nature, creates rules for human existence. In contrast to civilized cultures, primitives understand nature as freedom, as the place of God, while law is closely related to informal traditions.[10] Primitive law thus functions both as an attempt to adjust to the forces of nature and as a way of regulating social relations. The primitive, in attempting to come to terms with nature, constructs the bonds linking individuals to each other. Nietzsche praises the primitive religiosity of the ancient Greeks in their relation to nature over the modern civilized and scientific attitude because of the human bonds generated by the primitive, magical attitude. The directly lived relationship between individuals, built upon pledges and gratitude, provides the foundation for social relations. Aesthetically constructed as a collective reaction to the forces of nature, primitive law is "nobler" because it is not based upon a set of rational or universal truths but rather upon the practical necessities of everyday reality.[11]

REASON AND BARBARISM

If for Nietzsche myth and the primitive are the basis of human law and morality, reason and civilization become the sources of barbarism. This equation of civilization with barbarism not only conflicts with Benjamin's and Habermas's view that primitive myth must be replaced by philosophy and critique, but also with the aestheticist readings that oppose civilization to barbarism. In defending science as the only possible future for all art, Danto sets up a distinction between civilization and barbarism that is meant to take the place of the opposition between science and art. "The contrast is always between suffering and exultation, between barbarism and civilization," he writes, "and science, no *less* than art, is an instrument for the enhancement of life. He [Nietzsche] never opposed art in the narrow sense against art in the wide sense—the latter counting science as one of its forms."[12] For Danto, the primary conflict in *The Birth of Tragedy* is not between myth and reason but between civilization and barbarism. This opposition is the pendant to the similarly false opposition between human knowledge and the chaos of nature. If the only antithesis to rationality is formless chaos, the only alternative to a civilization based on the progress of rationality is barbarism.

Sloterdijk's analysis of the Dionysian also adheres to this logic by connecting the formlessness of nature to the chaos of the barbaric:

"Before our eyes, Nietzsche splits the Dionysian throng into two se-
verely differentiated, almost oppositional choruses, which relate to
each other like culture and nature or civilization and barbarism."[13]
While the barbarian Dionysus enacts a real Dionysian "regression"
into animality, the Greek Dionysus only enacts a representation of
a regression. Defending cultural representation against the chaos of
nature, Sloterdijk presents this distinction between Dionysus in reality and Dionysus in art as a progression from the barbarian to the
civilized. He further sees the Apollinian restriction of the original
Dionysian within the boundaries of the work of art as being the
"primal scene of civilization" and the original Dionysian festivals as
a lost state of nature that can only reemerge as a barbaric frenzy to be
avoided at all costs.[14] Recapitulating de Man's idea that Dionysus
"never *is*, in the full sense, an essence, but the possibility of an essence to exist in the guise of its represented appearance," Sloterdijk
argues that the structure of the tragedy is and must be an Apollinian
one, which allows a "Dionysian outburst" only to the extent that it
occurs within the "quotation marks" of an Apollinian artistic semblance.[15]

By imprisoning the Dionysian within the bounds of "its represented appearance," de Man and Sloterdijk attempt to force it to
cede its authority to the constructor of the appearance—philosophy. According to Sloterdijk, the chaotic masses depend upon the
Apollinian artist and the Socratic intellectual to maintain any existence at all. Sloterdijk states that the only possible appearance of the
Dionysian is as a representation within the Apollinian theater: "Dionysian revelers in place of Dionysian revelers, unification in place
of unification." He then goes on to equate Apollinian representation with philosophy, which also demonstrates this structure of replacement by replacing the thing with the concept.[16] The only possible manifestation of nature is thus as the object of reason in
philosophy, and anything outside of reason is considered either
chaotic or nonexistent.

The theoretical argument about the impossibility of creating any
bridge to the essence of nature becomes a practical argument about
the role of philosophy and science in human relations. Because the
creation of forms can only be a conscious human endeavor, even the

worst philosophy would be preferable to a "state of nature" that is chaotic, formless, and barbaric. Though philosophy is limited to the world of appearances and thus self-referential texts, Danto and de Man have in effect reduced the world to fit into these limits and deemed it possible and even necessary to ignore anything beyond.

This shifting of the terms in order to transform the myth-versus-science opposition into one between barbarism and civilization is precisely the move that Nietzsche attacks in his polemic against the "healthy-minded" onlookers who turn away "with contempt" from the Dionysian (BT 36–37, GT 29). Rather than opposing civilization to barbarism, Nietzsche's intimation that art might be a correlative or supplement to science is an affirmation of the limits of science and of the necessity of recognizing an antithesis to civilization that is not barbaric, but primitive: an artistic means for dealing with the metaphysical questions that lie outside of the authority of science. The very opposition of civilization to barbarism belongs to a scientific perspective. From Nietzsche's viewpoint, civilization and barbarism are intimately connected, and the true antithesis of barbarism is the primitive.

Nietzsche demonstrates this opposition between the lawful primitive and the barbaric civilized in his discussion of Greek tragedy. He sees his pessimistic, mythic view of tragedy in the work of Aeschylus and Sophocles while he interprets the Socratic tragedy of Euripides as an example of the optimistic, rationalist view of the world. Whereas pre-Euripidian tragedy is based on a Dionysian mimesis that opens up the drama to the antinomies of experience, the Euripidian tragedy accords with a scientific perspective by constructing a theoretical, cognitive representation with a critical purpose. But in comparing these two perspectives, Nietzsche argues that it is in fact the rationalist perspective and not the mythic one that leads to barbarism in human affairs.[17]

Barbarism only arises after the optimism of the Socratic perspective, which presents nature and life as ultimately comprehensible and sees cognition as the path to happiness (BT 91, GT 94), has destroyed the structures residing in the mythic dimension. The dramas of Euripides, for example, seek to develop a critical, philosophical attitude in the audience: "And so the Aristophanean Euripides prides himself on having portrayed the common, familiar, every-day life and activities of the people, about which all are qualified to pass judgment. If the entire populace now philosophized, managed land and goods, and conducted lawsuits with unheard-of circum-spection, he deserved the credit, for this was the result of the wis-dom he had inculcated in the people" (BT 78, GT 77). By attempting to break down the distinction between art and society to make art resemble the everyday, Euripides, like Benjamin, pursues a didactic purpose that assumes that critical discourse, when taught to the people, can change the world in such a way as to avoid the disasters of tragedy. This didactic goal suppresses the tragic Dionysian basis of art by depicting tragedy as avoidable through wisdom. This view recognizes neither the validity of an aesthetic organization of na-ture nor of the Dionysian approach to nature. Thus, the limits that fate sets upon human aspirations are interpreted, not as a conse-quence of nature as an independent force but of a lack of knowl-edge. This understanding, which immediately defines everything irrational as chaotic and barbaric and attempts to eliminate it, only succeeds in destroying the mythic structures that reside in this di-mension and guarantee the proper functioning of morality.

Eventually, Euripides is forced to admit the power of the irratio-nal and the futility of trying to destroy it, but he still remains within a rationalist perspective by interpreting this power as merely de-structive and arbitrary. As Nietzsche describes, late in his life Eurip-ides turns toward a pessimistic Socraticism in which the Dionysian is affirmed, but only as an unstoppable destructive force rather than a creative one: "In the evening of his life, Euripides himself pro-pounded to his contemporaries the question of the value and sig-nificance of this tendency, using a myth. Is the Dionysian entitled to exist at all? Should it not be forcibly uprooted from Hellenic soil? Certainly, the poet tells us, if it were only possible: but the god Dio-nysus is too powerful; his most intelligent adversary—like Pen-theus in the *Bacchae*—is unwittingly enchanted by him, and in this enchantment runs to meet his fate" (BT 81, GT 82). Despite the fact that *The Bacchae* depicts the "victory of Dionysus," it maintains a Socratic viewpoint, first, in its attempt to directly depict the Dionysian at all—thereby reifying it into a distinct entity—and, second, in its construction of the Dionysian as barbaric.

Yet in Nietzsche's view, the Dionysian is only barbaric when it has been distorted into the opposite of reason. Before Euripides, the Dionysian is not merely a nether sphere of darkness to be eliminated, but a dimension of traditions upon which ordered human relations are based. It is only when Euripides depicts the Dionysian in *The Bacchae* as the opposite of reason that it becomes barbarism. Even though Euripides stages this final tribute to Dionysus, Nietzsche argues that it was too late and that Euripides' dramas had already introduced the crucial shift from a Dionysian to a Socratic society. Euripides, in paying tribute to the Dionysian, distorts it and mistakes it for the barbarism that it would not have become if the Socratic had been defeated.

According to this evaluation of the Dionysian, Nietzsche attributes the causes of barbarism to the absence of Dionysus and myth rather than to their domination:

> Let us mark this well: the Alexandrian culture, to be able to exist permanently, requires a slave class, but with its optimistic view of life it denies the necessity of such a class, and consequently, when its beautifully seductive and tranquilizing utterances about the "dignity of man" and the "dignity of labor" are no longer effective, it gradually drifts toward a dreadful destruction. There is nothing more terrible than a class of barbaric slaves who have learned to regard their existence as an injustice, and now prepare to avenge, not only themselves, but all generations. (BT III, GT 117)

While the theoretical, scientific worldview believes that the burdens of nature, that is, the necessity of work and suffering, are surmountable with the aid of the intellect, Nietzsche argues that the limits of nature are in fact insurmountable and that the optimism of the theoretical worldview can only be maintained by banning the work and suffering of human existence into a slave class while at the same time ideologically denying the necessity of this class. Meanwhile, this class, itself infected with a scientific optimism, not only recognizes its own suffering as unjust (which it may well be), but is no longer contained in its behavior by the ethical restrictions that a properly functioning mythic culture can provide. The resulting barbaric vengeance of this class that Nietzsche fears is not a result of Dionysian myth but rather of its destruction.

THE SATYR CHORUS

The opposite of such barbarism is the communion with nature that Nietzsche locates in the tragedy's satyr chorus. This chorus acts as the mediator of a transcendent, spiritual experience for the audience, creating a bond between humans and nature and at the same time suspending social divisions in order to create a unified community. This creation of a Dionysian experience of unity depends on an imitation of nature in which the social boundaries constructed by culture are transcended and the entire community shares the experience of the power of nature. This experience occurs in the tragedy as a transformation of the entire audience.

Though a drama would normally be considered an example of Apollinian art because it enacts an imitation of human events on the level of "Apollinian appearances" (BT 66, GT 64), the chorus transforms the tragedy into a Dionysian experience: "the gulfs between man and man give way to an overwhelming feeling of unity leading back to the very heart of nature" (BT 59, GT 56). Unity is enacted not just as a representation but as a metaphysical activity in which "a whole throng experiences the magic of this transformation" (BT 64, GT 61). The goal of this Dionysian transformation is the replacement of the "person of culture" (*Culturmensch*) by the satyr chorus. This is a primitivizing movement from civilization toward, not barbarism, but an ideal archetype of man in a primitive state: "Nature, as yet unchanged by knowledge, with the bolts of culture still unbroken—that is what the Greek saw in his satyr who nevertheless was not a mere ape. On the contrary, the satyr was the archetype of man, the embodiment of his highest and most intense emotions" (BT 61, GT 58). The transformation of the Dionysian revelers into a satyr chorus is not a regression but a return of humans to themselves prior to the alienating structures of "culture." Nor is this mimesis of nature harmony. It is a dissonance arising out of the con-

74

tradictions of experience created by the conflictual relation between humankind and nature.

Nietzsche opposes the satyr chorus to the "person of culture," who does not recognize the validity of Dionysian truth nor the viability of primitive community: "The contrast between this real truth of nature and the lie of culture that poses as if it were the only reality is similar to that between the eternal core of things, the thing-in-itself, and the whole world of appearances" (BT 61, GT 58–59). The issue in the discussion of the thing-in-itself and appearances was the priority of the thing-in-itself as a dimension of forces that manifests itself as the world of appearances yet at the same time maintains this world in a state of flux. So too here, the issue is the chorus's ability to mediate an experience of the "truth of nature" so as to dissolve the fixed objectifications of "the lie of culture." According to the "person of culture," the only reality that exists is a static realm of appearances in which existing reality is frozen into its current structures and divisions, and the dissolution of these divisions would be a regression into chaos. Against this rationalistic understanding of reality, Nietzsche attempts to imagine a situation in which the breakdown of divisions would allow the community to view itself as a unity held together by the members' common experience of the forces that structure their existence. In seeking to defend "the sphere of poetry" as the expression of the truth of nature, Nietzsche attempts to imagine a collective experience of the forces of nature that exist behind all fixed structures.

The chorus functions as "a living wall against the assaults of reality" (BT 61, GT 58), separating the audience from its everyday reality and transforming it into a chorus of satyrs: "Such magic transformation is the presupposition of all dramatic art. In this magic transformation the Dionysian reveler sees himself as a satyr, *and as a satyr, in turn, he sees the god*" (BT 64, GT 61–62). As a mixture of human and animal, the satyr is the image of a human in communion with nature as the thing-in-itself. This communion in turn allows the human-as-satyr to experience a vision of the god: "In its vision this chorus beholds its lord and master Dionysus and is therefore eternally the *serving* chorus: it sees how the god suffers and glorifies himself and therefore does not itself *act*. But while its attitude to-

ward the god is wholly one of service, it is nevertheless the highest, namely the Dionysian, expression of *nature* and therefore pronounces in its rapture, as nature does, oracles and wise sayings: *sharing his suffering* it also shares something of his *wisdom* and proclaims the truth from the heart of the world" (BT 65, GT 63). That the human must be transformed into a satyr to see the god demonstrates for Nietzsche the proximity between natural forces and the power of the gods. To the extent that humans must constantly struggle with natural forces in order to attain their goals, they are at odds with nature. But in the mythic tragedy this recognition of the power of nature does not result in submission to nature but in sacrifice to the god. The transformation into the satyr chorus allows humans to experience a unity with nature that at the same time creates a vision of the god. For the recognition of the divine can only occur once humans attain a consciousness of their own weaknesses in their struggle against natural forces. Nature and the gods are the two aspects of a primal dimension closed to human understanding and only approachable through aesthetic experience.

NIETZSCHE'S UNIVERSALIST LEGACY

Though Nietzsche's ideas began the impulse toward primitivism in Europe, they must compete with the two modern understandings of the primitive that construct it either as a backward and barbaric state or as a pristine utopia. The first alternative is taken by anthropologists of the nineteenth and early twentieth centuries. The second alternative is exemplified in the early work of Paul Gauguin.[18] In addition to these two approaches to the primitive, other interpretations of Nietzsche's ideas often distorted his conception of the primitive by reading the primal unity as an objectified time or place and treating the Dionysian as a force in reality rather than an art force. These readings were encouraged by some of the gaps and inconsistencies in *The Birth of Tragedy* in which the prescriptive passages concerning German culture often contradict the ideas developed in the analysis of Greek tragedy. In arguing for the unity and the purity of German culture, Nietzsche overlooks several problems in the development and maintenance of a cultural tradition that arise in his discussion of ancient Greek culture.

Though Nietzsche mentions universal validity as a characteristic of science and implies thereby that mythic truth is anti-universal, he fails to investigate any further the issue of universal validity in his description of the tragic worldview. Though he later develops a critique of the universalizing tendencies of Christianity, for instance, he does not carry out a similar operation with his own Dionysian perspective. He never considers the extent to which a particular mythic tradition must be thought of as anti-universal (that is, valid only within a particular time and place). Consequently, interpreters have sometimes assumed that he developed a universal myth.

Neither does Nietzsche pursue the question of the size of a viable cultural community. He only goes so far as to say that the prerequisite for cultural unity is an experience of myth that places a limit on the horizons of a community: "only a horizon defined by myths completes and unifies a whole cultural movement" (BT 135, BT 145). In his investigation into the mechanisms for creating unity he limits himself to describing the tragic chorus, but even in this example the community cannot be much larger than the size of the amphitheater, particularly if a mythic tradition's validity is based on its connection to individual experience. His failure to inquire further into the difficulties of extending the size of a mythic community beyond the bounds of Athens leads to his simple assumption of a common mythic foundation for all of Germany and to the cultural nationalism of *The Birth of Tragedy*.

The universalist elements of Nietzsche's argument also cause him to place artificial limits on the mythic material available to a culture. In his defense of German culture he asserts the inability of one culture to utilize the works of art of another culture: "It scarcely seems possible to be continually successful at transplanting a foreign myth without irreparably damaging the tree by this transplantation. In one case it may perhaps be strong and healthy enough to eliminate this foreign element in a terrible fight; usually, however, it must consume itself, sick and withered or in diseased superfoetation" (BT 138, GT 149). The need for myth to form a plausible link to individual experience causes Nietzsche to reject the transplantation of foreign cultures into German culture. Myths that speak to individual experience must be tailored to the characteristics of a particular culture.

Yet Nietzsche contradicts himself by denying the principle of cultural specificity, first, in his nationalist fusion of all Germans into one culture and, second, in his inability to understand specific points of affinity between two different cultures. In its use of ancient Greek models for nineteenth-century German culture, *The Birth of Tragedy* itself is evidence that myths from one culture can resonate for people in another time and place. Especially in light of Nietzsche's support for efforts to "penetrate into the core of the Hellenic nature, to establish a permanent alliance between German and Greek culture" (BT 122, GT 129), his rejection of foreign influences must be considered a rejection specifically of "Romanic" civilized cultural models in a situation where no other current models are available. Yet to the extent that his privileging of the experience of Greek culture contains a claim for the universal validity of this culture rather than for the particular resonance between ancient Greek and nineteenth-century German culture, Nietzsche again falls into a universalist attitude toward myth rather than a particularist one.

This final point is crucial for understanding the effect of Nietzsche's ideas on the subsequent development of European art. Because the power of a myth is determined in the moment of reception, its source is not as important as the experiential basis of the recipients upon which the myth's validity is grounded. By merging myth with art, Nietzsche is able to argue that traditional forms such as myth and ritual are not simply arbitrary and prejudicial, but have an objective foundation that is based on their aesthetic reception. In this way, Nietzsche can defend tradition and myth against reason and enlightenment as organizers of social life. The only truly mythic art would be created, not so much in an artistic genius's act of production, though this creative moment still exists, but rather in the mythic reception. Aesthetic production in such a mythic, oral tradition would be subordinated to the "editorial" decision-making that remains in the receptive capacity of the community. The connection between myth and art leads to an understanding of art that links its forms to a metaphysical and communal framework usually reserved for myth and religion.

The primary danger in Nietzsche's vision of a mythic art, at least in *The Birth of Tragedy* where he still looks to Richard Wagner's work as the supreme example of this type of art, is that art threatens to become an autonomous and universal sphere detached from the kind of community determination that maintains the vitality of mythic forms. In spite of his attempt to emphasize the mythic aspect of tragedy, Nietzsche's concentration on "mythic tragedy" rather than myth *tout court* distinguishes art from myth in order to privilege art as a more consciously determined example of myth. The consequence is that, rather than pointing the way to a renewed appreciation of myth and tradition in their particularity, his work fed into a monumental attempt on the part of European artists and intellectuals to develop a *universal*, mythic art. On the one hand, such art claims a metaphysical significance, but on the other it remains separate from myths and rituals grounded in the *particular* oral traditions and community determinations that could justify the metaphysical pretensions.

2. Primitivism in Art

4

THE PRIMITIVE DIMENSION
IN SIGMUND FREUD'S
TOTEM AND TABOO

THE IDEAL AND THE REAL

In 1912 Sigmund Freud published "Some Points of Agreement between the Mental Lives of Savages and Neurotics," which was collected with three later articles a year later under the title *Totem and Taboo*.[1] Freud's text appeared in the same period, immediately before World War I, in which primitivism was being developed by the cubists in France and the expressionists in Germany and marks a turning point in the scientific analysis of "primitive" culture. Though it still retains much of the evolutionary framework of the anthropologists active at the time, *Totem and Taboo* develops the categories needed to reject this framework and radically alter the European perspective on both primitive culture and modern science.

In discussing this text in the context of primitivism, however, subsequent commentators have often equated Freud's views with those of anthropologists whom he cites, assuming that his primitivism simply reproduces their association of tribal cultures with instinctual behavior and an early stage in human development. Hal Foster writes, for instance:

> By *primitivism* I mean initially an association of racial others with instinctual impulses (the Rousseauist legacy in Freud) and/or with symptomatic conflicts (as in the subtitle of *Totem and Taboo: Some Points of Agreement between the Mental Lives of Savages and Neurotics* [1913]). But in a way that is both less obvious and more problematic I also mean an association of tribal peoples with *pregenital* orders of the drives, especially

oral and anal stages, an association in which genitality is often correlated with civilization as achievements beyond "the primitive." (An early line from *Totem and Taboo*: "the savage [is] a well-preserved picture of an early stage of our own development.")[2]

It is clear that European ethnocentric views of other societies were dominant in the nineteenth and early twentieth centuries and that Freud borrowed many of the ideas in *Totem and Taboo* from anthropological accounts that maintained such an evolutionary view of society.[3] However, his work was intimately connected with the advent of primitivism in that it did not simply follow but also overturned the assumptions underlying these views.

If the primitive were related to the uncanny or the repressed or pregenital stages of development as Foster argues, the primitive would indeed be reduced to a projection of a progressivist consciousness. But instead of performing such a reduction, Freud's work delineates a concept of the primitive in which it is an independent dimension in its own right that is active in every culture, not merely a projection of the European mind. Once this argument is uncovered, *Totem and Taboo* can be read as asserting that neurosis is a symptom of a modern culture in which the primitive dimension is ignored rather than of a "tribal" culture where the myths and rituals of the primitive dimension have a collective space in which to develop.

The difficulty in deriving such a view of the primitive from *Totem and Taboo* is that this view contradicts the anthropological theories of Edward B. Tylor and James George Frazer, whom Freud relied upon for support. But as this section will show, Freud's text is divided against itself, riven by an inner conflict between the primitivism of his psychological approach and the progressivism of the anthropological theories he is unwilling to directly contradict. Freud begins by citing Tylor, who used the opposition between the ideal and the real to demonstrate the inferiority of the fantastic and superstitious beliefs of "primitive" peoples when compared with modern science. Quoting Tylor, Freud describes the spiritual emphasis behind the magic of the "primitives" as a case of "mistaking ideal analogy for real connexion."[4] Freud then connects the concentration on the ideal over the real to a pathological view of the world by linking it to the thought of the mentally ill. He describes the primitive focus on the ideal as similar to the confusion between the real and the fantastic amongst the mentally ill and employs a term coined by one of his patients, the "omnipotence of thoughts," to describe this state.[5]

Although both Tylor and Freud affirm the value of ideas over things in primitive thought, their differing attitudes toward the primitive can be distinguished by the degree to which each is willing to affirm a continuity between primitive and modern thinking. Whereas Tylor considers the emphasis on the ideal a "mistake," Freud sees it as a psychologically plausible though pathological perception of the world. The third essay of *Totem and Taboo*, "Animism, Magic and the Omnipotence of Thoughts," is consequently built upon two opposing theses. On the one hand, Freud describes the primitive relation to the spiritual as a pathological state of fantasy production in both the primitive and the mentally ill. On the other hand, he recognizes that the structures of primitive thought are not necessarily "backward" and in fact have an important cultural value for modern culture. Freud constantly wavers between rejecting the validity of the spiritual aspect of primitive culture and attempting to explain the psychological necessities that create this aspect.

Freud quotes Tylor's arguments in order to revise them by providing his own interpretation of the difference between the ideal and the real. Freud consistently argues that the progressive evolution away from spiritual and superstitious explanations of the world and toward materialist, scientific ones traces a movement from the primitive to the modern. However, he revises the meaning of the terms *ideal* and *real* to explain their psychological significance. Instead of speaking of the ideal and the real, he investigates the tension between wishes and reality. By emphasizing the wish character of ideas, Freud transforms ideas into forces that act upon reality: "It is easy to perceive the motives which lead men to practise magic: they are human wishes. All we need to suppose is that primitive man had an immense belief in the power of his wishes."[6] By arguing that the ideal is actually another word for the wishes of the individual, Freud maintains the dichotomy that Tylor sets up, but alters the terms. Instead of concentrating on the human ability to match ideas with reality, Freud investigates the constant conflict between wishes and an outside reality. This revision transforms the opposition between ideal and real. Where Tylor distinguished the ideal and the real as two mutually exclusive worlds, Freud sees a constant conflict between the forces of desire and the forces of external necessity. But once Freud makes this shift, he sets the stage for an entirely new epistemology that is no longer based on the idea of universal and objective knowledge but rather on the primitivist idea that knowledge arises as a projection of human wishes.

Because it both relies on Tylor's thesis and alters it, Freud's *Totem and Taboo* demonstrates aspects of both a representational and a mimetic conception of cognition and cultural production. On the one hand, the representational model of culture is dominant when Freud uses the terms *fantasy* and *illusion* to describe the deficiencies of primitive thought. The basis of such deficiencies is the inability to distinguish between wishes and the real world: "We are thus prepared to find that primitive man transposed the structural conditions of his own mind into the external world."[7] Assuming a separation between idea and reality and using correspondence between the two as the measure of validity, Freud concludes that the primitives' belief in their ability to influence nature through their wishes is proof of their childish inability to distinguish between ideas and things. He describes the magical system of the primitives as an example of a narcissistic belief in the "omnipotence of thoughts" and characterizes the primitive worldview as a delusional one in which the primitive takes structures of the psyche and projects them onto the outside world. Following Tylor, Freud emphasizes that the structures of primitive thought are arbitrary and fantastic, replacing an objective outside reality with a desired one.

On the other hand, Freud's transformation of ideas into wishes as the primary category of analysis shifts the criteria for determining the validity of primitive beliefs. His revision of Tylor's theories moves him toward a mimetic understanding of culture that does not distinguish ideal objects from real objects and concentrates instead on a mediation of the forces of the psyche with the forces of the outside world. From this perspective, primitive beliefs should not be judged according to their correspondence to the world but according to how they function practically to structure behavior.

Freud agrees with Tylor in favoring a scientific materialism in order to reject primitive culture. Yet, while Tylor characterizes the primitive as a rejection of the real (or material) in favor of the ideal (or spiritual), Freud understands this "mistake" as psychologically justified and thus to a certain extent legitimate. Despite his dim view of the fantastic character of primitive thought, Freud's attempt to take primitive thought seriously and on its own terms allows him to uncover the psychological mechanisms that give validity to beliefs and rituals in primitive societies. Arguing that magic finds its latent justification in unconscious desires and restrictions, he shows how primitive modes of thought are not simply results of faulty thought processes. In ignoring the distinction between ideal and real, spiritual and material, primitive thought does not simply commit an error but develops according to an alternative logic in which the opposition between desires and necessities is more important than one between ideas and objects.

Freud not only describes such a logic, but in fact adheres to it in his arguments. Just as Nietzsche postulates a dissolution of the boundaries between subject and object and between thing-in-itself and appearances to uncover a realm of forces governing appearances, Freud integrates the material with the spiritual by conceiving the world as a conflict between human desires and external necessities. He is consequently able to uncover the psychological realities behind spiritual ideas in order to establish a material foundation for the spiritual in culture. Yet Freud's attempt to simultaneously maintain both a correspondence theory of knowledge and a psychological theory of oppositions between forces leads him toward the constantly equivocating statements about the primitive that mark his writing.

In redefining the real as the reality principle (that is, external necessity), Freud undertakes an analysis of primitive thought that attributes to it a latent coherence that can be discovered behind the manifest superstitions. His emphasis on the wish character of magic highlights the relation of these wishes to the mechanisms of the unconscious, which leads him to compare the primitive with the neurotic. As in his investigation of psychological illness where he attempts to understand how seemingly irrational behavior can make psychological sense within the consciousness of the neurotic taken as a logical system, he does not reject the ideas and wishes of the primitive out of hand. Recognizing the validity and significance of an "imagined reality" for the thought and behavior of the primitive as well as the neurotic, Freud treats the desired reality of the primitive as something coherent and sets out to investigate the psychological motivations for the details of primitive thought and behavior.[8]

Freud has two ways of validating the ideas of primitive magic. First, he maintains that the beliefs of the primitives gain credibility from the fact "that in the former instance [of the primitive], too, psychical reality—as to the form taken by which we are in no doubt—coincided at the beginning with factual reality; that primitive men actually *did* what all the evidence shows that they intended to do."[9] Here, Freud resorts to a correspondence theory of legitimation. To be valid the psychic reality must correspond to a real event in an outside factual reality. This materialistic method of explanation is analogous to Freud's attempt to explain neurotic behavior as being the result of past traumas that actually occurred during the childhood of the neurotic. This mode of explanation leads Freud to his dubious anthropological theory that humanity originates when the primal horde kills the father.[10]

At the same time, however, Freud also tries to legitimate primitive beliefs by demonstrating how they function as a complete psychological system on their own, regardless of whether they express a directly verifiable truth about factual events. He explains, for instance, that the rules of taboo are a set of restrictions on libidinal fulfillment that follow strict psychological rules when considered within the cultural system where they arise. To demonstrate this mechanism, he takes up James George Frazer's description of the rules of cleanliness and chastity that warriors of a particular tribe impose upon themselves in preparation for battle. Frazer demonstrates how these rules derive from the obviously false superstitions of the tribe. Freud, however, treats the superstitious explanation as the "manifest" one and then goes on to provide a "latent" psychological motivation for such rules: "None the less the fact remains that they have made an instinctual renunciation; and we can understand the position better if we suppose that the savage warrior submits to these restrictions as a counter-measure because he is on the point of yielding completely to the satisfaction of cruel and hostile impulses which are as a rule prohibited to him."[11] In this example, Freud demonstrates that the magic and superstition of primitives function in fact more like restrictions on their own activity than an exertion of power over nature. By understanding magic as a system of rules, Freud here begins to consider this system, not as a way of immediately gratifying wishes through fantasy, but exactly the opposite—as a means of restricting immediate inner desires in order to pursue long-term goals: "Though the grounds alleged for these prohibitions may belong to a magical context, yet the fundamental idea of gaining greater strength by renouncing some instinctual satisfaction remains unmistakable; and the hygienic root of the prohibition which lies alongside its magical rationalization must not be overlooked."[12] Freud characterizes this ability to recognize the limits of human desire and the necessity of repression—the reality principle—as the true measure of the development of a culture. According to this interpretation, primitive thought incorporates the reality principle through its system of restrictions and creates a mediation between desires and necessities rather than a projection of wishes onto reality. This process is not limited to tribal cultures but must take place in modern cultures as well, and Freud even goes so far as to relate the taboo restrictions of primitives to Kant's categorical imperative: "taboos still exist among us. Though expressed in a negative form and directed towards another subject-matter, they do not differ in their psychological nature from Kant's 'categorical imperative,' which operates in a compulsive fashion and rejects any conscious motives."[13]

The projection of psychic processes onto the outside world does not simply create delusions but leads to a "mental relief" of the tension of inner psychological conflicts.[14] If this is true, then the primitive projection of inner psychological conflicts can be interpreted as an attempt to create a juncture between inner psychology and the outside world of natural and social restrictions on individual desires. The primitive mediates the ideal with the real by relating to the real, not as a set of objects to be understood, but as a set of forces to be confronted on both an individual and a communal level. By understanding individual problems as collective ones, the primitive is able to integrate the outside world into the totality of individual experience.

REDEFINING PROGRESS

Freud's psychological reading of the primitive leads him toward an understanding of progress that diverges markedly from that articulated by Frazer. Freud begins by appropriating Frazer's characterization of primitive thought as a situation in which "men mistook the order of their ideas for the order of nature, and hence imagined that the control which they have, or seem to have, over their thoughts, permitted them to exercise a corresponding control over things."[15] Frazer concentrates on ideas as a set of given objects and then compares these ideal objects with real objects to determine if there is a direct correspondence. By doing so, he condemns primitive magic for being incapable of accurately matching the ideal signs of the psyche to the real referents of nature. He depicts an evolution of human culture from magic to religion to science in which an increasingly accurate perception of the real coincides with advances in the manipulation of nature: "Meanwhile the magicians, who may be repressed but cannot be extirpated by the predominance of religion, still addict themselves to their old occult arts in preference to the newer ritual of sacrifice and prayer; and in time the more sagacious of their number perceive the fallacy of magic and hit upon a more effectual mode of manipulating the forces of nature for the good of man; in short, they abandon sorcery for science."[16] The primary criterion for choosing science over sorcery is the ability to manipulate nature. Whereas primitives confuse the ideal with the real, the scientific mind can distinguish the ideal order of the mind from the real order of nature for the purpose of controlling nature more efficiently. The two assumptions that underlie this representational view are that the natural order is an objective and universally valid set of objects and relationships and that it is possible to directly perceive and depict this order. The validity of a system of thought is to be judged by whether it allows one to construct a mirror image of the real world so as to then control it.

Freud constructs a development that names Frazer's same three stages of magic, religion, and science but alters the criteria for categorizing these three stages. Whereas for Frazer the progress of a culture can be measured by its ability to manipulate the forces of nature, Freud emphasizes exactly the opposite—the ability to recognize the power of nature and necessity. Freud places the primitive at a lower stage of an evolutionary progression because the primitive lacks a sense of the limits that nature sets upon human desires.

> At the animistic stage men ascribe omnipotence to *themselves*. At the religious stage they transfer it to the gods but do not seriously abandon it themselves, for they reserve the power of influencing the gods in a variety of ways according to their wishes. The scientific view of the universe no longer affords any room for human omnipotence; men have acknowledged their smallness and submitted resignedly to death and to the other necessities of nature. None the less some of the primitive belief in omnipotence still survives in men's faith in the power of the human mind, taking account, as it does, of the laws of reality.[17]

Freud constructs a philosophy of history that describes the evolution from primitive to religious to scientific worldviews as an increasing ability to recognize the power of necessity as a limitation on human desires and needs. At this point, it is no longer the ability to match ideas with real objects that determines the sophistication of a system of thought. Rather, the crucial issue is whether one recognizes the limits that necessity and death place on human wishes and aspirations. The recognition of the power of the forces of nature determines progress and not, as Frazer argues, a knowledge of and manipulation of the objects of nature.

Freud reinterprets the meaning of the "real" by relating it to the necessities that nature imposes upon humankind, death being the primary exigency to which the individual must submit him or herself. At the end of the passage just quoted, Freud even notes that the modern individual's confidence in his or her own ability to manipulate nature is a sign of the persistence of primitive ideas in modern society. At the same time, he notes that primitive cultures can recognize limits on human endeavor just as well as modern cultures can: "If the survivors' position in relation to the dead was really what first caused primitive man to reflect, and compelled him to hand over some of his omnipotence to the spirits and to sacrifice some of his freedom of action, then these cultural products would constitute a first acknowledgment of Ἀναγχη [Necessity], which opposes human narcissism. Primitive man would thus be submitting to the supremacy of death with the same gesture with which he seemed to be denying it."[18] At this point, it becomes increasingly unclear just what constitutes a modern and what a primitive relation to reality because Freud, in the course of his essay, has revised the meaning of "recognition of reality." He begins with Frazer's and Tylor's understanding of it as the ability to match an ideal image to an outside reality and uses this understanding to describe the primitive "omnipotence of thoughts." However, Freud later suggests that the ability to recognize the limits that nature and, particularly, death place on human aspirations is the guiding factor in determining the primitivity or modernity of a system of thought. This new understanding of reality as "reality principle" brings confusion into the neat evolution from primitive to scientific outlined by Frazer. Freud himself notes that elements of primitive consciousness exist in modern society and vice versa. Yet, if we take Frazer's view ("manipulating the forces of nature for the good of man") as being typical of a modern consciousness, we find that Freud's redefinition of the real creates a reversal in the evaluation of primitive and modern, even though Freud himself does not point this out.[19] The primitive worldview that recognizes the limitations of human aspiration and the power of nature is more sophisticated for Freud than the modern idea of a domination of nature.

But rather than simply reversing the direction of development, positing "primitive" culture as more advanced than "modern" ones, Freud's theories ultimately overturn the entire idea of evolution as a concept that can be meaningfully applied to compare different human cultures. This does not mean that *primitive* and *modern* lose their meanings entirely. Instead, *primitive* is redefined to refer to a particular dimension of every culture in which psychological conflicts such as the recognition of death are played out and given collective expression. The "primitive" becomes important in a culture in all those cases, such as death, when human endeavor is frustrated by natural limitations. By contrast, "modern" would refer to cultures in which there exists such a faith in the technical abilities of humans that the primitive dimension is thought to be no longer relevant. Because its belief in the unlimited abilities of human problem-solving leads to the idea of the obsolescence of the primitive dimension of myth and ritual, the "modern" attitude is, according to Freud's categories, the pathological one—a state of delusional belief in the "omnipotence of thoughts."

BEYOND FREUD

Despite the conclusions that can be drawn about the primitive from Freud's investigation of the relation between individual psychology and primitive culture, his own evaluation of this relation assumes that nonmodern cultures are the pathological ones. Though he recognizes and describes the mechanisms that motivate the "pathologies" of the primitive, he still maintains the superiority of a scientifically based culture. In contrast to this view, later commentators have suggested that Freud's uncovering of psychological explanations for cultural productions points rather to the sophistication of "primitive" cultures, which are able to produce a continual communal "cure" for otherwise endemic individual maladies.

This line of reasoning is already implicit in Freud's argument about the relation between neurotics and primitives. In his description of the centrality of death for neurotics, for instance, Freud describes how primitive beliefs, in addressing the issue of death, create a collective reaction to a problem that affects the psychology of each individual member simultaneously: "Schopenhauer has said that the problem of death stands at the outset of every philosophy;

93

and we have already seen that the origin of the belief in souls and in demons, which is the essence of animism, goes back to the impression which is made upon men by death."[20] Because death is not just a primary issue for every individual's psychology but a defining one for a culture, the link between individual psychology and the beliefs and constructions of a culture leads to a collective mediation between the inner world of the psyche and the outer world of nature.

Developing this relation between individual psychology and communal myths, Harold Bloom insists on "the sad, simple, and truthful translation of totem into psychoanalyst and of taboo into transference."[21] According to this translation, the cultural constructions of a primitive community perform the same function that psychoanalysis has taken over in modern society. A. L. Kroeber elaborates on this possibility:

> The experience of first-hand observers will probably be unanimous that primitive communities, like peasant populations, contain very few individuals that can be put into a class with the numerous neurotics of our civilization. The reason seems to be that primitive societies have institutionalized such impulses as with us lead to neuroses. The individual of neurotic tendency finds an approved and therefore harmless outlet in taboo, magic, myth, and the like, whereas the non-neurotic, who at heart remains attached to reality, accepts these activities as forms which do not seriously disturb him. In accord with this interpretation is the fact that neurotics appear to become numerous and characteristic in populations among whom religion has become decadent and "enlightenment" active, as in the Hellenistic, Roman Imperial, and recent eras; whereas in the Middle Ages, when "superstition" and taboo were firmly established, there were social aberrations indeed, like the flagellants and children's crusade, but few neurotics. Much the same with homosexuality, which the North American and Siberian natives have socialized. Its acceptance as an institution may be a departure from normality, but has certainly saved countless individuals from the heavy strain which definite homosexualists undergo in our civilization.[22]

Though Freud himself does not develop this line of reasoning, Kroeber demonstrates that Freud's arguments can be extended to reveal possible therapeutic properties of various cultural productions. The psychological argument about the relation between individual psychology and cultural constructions such as myths and rituals opens the way to an understanding of the primitive that sees it as a constant aspect of human culture.

Claude Lévi-Strauss goes even further than Kroeber in order to completely dissolve the distinction between neurotic and nonneurotic and between myth and reality in the primitive condition. On the one hand, myth is a means for preventing individual neuroses by collectively expressing and addressing conflicts that arise in *every* individual consciousness and not just among neurotics. On the other hand, the justification for myth rests, not on a relation to certain historical events or primal archetypes, but on the continual repetition of particular conflicts within the consciousness of each individual to whom a myth might speak. Lévi-Strauss formulates this possibility in terms of a critique of Freud's analysis:

> The failure of *Totem and Taboo*, far from being inherent in the author's proposed design, results rather from his hesitation to avail himself of the ultimate consequences implied in his premises. He ought to have seen that phenomena involving the most fundamental structure of the human mind could not have appeared once and for all. They are repeated in their entirety within each consciousness, and the relevant explanation falls within an order which transcends both historical successions and contemporary correlations. Ontogenesis does not reproduce phylogenesis, or the contrary. Both hypotheses lead to the same contradictions. One can speak of explanations only when the past of the species constantly recurs in the indefinitely multiplied drama of each individual thought, because it is itself only the retrospective projection of a transition which has occurred, because it occurs continually.

As far as Freud's work is concerned, this timidity leads to a strange and double paradox. Freud successfully accounts, not for the beginning of civilization but for its present state; and setting out to explain the origin of a prohibition, he succeeds in explaining, certainly not why incest is consciously condemned, but how it happens to be unconsciously desired.[23]

According to Lévi-Strauss, the present significance of myth is not its ability to recount actual events in a culture's history, as Freud argues, but its ability to reenact conflicts that recur in the development of each individual belonging to the culture.[24] Thus, the reality of the myth is not to be understood literally and representationally, as a recounting of factual events in a history, but rather psychologically and mimetically, as a reenactment of conflicts that recur as a result of competing forces acting upon all members of a community. Lévi-Strauss locates the identity of nonmodern and modern culture in the fact that both share a certain "primitive" sphere of consciousness in which conflicts between desires and external necessity meet and demand resolution in each individual. The resolution consists of a formal reenactment that is carried out, ideally, in myth and ritual and, alternatively, in art and psychoanalysis.

If one follows Lévi-Strauss in drawing out the consequences of Freud's premises in *Totem and Taboo*, it becomes clear that Freud's accomplishment was to discover that the purely "psychic" processes such as those found in primitive myths are not arbitrary. They are actually structured according to those unresolved conflicts of human life that continue to recur in individual consciousness. This insight leads to the recognition of the value and continuing significance of myth as a collective depiction of these conflicts.

Life's unresolved conflicts continue to afflict individual consciousness even when modern society denies the validity of myth. The primitive dimension does not disappear with modernity; the forces that dominate it are still active, but they are compelled to find alternative forms of expression. Freud notes that modern art still operates with the structures of primitive thought: "In only a single field of our civilization has the omnipotence of thoughts been retained, and that is in the field of art. Only in art does it still happen that a man who is consumed by desires performs something resembling the accomplishment of those desires and that what he does in play produces emotional effects—thanks to artistic illusion—just as though it were something real. People speak with justice of the 'magic of art' and compare artists to magicians."[25] Freud points out a connection between the magical practices of the primitive and the creative imagination of the artist that is based on the ability of both to present inner ideas and wishes as if they were real. At the same time, he notes a crucial difference between myth and art: "But the comparison is perhaps more significant than it claims to be. There can be no doubt that art did not begin as art for art's sake. It worked originally in the service of impulses which are for the most part extinct to-day. And among them we may suspect the presence of many magical purposes."[26] In comparing the magical art of the primitive with modern "art for art's sake," Freud assumes that there is a progression from the former to the latter. He places the different styles of art (primitive magic, representational, art for art's sake) into an evolutionary development that progresses further and further from the original "impulses which are for the most part extinct to-day." Freud describes this evolution as one from a belief in the importance of the ideal to an admission that the ideal in art is merely an "illusion." Magic's original claim to reality has been rejected in favor of an art that denies all relation to reality. Yet the progression from primitive magic toward art for art's sake was precisely the trend against which expressionist artists were revolting as Freud was writing *Totem and Taboo*. Rather than as a development, they saw this progression as art's abdication of its social role. To reconstruct this role, the expressionists sought to recover a mythic function for art in contemporary society.

5

ABSTRACT ART AND THE
PRIMITIVE SPIRIT IN THE WORK
OF WASSILY KANDINSKY

The first studies of primitivism concentrated on the formal structures common to both twentieth-century European and primitive art. This led art historians and then anthropologists to take an interest in these formal aspects of African art rather than using this art merely as a source of anthropological documentation of cultural practices. Robert Goldwater's seminal work on primitivism describes this interest in form as an important step toward gaining a genuine appreciation of foreign cultures, a step that was enabled by the European attack on inherited classicist aesthetic ideals.[1] More recently, William Rubin has described primitivism as an "affinity of the tribal and the modern" because, on the one hand, primitive and modern art share formal affinities that make them comparable and equally valid and because, on the other, both primitive and twentieth-century European aesthetics emphasize the inner form of the work of art rather than its ability to imitate reality.[2]

Many writers have criticized this concentration on the formal qualities of both twentieth-century European and "tribal" works of art because focusing on form decontextualizes the works, obscuring the specific social context within which all art is produced as well as the imperialist violence that was the prerequisite for the West to be in a position to appreciate primitive art. Patricia Leighten disputes the formal character of cubist primitivism by arguing that the subject matter and social context of Picasso's *Les Demoiselles d'Avignon* are at least as important to its revolutionary effect as the formal qualities.[3] Similarly, for Hal Foster the formal affinities that Rubin notes between the primitive and the modern "seemed derived in equal part from the formalist reception of the primitive read back into the tribal work and from the radical abstraction performed on both sets of objects."[4] According to this viewpoint, the Museum of Modern Art's emphasis on form is a denial of the particularity of other cultures and a means for commodifying primitive art. As a possible alternative to such an imperialist stance, Marianna Torgovnick and James Clifford stress the differences between the origins of African art and their function within Western culture.[5] Thomas McEvilley develops this argument by emphasizing the distinction between the Western "making of objects whose only or primary function is pure contemplation and aesthetic appreciation" and the "functional types of image-making and craftsmanship" that prevail in "[m]ost of the world's cultures."[6]

Yet because these attempts to illuminate social context are framed within a critique of a formalist approach, they have lost a consciousness of the intimate relation between form and social context. Jill Lloyd's book, for instance, places expressionism within a social context of primitivizing attitudes that were prevalent in early-twentieth-century Europe, and it consequently depicts expressionist primitivism more as a question of social attitudes than of aesthetic form. She focuses on *Brücke* artists such as Max Pechstein and Emil Nolde to the exclusion of artists connected with *Der Blaue Reiter*, such as Kandinsky and Marc. Doing so enables her to show that the expressionist fascination for the primitive is merely an inversion and not a subversion of the older evolutionist denigration of the primitive.[7] In her account, both expressionist fascination and evolutionist denigration lead to a view of Oceanic and African cultures as original and undifferentiated states that are to be strictly differentiated from European culture. She never presents the possibility of perceiving these cultures without the prejudices of a colonialist perspective.

Lloyd's critique of expressionist exoticism depends on a rejection of the concentration on form characteristic of cubist primitivism, or at least of the Museum of Modern Art perspective on it.[8] For this reason, she and most of the other critics who have taken this approach in recent years are left in a difficult bind when they evaluate the primitive. Their critique of both exoticism and the concentration on form results in a general suspicion toward attempts to recuperate primitive art as a valid model for European art. But to the extent that they deem such recuperations to be impossible, they must insist on the radical difference between primitive and Western and deny the specificity of the term *primitive*. They must equate the civilized/primitive distinction with the Western/Other distinction. As a result, the primitive dimension is either denied as a valid category in itself, or this category is relegated to other cultures defined as "Other." Either way, the specifically primitive dimension of European culture is ignored, which further exoticizes both the primitive and the non-European.

In contrast to this approach, the analysis of Kandinsky's primitivism that follows will develop an idea of the primitive that is cross-cultural, in which the primitive is defined as a dimension of every culture rather than a label for foreign ones. In his 1993 essay, Foster begins to move toward such a perspective by recognizing that primitivism, for all its racist and sexist overtones, nevertheless delineates a space of critique within European culture: "Its [the avant-garde's] identification with 'the primitive,' however imaged as dark, feminine, and profligate, remained a *dis*identification with white, patriarchal, bourgeois society."[9] As Torgovnick later attempts to show, the "disidentification" contained in primitivism was not simply a negation; it had a positive content as well. She uncovers a critical dimension of primitivism in her comparison of male and female perspectives on the primitive and in her recognition that "primitivism is much more about 'us' than about them.' "[10] However, Torgovnick does not consider the formal structure of the primitive but rather equates the primitive with "the oceanic" and a "sense of coming out of the self and interdependence with the universe."[11] For this reason, her study remains within the bounds of a rationalist perspective in which the primitive is seen as either an idyllic harmony with the universe or as a violent and dangerous void.[12] As I hope to show, an alternative view of the primitive, unencumbered by this rationalist approach, can only be discerned by considering form.

Peg Weiss's book *Kandinsky and Old Russia: The Artist as Ethnographer and Shaman* begins to describe such an alternative primitivist perspective in expressionism by documenting Kandinsky's intimate familiarity with primitive cultures and his desire to emulate primitive art in his painting. For Weiss, "The healing role of the shaman in primitive society became a metaphor for the role Kandinsky felt the artist should play in the modern world."[13] She not only demonstrates the enduring importance of Kandinsky's ethnographic encounters with the shamanistic cultures of northern Russia for the development of motifs in his painting.[14] She also provides a convincing argument for the formal similarities between his paintings and primitive works of art such as the drawings on Siberian Lapp shaman drums.[15]

From Weiss's discussion, one can infer that Kandinsky combined the primitivism of cultural goals associated with the *Brücke* artists with the "formal" primitivism of the cubists to promote an aesthetically based, yet broad social project that envisions a fundamental transformation of European culture away from materialism and toward spirituality. Artists such as Pechstein and Nolde understood the primitive to be a characteristic of certain exotic cultures that they visited, and their work demonstrated a thematic interest in South Seas cultures. Expressionists connected with *Der Blaue Reiter* on the other hand attempted to understand the primitive as a certain spiritual dimension of all human culture. They did not work with dichotomies of Western versus non-Western or primitive versus modern but with the distinction between the spiritual and the material. They thereby retained a cultural understanding of primitive forms, not in order to distinguish between European and primitive, but to distinguish between primitive and civilized tendencies within European culture.

At the same time, the artists of *Der Blaue Reiter* saw a formal connection between their primitivism and the goals of primitive artists working in other cultures.[16] How did Kandinsky define this formal connection? Though Weiss documents the formal affinities between Kandinsky's work and that of "primitive" cultures, she does not provide an explanation for the connection between primitivism and abstraction. Yet such an explanation is crucial for understanding not just how primitive art influenced Kandinsky's work but to show, as I will attempt to do, how his most advanced techniques of abstraction were inconceivable outside of a primitivist project.

Wassily Kandinsky, Motley Life (Das bunte Leben)*, 1907, tempera and gouache on canvas, 130 × 162.5 cm. Städtische Galerie im Lenbachhaus, Munich. © 2000 Artists Rights Society (ARS), New York/ADAGP, Paris.*

PRIMITIVISM AND ABSTRACTION

Kandinsky's interest in integrating a spiritual element into art began very early in his career, and his development as an artist can be interpreted as a systematic appropriation of the techniques of primitive religious art. Before becoming a painter, his ethnographic work in Russia dealt with folk culture and legends, and his early primitivism was very similar to that of Pechstein and Nolde in its borrowing of Gauguin's techniques.[17] While Gauguin painted colorful scenes of Breton and Tahitian traditional life and Pechstein and Nolde depicted folk life in Germany and the South Seas, Kandinsky painted similar images of folk gatherings in the Russian empire in works such as *Arrival of the Merchants* and *Motley Life* (see

Wassily Kandinsky, Sketch for "Composition II" (Skizze für Komposition II), *1910, oil on canvas, 97.5 × 131.2 cm. Photograph by Robert E. Mates, © The Solomon R. Guggenheim Foundation, New York. © 2000 Artists Rights Society (ARS), New York/ADAGP, Paris.*

above, left).[18] As he himself describes, these two paintings were steps in a development that led toward the creation of one of the first paintings demonstrating his more abstract style, *Composition II* (see above, right).[19] By 1911 Kandinsky's use of both Christian and Russian pagan religious iconography as the basis of several paintings was combined with a move toward abstraction, signaling a shift from the type of primitivism pursued by Gauguin or Pechstein.[20] These paintings use religious themes and symbols to express a spiritual content, yet they also demonstrate Kandinsky's attempt to appropriate the techniques of primitive art.

Will Grohmann notes that the religious paintings of 1910–1912 were influenced by the Bavarian paintings on glass, not only in terms of theme but also style and technique.[21] These paintings, which deal almost exclusively with religious themes, herald Kan-

Wassily Kandinsky, All Saints I (Allerheiligen I), *1911, glass painting,
34.5 × 40.5 cm. Städtische Galerie im Lenbachhaus, Munich. © 2000 Artists
Rights Society (ARS), New York/ADAGP, Paris.*

dinsky's turn toward abstraction through a gradual effacement of
recognizable objects and symbols. Many of the paintings that have
religious themes in their titles Kandinsky painted twice—once as
paintings on glass based on the Bavarian primitive models and a
second time as oil paintings in which the clear and recognizable
forms from the glass paintings become much less recognizable as
objects, though the general outlines and color schemes remain similar. Commentators have noted this pattern in order to "decipher"
the forms depicted in the oil paintings. For instance, Grohmann
notes the more realistic quality of the glass paintings of *St. George*,
All Saints, and *Small Pleasures* as compared with the oil versions of
the same paintings.[22] Rose-Carol Washton Long uses the close rela-

Wassily Kandinsky, All Saints II (Allerheiligen II), *1911, oil on canvas,
86 × 99 cm. Städtische Galerie im Lenbachhaus, Munich.*
© *2000 Artists Rights Society (*ARS*), New York/*ADAGP*, Paris.*

tion between the abstract oils and the more representational paintings on glass to argue that the shapes of the oils are derived from real
objects that are clearly defined in the glass paintings. In also emphasizing the predominance of religious themes in the work accompanying Kandinsky's move toward abstraction, Long shows that his
use of Christian religious symbols is the key to understanding his
more abstract works.[23] Thus, she too points out how paintings such
as *Sketch for "Composition II"* demonstrate the same religious iconography as the paintings on glass based on Bavarian models.[24] Her
explanation of Kandinsky's method of abstraction is that he sought
to hide the meaning of the images in order to achieve a more mysti-

Wassily Kandinsky, Composition V, *1911, oil on canvas, 190 × 275 cm. Private collection.* © *2000 Artists Rights Society (ARS), New York/ADAGP, Paris.*

cal effect. Describing how a painting such as *Composition V* repeats in a "veiled" manner the motifs presented in the watercolor *Sound of Trumpets* and the oil painting *All Saints II*, Long argues that Kandinsky's development toward abstraction was both an attempt to hold onto religious symbols so as to maintain a metaphysical meaning and a method of hiding the religious images in order to create a sense of mystery.[25]

Weiss uses a similar method to uncover in these paintings the shamanistic motifs that Kandinsky borrowed from his ethnographic knowledge of Siberian folk cultures. Of *Composition V* she writes: "Inspired by the example of primitive pictography, the artist adroitly compressed bits and pieces from his own syncretic iconography together with borrowings from the Persian miniature, a shaman's drum, and motifs of the *Kalevala*, reducing his pictorial universe to an iconography of skeletal remnants floating freely in an explosive constellation of events shrouded in a nebulous haze."[26]

She goes on to provide examples of correspondences between figures in the painting and similar figures from Lapp shaman drums.
When combined with Long's analysis, Weiss's description of Kandinsky's borrowings from Siberian folk culture demonstrates how
his syncretic vision brought together Christian and pagan motifs
into a single image.[27]

But while Long and Weiss provide convincing arguments for the
thematic continuity of Kandinsky's development and the persistence of Christian as well as Russian folk motifs in his paintings,
they do not provide an adequate explanation for the formal break
that separates *Motley Life* and *Arrival of the Merchants* from *Sketch
for "Composition II"* or *All Saints II* from *Composition V.* The crucial
issue in a comparison of the earlier and later paintings is the change
from one aesthetic to another. *All Saints II*, for example, exemplifies
a primitivist aesthetic through Kandinsky's use of religious motifs
and symbols such as the clearly recognizable images of saints and
angels. The primitivist element is also evident in a use of perspective
that does not depict the figures according to naturalistic size and
distance. Like the primitive and medieval models to which Kandinsky refers, the figures seem to float in an imaginary landscape in
which size and distance become measures of spiritual importance
and a gauge of spiritual relationships rather than of "accurate" physical perspectival relationships. Reorganizing figures within a spiritual rather than material landscape is for Kandinsky an intermedi-
ate step toward an "abstract" work of art that only depicts spiritual
forms and has done away with material objects.

Composition V presents another stage in this development toward
the depiction of a spiritual content. Here Kandinsky maintains the
color scheme and the general shapes of *All Saints II* but has transformed the recognizable figures into abstract shapes. His efforts result in a painting that demonstrates the same sense of movement,
complexity of form, color scheme, and decenteredness as *All Saints
II* but without the allegorical reference to specific recognizable objects. The recognizable figures of *All Saints II* have been transformed in the second painting into an ensemble composed more of
lines and color than of distinct and recognizable objects.

The point of Kandinsky's efforts to dissolve both the empirical objects and the religious symbols into less and less recognizable forms is not simply to create "a sense of mystery" or a "nebulous haze." It reflects his move away from the idea of representation as the basis of his aesthetic. As Jelena Hahl-Koch points out with regard to other paintings of the same period, "the quest for a motif is unimportant in comparison with the composition of the picture."[28] Kandinsky attempts to replace a representational aesthetic with a musical, compositional one in order to create a spiritual significance in a painting while eliminating the symbolic meaning that inevitably detracts from the pure image by diverting attention toward a narrative content.

This movement toward abstraction is intimately connected with Kandinsky's primitivism. With regard to the set of paintings that culminated in the abstract forms of *Composition VI*, Sixten Ringbom concludes: "The ultimate goal of the preliminary work was the elimination of the corporeal forms and the expression of a spiritual content."[29] Abstraction is not a purely formal innovation but a means for attaining a spiritual goal. As such, the abstract paintings attempt to follow the same path as primitive works of art that are not created as representations of material objects but as receptacles for spiritual forces.

THE PRIMITIVE SPIRIT

Kandinsky's rejection of material objects on the canvas stems from his conceptual rejection of material objects in culture in favor of a spiritual dimension. But once the relation to material objects and religious symbols is dissolved, it is necessary to find another way to lend "objectivity" to the work of art if it is not to remain a totally private construction. Kandinsky's search for an alternative understanding of art in which it could express a spiritual meaning without depending on objects or symbols for its effect coincides with his approach toward a primitivist aesthetic.

Kandinsky's primitivism is based on a philosophy of history that is cyclical not evolutionary, in which return and repetition are more important than continual progress away from an original source. He emphasizes that the important influences on an artist depend less upon the unity of a particular national tradition than "a similarity of the 'inner mood'" between one period and another. An artist's particular spiritual goals may correspond to the goals of artists of a totally different time and place. By opening up the possible range of models for artists to follow and by rejecting an evolutionary model of artistic development, he places the modern and the primitive artist on an equal footing and is able to recognize the possibility of learning from the latter. At the same time, he limits the arbitrariness of possible influences upon the modern artist by insisting that a congruence of inner goals must decide the relevance of one artistic style for the work of another time and place. In *On the Spiritual in Art* Kandinsky describes the orientation toward a substantive spirituality outside of art as the goal that links European artists to primitive ones:

> There exists, however, another outward similarity of artistic forms that is rooted in a deeper necessity. The similarity of inner strivings within the whole spiritual-moral atmosphere — striving after goals that have already been pursued, but afterward forgotten — this similarity of the inner mood of an entire period can lead logically to the use of forms successfully employed to the same ends in an earlier period. Our sympathy, our understanding, our inner feeling for the primitives arose partly in this way. Just like us, those pure artists wanted to capture in their works the inner essence of things, which of itself brought about a rejection of the external, the accidental.[30]

In arguing that both the primitive and the expressionist are more concerned with an inner spiritual essence than with external material appearances, Kandinsky describes a modern return to a primitivist aesthetic after a period of a materialist suppression of the spiritual. Rather than characterizing his own culture as having a primitive spirituality, he describes it as a period "in which the soul is neglected and deadened by materialistic views, by disbelief, and their resultant, purely practical strivings."[31] By developing what Richard Sheppard denotes as a "quasi-religious aesthetic," Kandinsky seeks to mobilize his art as a means for providing a spiritual antidote to the materialist deadening of the soul. As Sheppard explains, "After 1909, Kandinsky's 'struggle between the material and the spiritual' was shorthand for a struggle between the forces of religious spirituality on the one hand and the unholy alliance between demonic and materialistic forces on the other."[32]

According to Kandinsky, materialism has three unfavorable consequences for European art, which his art seeks to overcome. First, it leads to a "materialist" art based on the representation of material objects. Kandinsky interprets the rise of a realist aesthetic in the fifteenth century as a sign of decline in which art becomes lifeless: "Yesterday had a proper look at the wood carvings in the 'Germanic.' I realized quite clearly that you can see a definite striving to depict reality as early as the fifteenth century. And the more real a thing becomes, the more lifeless. Rococo looks like spasm of despair in the face of approaching mindless Realism."[33] Kandinsky sets up a history of European art in which the realist aesthetic that develops from the Renaissance through the nineteenth century must be seen as a steady diminishment of art's functions.

Second, materialism results in a concentration on the technical questions of art rather than on the substantive value questions that concern the entire society. He therefore rejects the purely ornamental as too technically oriented and locates the primitive tendencies of art in the construction of spiritual goals and values—the "what" of values as opposed to the "how" of techniques: "If, even today, we were to begin to dissolve completely the tie that binds us to nature, to direct our energies toward forcible emancipation and content ourselves exclusively with the combination of pure color and independent form, we would create works having the appearance of geometrical ornament, which would—to put it crudely—be like a tie or a carpet. Beauty of color and form (despite the assertions of pure aesthetes or naturalists, whose principal aim is 'beauty') is not a sufficient aim of art."[34]

Finally, he interprets the idea of "art for art's sake," in which art is cut off from reality, as a final desperate defense of an art that is surrounded by a materialist attitude. Because the real is equated with the material and the technical in a materialist age, the spiritual has no alternative but to express itself in the realm of a "pure" art having no relation to reality: "the opinion arises that 'pure' art is not given to man for a special reason, but is purposeless; that art exists only for art's sake (*l'art pour l'art*)."[35] Kandinsky criticizes the isolation of art from substantive goals but sees art for art's sake as the only escape for an art that is threatened by a subjugation to an instrumental rationality.

In opposition to these three characteristics of art in a materialist age (realist representation, concentration on technical questions, art for art's sake), Kandinsky attempts to conceive of an art that is both nonrepresentational and intimately connected with the society's construction of substantive values. As a consequence, when he discusses the importance of inner form as a replacement for representational accuracy when evaluating the work of art he subordinates inner form to a higher, spiritual value. Though Kandinsky judges painting according to inner form rather than representational accuracy, the form itself is not the goal: "It is not form (material) that is of prime importance, but content (spirit)."[36] The artist's task is to discover the form that can best mediate the desired spiritual content.[37] Rather than a mechanism that reproduces the appearance of things in nature, art is "a power that has a purpose and must serve the development and refinement of the human soul —the movement of the triangle."[38]

This employment of art as a spiritual tool for a culture establishes the primitivist direction of Kandinsky's art. For both the primitive and the primitivist the work of art is only the tangible form of the intangible spirit of a thing.[39] Thus, it is not a "tree" that one paints, but the "spirit" of the tree. Abstraction and inner form function as the means for mediating the spiritual aspect of a work of art, and art's cultural mission is to be a mediator of values through form.

Because goals and values belong to a realm of the nonmaterial that cannot be discussed scientifically, Kandinsky's critique of materialism leads him to affirm the role of art as the only viable mediator of values in a society.[40] Believing that the art of Europe has been trapped within a stifling materialism that has diverted it from its true role as this mediator, he looks to the art of primitives as the model for an art that might construct an approach to the spiritual:

"On the other hand, the number of people who set no store by the methods of materialistic science in matters concerning the 'nonmaterial,' or matter that is not perceptible to our senses, is at last increasing. And just as art seeks help from the primitives, these people turn for help to half-forgotten times, with their half-forgotten methods. These very methods, however, are still current among those people we have been accustomed to look upon with contemptuous sympathy from the heights of our knowledge."[41] To avoid a turn away from the real world and toward a purely aesthetic reality, Kandinsky claims that his focus on the spiritual is not a rejection of art's relation to the real world but rather an emphasis on a "nonmaterial" reality inaccessible to natural science. His opposition to science as a source of values and his affirmation of art as the only mediator of the spiritual defines his conception of culture as primitivist.

INTERNAL NECESSITY

Because the definition of the spiritual depends as much upon how the imagination constructs it as upon any objective reality that the spirit may have, the creation of Kandinsky's abstract work of art is in danger of becoming a highly subjective process. In the models of primitive art from both Christian and Russian folk traditions upon which Kandinsky relies, the work of art is embedded within a system of beliefs and values that is already familiar to the viewers and rules out an idiosyncratic reception. But the syncretic nature of the influences that Long and Weiss document also indicate that the beliefs of one particular religious tradition are not sufficient for determining the spiritual context of Kandinsky's paintings. Because they are not limited to an iconographic context, the Theosophical influences on Kandinsky's development outlined by Ringbom provide a better indication of the intellectual context of the abstract method.[42] But even here, it is fairly clear from Kandinsky's theoretical statements that his art is not meant just for Theosophists but for his entire epoch. As Ringbom recounts,

Kandinsky assumed an affinity between Theosophy and his own generation of artists who both turn to the primitives in search of *inner* knowledge; we can now sense the extent of this affinity. Mme Blavatsky's "eternal truth"—to which Kandinsky explicitly refers—has an exact counterpart in his own "purely and eternally artistic." The former is present in all religion, the latter in all art. Both represent an inner spiritual core, and both are now, on the threshold of the Spiritual Era seeking expression, the former as Theosophy, the latter as abstract art. Together with Theosophy abstract art will prepare mankind for a spiritual renewal.[43]

In following the Theosophical idea that there is a universal basis for spiritual forms and in seeking to arrive at this basis in his art, Kandinsky begins to ignore the specific external context. His primitivism is thus marked by a universalist project, which both sets it apart from the primitive art he emulates but also ends up stifling the very spiritual aspect he sought to revive by isolating it from the community context that would give it meaning.

Because the primitive art Kandinsky emulated was always embedded in a specific tradition, abstract forms did not exist for themselves but were always implicitly augmented with associations from the cultural context in which they were produced. As a consequence, abstraction was not a means for banning external reality from the work of art but the opposite: a way of integrating this reality into the fixed form. The specific assumptions of a cultural tradition served to bind the abstract forms into their context. Though a representational content is often absent in these works of art, the context fills in the content, and the abstract form becomes a vessel in which the context unfolds.[44]

Kandinsky, however, did not see himself as working within a particular belief system or religious tradition. Rather, he sought to develop through abstraction a universal language of art that would provide a direct link between artist and viewer without the detour through a specific cultural context. He saw in Theosophy, not a particular creed, but a universal theory of colors and forms that could help him arrive at such a universal language. Here, Kandinsky does not accept the symbolic meanings attached by Theosophists to specific colors: "The influence worked on a more general and fundamental level than in isolated details such as the meaning of single colours."[45] Using Theosophical theories of the spiritual world as a model, Kandinsky developed ideas of form and color in which they became separated from the representational subject of the painting so they could exist on their own. Rather than a specific system of beliefs and experiences, an "internal necessity" governs the formal constructions of the artist and determines their aesthetic beauty: *"Whatever arises from internal, spiritual necessity is beautiful. The beautiful is that which is inwardly beautiful."*[46]

Kandinsky's two explanations for how internal necessity functions lead him to two opposing theories of the way in which the work of art establishes its legitimacy for an audience. The first explanation is similar to Carl Einstein's in that it is able to integrate form with social context. In it, the ensemble of elements in an image constructs a set of oppositions that, taken together, form a unified whole organized according to an internal necessity.[47] Kandinsky takes music as his model of a pure art in which the organic whole is more important than the representation of reality.[48] He then extrapolates from the compositional form of music in order to apply the idea of composition to painting. He struggles against the prejudices that favor realist representation in art to concentrate on the compositional aspects of a work of art, which are defined by the oppositions between colors and by the abstract images of graphic form. As an example he describes the effect of a red dress as a function of its place in the ensemble: "The effect produced, however, is reciprocal, since the red of the dress acts upon the figure clothed in this same red, and vice versa."[49] By defining inner necessity in terms of an ensemble of relations within the work of art, Kandinsky opens the possibility that this ensemble might reenact a particular structure of relations outside of the work of art, in the consciousness of the viewer. In this case, the composition creates an aesthetic structure that is analogous to a structure of consciousness. While this means that the work of art depends upon a prior context in order to be understood, it also implies that the relation to experience and external necessities is crucial for the unfolding of the work of art.

In contrast to this first explanation, the second explanation of inner necessity is based on a theory of color and form that closes off the relation to an outside context by assuming that each specific color and shape has an "inner sound" that is "self-sufficient and completely independent."[50] Kandinsky describes, for instance, the inner values of various colors:

> Yellow easily becomes acute and cannot sink to great depths. Blue becomes acute only with difficulty and cannot rise to great heights.
>
> The ideal balance of these two colors—diametrically opposed in every respect—when they are mixed, produces green. The horizontal movement of one color cancels out that of the other. The movement toward and away from the center cancels itself out in the same way. Tranquility results. This logical conclusion can easily be arrived at theoretically. And the direct effect upon the eye and, finally, through the eye upon the soul, gives rise to the same result. This fact has been known not only to doctors (and in particular to oculists), but to everyone for some time. Absolute green is the most peaceful color there is: it does not move in any direction, has no overtones of joy or sorrow or passion, demands nothing, calls out to no one.[51]

This attempt to assign fixed values to different colors is an attempt to emancipate colors from a strict adherence to "realistic" renderings of colors in nature, making it possible for instance to paint a "red horse."[52] But at the same time Kandinsky's spiritual catalog of color effects runs the risk of arbitrarily pinning down the spiritual value of colors according to a private schema that he understands to be universal.

Ringbom points out that Kandinsky's notion of inner necessity depends upon a supernatural schema in which colors and forms have specific "vibrations" that resound in the entire cosmos, thus guaranteeing that the artist's vision will be reproduced in the consciousness of the viewer:

> The world sounds, the artist participates in the inner world with his inner element, the soul of the artist vibrates, and by means of colours, sounds and words the artist evokes corresponding vibrations in the soul of the beholder. Art, in the last

resort, is *knowledge* achieved by fine vibrations in the soul; this is the "ultimate goal" which Kandinsky shared with Theosophy and the answer to what we have called the "problem of information." The abstract artist does not observe his subject in the way a realist looks at the reality he is reproducing on his canvas; nor does he "see" the spiritual reality in the clairvoyant manner which the Theosophists claimed to be able to do. The abstract work instead emerges "out of the artist" shaped by the soul vibrations which are a resonance of the sounding cosmos, and this process in [*sic*] the guarantee for the connexion between the inner, spiritual content of the work and the inner, spiritual element of the world.[53]

This limiting of color and form to an "inner sound" fixes the meaning of an abstract shape or color as an objective entity whose significance is determined prior to the encounter with the experiences of a specific viewer. By postulating a set of inner sounds that retain values in and of themselves, Kandinsky's theory of art seeks to establish a universal theory of color and form applicable to all art. But in doing so, it undermines the relationship between the composition and the specific cultural context of the viewer. If the meaning of color and inner form are defined prior to the concrete viewing experience, this encounter becomes superfluous for the significance of the work of art.

EXTERNAL NECESSITY

Unless one accepts on faith the supernatural explanation of a "sounding cosmos," a particular color or image cannot have a universal significance.[54] Rather, the significance of a color or an entire painting will depend on the associations it forms within a particular viewer. Because a color or a form depends upon the viewer's associations to attain its final determination, objectivity is not universal but communal, dependent upon a set of common cultural experiences that unite the viewer with the creator of the work of art. Realist art could claim to be universal because a viewer from any culture could recognize the content of the painting. But this universality was purchased at the price of reducing art to the function of being a representation of material objects. When Kandinsky's art abandons the reference to empirical objects as its link to the viewer and becomes abstract in order to mediate a spiritual content it becomes far more dependent upon a cultural context to create its significance for the viewer. The work of art becomes the nexus at which the parameters of this context manifest themselves, and abstract art depends much more on an external context to gain meaning than does realist art. This is true because for abstract art the external world does not consist of material objects (as with realist art), but of the external, natural forces that are beyond human control and that shape the construction of meaning for a particular culture.

In his critique of art's isolation from substantive goals, Kandinsky does not recognize the importance of external necessity to the creation of art. Instead, he proposes inner form and internal necessity as the determinants of nonrepresentational art, a conception that depends, as Ringbom shows, on supernatural explanations of art's effects. In concentrating on art as a creator of goals and values, Kandinsky neglects art as a mediator between these goals and external necessities.

By rejecting any connection to external necessity in abstract art and by searching for an internal necessity to guarantee art's objectivity, he runs the risk of trapping his art within a private hermeticism that underrates the central role that cultural context plays in determining the exigencies that define the meaning of art. As Carl Einstein remarks: "His [Kandinsky's] spiritual purism retains a piece of old Christian metaphysics: the doctrine of the absolute, hermetic spirit."[55] An inner sound that emanates from a color or shape and is independent of its context remains trapped in an absolute, hermetic world. This aspect of Kandinsky's theory of form prevents the mediation of inner with outer forces that can only arise parabolically out of the relationship between individual elements in a composition. As Einstein notes, "Kandinsky concerns himself too little with the overall relation of colors and overlooks the relationships by which those colors first attain a meaningful determination."[56]

The danger of a private hermeticism in Kandinsky's work leads to both a notion of relativistic truth that changes with each viewer and a universalist mysticism that claims that the work of art has a direct access to a transcendent and metaphysical state of "being" preceding external reality. Kandinsky demonstrates the relativist implications of his theory in his description of beauty and truth: "The ear has to capture what is necessary to it. This necessity comprises beauty and truth. For that reason there is neither a single beauty nor a single truth. There are as many of each as there are souls in the world."[57] In contrast to this relativist stance concerning truth, where it becomes independent of collective determinations, Einstein emphasizes that aesthetic truth is a collective construction that must legitimate itself through the development of a group consensus.[58] For Einstein, this latter view of aesthetic truth is the only valid one if one is to maintain the idea that art has a spiritual function. Outside of such a group consensus, aesthetic truth becomes a private neurosis rather than a collective myth.

Kandinsky's denial of cultural context as the final bearer of significance in a work of art also leads to a universalist vision of art. This vision has been praised by Philippe Sers because it constructs "metaphysical images," but it has been criticized by Mark Cheetham for its "essentialism." For Sers, the inner necessity of a work of art is grounded in an ontological structure of "Being," which exists as a unified objective reality behind all appearances and is expressed directly in the abstract work of art.[59] But to the extent that the existence of this inner content cannot be proved and must be taken on faith, it is actually just a cultural construction shared only by a small community rather than a universal foundation for art and spirituality. The belief in a universality prior to external appearances allows Kandinsky and interpreters such as Sers to discount both external limits and cultural context as being constitutive for the work of art. The result is the false belief that the soul vibrations pointing to an inner necessity are the source of art rather than an effect.

Though Kandinsky cannot be held directly responsible for Sers's metaphysics of "Being" (the relativist reading of his theories, for example, is also a possibility), this reading of Kandinsky's theories is certainly compatible with his own radical rejection of external reality in favor of inner necessity.[60] In moving away from material objects and toward abstract objects, Kandinsky's understanding of the abstract as an inner sound recreates on the ideal level of abstract objects the static objectification that he criticizes in the material world. His rejection of material objects ends up defining the work of art as the representation of spiritual objects.

Kandinsky's limiting of the spiritual to an abstract inner sound results from his tendency to differentiate strictly between the spiritual, inner world and the material, external world.[61] In setting up this strict differentiation, Kandinsky according to Einstein "retreats into a tenderly submissive fear of things, which he supports through the old opposition of spirit and worldly materiality without however mentioning the fruitfulness of material resistance (one of his most typical advantages). The freedom of expression after which he strives is founded upon a constrictive negation."[62] As Einstein emphasizes, the artist's attempt to turn away from the world and create out of an inner subjectivity will never accomplish a break with materiality. The subject itself after all can never escape its own bodily existence, and the retreat into interiority will perforce recreate on the subjective level the materiality and exteriority that Kandinsky seeks to leave behind.

Yet this inescapable corporality of the subject also guarantees that, in spite of his flawed theories of form and color, Kandinsky's paintings can still attain the type of spiritual effects that he seeks as long as he retains his commitment to following his subjective impulses. For the idea of internal necessity does not necessarily lead to an "essentialist" position, as Cheetham contends. It can also make sense within a vision of art in which the subjective impulses directing its creation exemplify the play of forces that govern an external reality outside the subject and the work of art.[63] Kandinsky's focus on internal necessity can thus function to create a mimesis of the forces of nature that maintains the primitivist element in the work of art. This is especially evident in many of the later paintings such as *Division-Unity*, *Animated Stability*, *Dusk*, and *Circle and Square*.[64] As a consequence, Kandinsky's work cannot be understood only within the context of a Western, Platonic tradition that applies an "essentialist metaphysic" to art. Nor can it be understood as part of civilization's "separation between the image and the prototype," the antithesis of a primitive merging, based on analogy, of subject and object, image and reality.[65]

Kandinsky's work is marked by a constant conflict between a primitivist and a universalist impulse. On the one hand, he attempts in his art to create compositions that operate according to a primitive aesthetic in that they attempt to gain meaning through the relations between elements, allowing a parabolical or analogical relation to the viewer's experience. Working within this aesthetic, his art may reject mimesis of material objects as its organizing principle, but it nevertheless maintains a connection to nature by imitating external forces as they express themselves through internal necessity.[66] In this conception, the work of art can only make sense within a particular cultural context, and its meaning cannot be universal. On the other hand, Kandinsky also sees abstraction as the attempt to discover a set of universal and objective inner sounds that emanate from specific forms such as the color yellow or the shape of a circle. This approach tends to objectify the spiritual, transforming it into the "dead" matter that Kandinsky seeks to overcome. His career is determined by this tension between the primitivist and the universalist understandings of the spiritual significance of abstract form. Yet, within the larger context of European primitivism, Kandinsky's work is unique in its power to link abstraction to primitivism in a way that renders European art into an enactment of the primitive rather than an objectification.

6

CONSTRUCTION AND MIMESIS
IN CARL EINSTEIN'S
THEORY OF ART

At the beginning of his seminal work on African sculpture, *Negro Sculpture* (*Negerplastik*, 1915), Carl Einstein criticizes the European prejudice against African art, which either denies its status as art or relegates it to a position of inferiority.[1] This prejudice is connected with two different but equally inadequate philosophies of history. On the one hand, evolutionary theories of art lead to the idea that primitive art is the most rudimentary level of a progression. On the other hand, the romantic interest in the primitive results in a static notion of the primitive that limits it to specific cultures and separates it from European art.[2] In contrast to these two notions, Einstein's own perspective on primitive art is distinguished by his alternative philosophy of history, which allows for a congruence between the primitive and twentieth-century European.[3] For Einstein, history does not evolve according to an overarching logic or follow the fixed categories of a mythic past. It is a constant reconstruction determined by the particular exigencies of the present moment, and he describes the new interest of European artists in African art as the construction of "a newly conceived object."[4]

As Einstein points out, for Europeans to be able to perceive African art as a possible object of study they have to develop an interest in the formal problems of three-dimensional space: "That which earlier seemed to be meaningless gained meaning in the recent efforts of artists. There was an impression that virtually no one besides the Negroes had constructed with such purity certain problems of space and a particular way of creating art."[5] The particular problems of space encountered by the cubists were also investigated in African sculpture, and this similarity of interests made African sculpture important for Einstein and his time. Since the way the past is received is a function of a society's current problems, European art could only receive African art properly after it had begun to pose the same questions.[6]

As a result, the fundamental role that art plays in the construction of reality for cubism determines Einstein's interest in primitive cultures. Einstein's discussions of twentieth-century European and primitive art are intimately connected, and he uses many of the arguments he develops in *Negro Sculpture* in his analysis of cubism in *Twentieth-Century Art* (*Die Kunst des 20. Jahrhunderts*, 1926).[7] Just as Einstein does not interpret cubism as deformation or regression, so he refuses to define primitive cultures in terms of their backwardness or their proximity to an eternally archaic. Rather, he considers both in terms of their ability to integrate individual experience into social structures and cultural life.

Einstein links his discussions of cubism and African sculpture with his earlier theoretical considerations of the way art fits into a cultural system. In so doing, he describes how the formal experimentation with space in African sculptures and in cubist paintings corresponds to an implicit metaphysics of perception in which space itself is represented so as to integrate the psychology of the spectator into the construction of laws of three-dimensional space.[8] This breakdown of the distinction between subject and object forms the mediation between humans and nature that is crucial to primitive art, whether it is produced in a traditional or in a modern society. Einstein redefines *primitive* to describe this aesthetic mediation between consciousness and nature. To the extent that this mediation is a foundational experience for every culture, the word *primitive* designates a particular dimension of all cultures rather than indicating specific cultures perceived to be premodern or antimodern.

Once the primitive is understood to be a specific dimension of society, cubism and African sculpture become two manifestations of the same primitive aesthetic. Primitivism no longer consists of an interest in particular "tribal" cultures but in locally organized aspects of all social life. Through the connection between primitivism and an interest in the local, the dichotomy between Western and Other becomes a dichotomy between universal and local. Since the local cannot be separated from the everyday, primitivism entails the attempt to rethink the relation of art to everyday life, and the term *primitive* could apply to any situation in which the local dimension of reality is decisive in determining the structure of social relations. A primitivist aesthetic involves not so much seeking a primitive culture as allowing the local dimension of any culture to develop. This project determines Einstein's idea of the primitive.

His engagement with the primitive art of Europe as well as of Africa, Asia, and the South Seas spans his entire career. His two most important studies of African sculpture are *Negro Sculpture* and *African Sculpture (Afrikanische Plastik*, 1921).[9] The former concentrates exclusively on formal problems presented by African sculpture and does not concern itself with the cultural context out of which these works originated. In fact, Einstein does not offer any information regarding provenance or current location for the sculptures he presents in *Negro Sculpture* and obscures the fact, for instance, that some of the sculptures he describes as African are actually from the South Seas.[10] Yet *Negro Sculpture* presents the theoretical foundations from which all of Einstein's later work would develop. As Georges Didi-Huberman has demonstrated, the primitivist arguments of Einstein's early work in fact build the foundation for his later critique of European aestheticism.[11]

Einstein's later writings concerning primitive art differ from *Negro Sculpture* only in that he is able to integrate a discussion of the history and customs of other cultures into his later analyses of primitive art. Though in *Negro Sculpture* he can only lament the general dearth of reliable information about the cultural context of African art, in *African Sculpture* Einstein includes the results of the research into African art and culture that he undertook in the years since the first book was published (1916 through 1921).[12] Later, Einstein expanded his research into primitive art by looking at the art of a "primitive" period in Japanese art, in *The Early Japanese Woodcut (Der frühere japanische Holzschnitt*, 1923), and the sculpture of the South Pacific, in *South Seas Sculptures (Südsee-plastiken*, 1926).[13] After his move to Paris in 1928, Einstein continued to publish articles concerning primitive art of Africa, central Asia, and the pre-Hellenic Mediterranean cultures.[14]

Einstein's selection of objects of study was not the result of a simple exoticist taste but rather of his interest in primitive forms of art in which the aesthetic realm is not isolated but inseparable from everyday life. He does not consider this integration of art with everyday life to be a reduction of the sacred, auratic quality of art but a form of emphasis on the sacred aspects of human experience. In his 1933 preface to the catalog for a New York exhibition of pre-Hellenic bronze statuettes, Einstein writes: "Art was a surety of pious living; it was significant since it was emblematic of a world attitude and a cult upon which the existence and destiny of the people depended. The character and attitude of this sacred early antique art was not determined by aestheticisms, but was derived from far more significant and non-aesthetic considerations."[15] As this passage demonstrates, Einstein's interest in linking art to "non-aesthetic considerations" was not an attempt to collapse art with the everyday, as Peter Bürger argues concerning the historical avant-garde. Instead, it was an effort to investigate the sacred qualities of art and their relation to "pious living." This interest in the sacred distinguishes Einstein's anti-aestheticist attitude from the historical avant-garde's nonsacred attempt at a "sublation of art in the praxis of life."[16]

Yet Einstein's work does not fit into Bürger's description of aestheticism either. Einstein's critique of aestheticism was determined by his continual interest in primitive art forms that are integrated into the cults and rituals of a culture. In this critique, Einstein opposes the empty formalisms of twentieth-century European art with the integration into community structures characterized by primitive art. In the same preface to the exhibition of bronze statuettes he says of aestheticism:

> Similarly art has evaporated into vague cloudiness, and works of art sink into a swamp of circumspections. Prophets may be heard who speak of the value of a confined red that emphasizes the flowing blue in the right hand corner. Let us frankly admit that art has forfeited its spiritual power since it is no longer harnessed to the service of a great and well-disciplined scheme

of things. Art, by itself, can never create this scheme of values, and purely aesthetic and formal criteria reveal precisely the spiritual poverty of a large part of contemporary "artistry."[17]

Einstein's antagonism toward aestheticism is not a critique of form itself, but of idiosyncratic forms that are not integrated into "a great and well-disciplined scheme of things" and thus lack a spiritual significance. This primitivist critique of an abstract formalism (also present in Kandinsky's work, though less consistently than with Einstein) forms the basis of the primitivist aesthetic that is crucial to Einstein's work from the very beginning.[18] This perspective considers form, not as a category limited to the individual work of art, but as a communal structure that determines perception and behavior. This view, already apparent in Einstein's early work on African sculpture and remaining constant throughout his career, reveals that the other debates of early-twentieth-century art between aestheticism and avant-garde, high and low, fascism and liberalism were mere side notes to the primary conflict between primitivist traditionalism and universalist modernism.

AESTHETIC TOTALITY

Einstein's early primitivist aesthetic develops out of a critique of natural science and the subject/object split. Objecting to the alienation between consciousness and the world around it that this split entails, he proposes an art in which the boundary between subject and object does not exist.

In his essay, "Totality" ("Totalität," 1914), he develops a critique of natural science in which he distinguishes between a totality based on the unity of natural laws and an aesthetic totality founded on a unity of subject and object. He describes the organization of the natural world according to natural laws as being a specifically scientific mode of totality based on a quantitative determination of things. Because the unity of the empirical world constructed by natural science is determined from the point of view of reason, which exists outside of the objects, its unity is a static one imposed by the subject. Empirical objects are reduced to interchangeable elements and raw material to be organized by the identity logic of reason. Consequently, the individual elements that exist in empirical reality are not considered as specific entities but are defined in terms of how they fit into the outside unity constructed by rational laws. Anything that does not fit into these laws is considered chaotic (that is, random).[19]

Instead of starting from the point of view of a universal reason, Einstein's own model of an aesthetic totality begins with the individual consciousness and its specific memories. His theory of art is based upon an investigation of the creation and structure of the memories that determine how an individual consciousness is organized. Einstein considers an individual consciousness not as an abstraction but as a social entity having a specific history that functions according to collective rules. Referring to the specific organization of the psyche as "totality," he differentiates this psychic totality from the quantitative totality of natural science.

He describes the difference between objects of natural science and psychic phenomena as a contrast between a quantitatively organized system and a qualitatively organized one: "We no longer consider a system to be the classification of a multiplicity demonstrating certain one-sided characteristics, we do not take it to be any kind of quantitatively defined organization, i.e. one which includes a certain number of objects; rather we designate as a system every concrete totality which does not derive its organization or structure from an outside instrument, but which is already in itself organized."[20] In contrast to a scientific system that is organized quantitatively as a specific number of objects all related to an outside law, a concrete totality has its own inner organization. This organization is determined by the qualities that make up the totality.

Einstein's description of experience is similar to that of Edmund Husserl's in that for Einstein the basic starting point for a conception of time is naive human experience.[21] Human experience according to Husserl has in itself no periodicity that could be related to a quantitative sequence of time. Every object of consciousness is a fleeting experience in a flow that is only experienced as the immediate present, already disappearing into the past and immediately replaced by another experience in the constant flow: "The psychical is simply not experienced as something that appears; it is 'vital experience' and vital experience seen in reflection; it appears as itself through itself, in an absolute flow, as now and already 'fading away,' clearly recognizable as constantly sinking back into a 'having been.'"[22] To differentiate between elements in the flow one must first find a basis for identity. The only such basis available in a constant flow is repetition.

The construction of objects occurs as a recognition that the flow of experience repeats itself according to certain patterns. These repetitions give the impression of the continuity of objects, and the recognition of a repetition is the creation of a specific quality. For this reason, a measurable atomic unit of experience cannot exist because each unit of experience must always be constructed as a remembered pattern perceived as a quality rather than a unit of quantitative time.[23] It is not possible to split up experience into basic quantitative units because doing so would destroy the patterns that define experience as a set of qualitative differentiations.

The creation of qualities out of repetitions occurs as the association of each single psychic event to a totality of remembered psychic experience. Each psychic event exists as a function of the associations that are made to past experiences and thus to the totality of consciousness.[24] The totality of consciousness separately defines the parameters of each unique experience by relating it to a store of latent qualities. Experience is only made possible through the creation of the specific qualities through which experience is organized. If consciousness did not create these qualities the phenomena could not exist.[25] The creation of specific objects occurs as an associative process in which immediate sensations activate latent memories of consciousness. When these memories are associated with the initial sensations the resulting complex defines a specific quality for the mind. The system of specific qualities according to which both objects and consciousness are organized defines a totality for Einstein.[26]

The malleability of this totality prevents it from becoming a rigid system of constant repetition.[27] Because totality in Einstein's conception is a creation of qualitative differentiations rather than a continually recurring structure, the particularity of an object, its specific quality, is not destroyed as in a rational totality, but enabled in this constantly changing aesthetic totality.

Instead of being based on fixed categories of reason, Einstein's model of totality depends upon the shifting patterns of memory. Experience occurs as a transformation of sensory information into qualities that are constructed through a constant relation of perception to the store of latent memories that can be recalled by consciousness.[28] Each specific experience can only gain form through its association with latent experiences—memories—which have either a similar or perhaps opposing qualitative value vis-à-vis the initial experience. Every moment of experience differentiates itself through its relation to an organizing totality, which includes all of the qualitatively different memories that bear on the particular moment.[29]

While memory is crucial to the construction of objects, this process of construction is also indispensable for the development of consciousness. The flow of experience occurs as a constant reconstruction of the totality of consciousness. Just as a new experience cannot be formed without a relation to the totality, the totality of consciousness could not itself exist without a constant redefinition of itself through the relation to each new experience. Each moment of experience is a new creation of the totality of experience out of a meeting of new perception and latent memories.

This dialectical relation between phenomena and consciousness combines the construction of both into a single process. Because consciousness defines the qualities that make up each individual experience, psychic phenomena are not objective entities. Instead, objects must be understood as always "conceived" in consciousness. Likewise, consciousness cannot be considered in the abstract but must always be considered as "consciousness-of."[30] Objects and consciousness exist within a single continuum rather than separated into two separate dimensions, and the distinction between subject and object does not exist except as an artificial separation of objects from the psychic totality that creates them. Since perception depends upon the construction of this totality, it is not a passive reception but an active construction. The rules by which objects are constructed do not come from the objects themselves nor from the laws of reason, but from the memories of each individual consciousness.

CONSTRUCTING CONSCIOUSNESS

In this context, art's significance for life lies in its ability to structure perception by shaping the structures of memory. Einstein's essay "Totality" begins with the following explanation of the role of art in perception: "Beyond its specifically defined role, art determines vision itself. The memory of all previously seen art weighs upon the viewer when he sees a particular image or perceives an impression from nature. Art transforms all vision, and the artist determines the general visionary imagination."[31] Because for Einstein particular experiences are the result of a creation of qualitative differentiations, artistic form becomes more than a "merely" aesthetic process. It is the basis of all perception and thus of all consciousness. The memory of structures presented in art provides the framework for perception in everyday life. Even when viewing objects other than works of art, the viewer's perception is shaped by the structures of seeing established by works of art. By creating a model of totality, art determines how one sees.

Einstein's particular conception of psychic totality thus forms the basis of his primitivist aesthetic. He develops this aesthetic in terms of the visual arts of painting and sculpture in his reading of African sculpture in *Negro Sculpture* and of cubist painting in the Picasso section of *Twentieth-Century Art*.[32] These two texts sum up Einstein's early theory of art by approaching the question of aesthetic totality from the point of view of the creation of three-dimensional space.

Einstein's analyses of cubism and African art presume an understanding of visual perception that takes into account the psychological components of perception.[33] For the mind to perceive a three-dimensional object as a single entity, it must synthesize both the visible elements of the object and the remembered elements into a single image of the object. Since an object can only be viewed from one angle and distance at a time, the consciousness of three-dimensionality only arises when the subject is able to combine different views separated by time into one object. The memory of aspects of a three-dimensional object that are not visible from a particular angle are combined with the visible aspects into a total form, which determines the visual experience of the viewer according to a particular conception of three-dimensional space. The choice of which views are used to conceptualize a three-dimensional object cannot be determined by any objective standard inhering in the viewed object itself and necessarily depends upon the psychology of the viewer. The psychological qualities of an individual consciousness function in tandem with the visual sensation in order to construct the object in the psyche, and an object cannot exist without the organization of memories that construct the object within the psyche.[34]

The conception of three-dimensional space presupposed by primitive art recognizes the role that psychic forces play in constructing objects. There can be no objective three-dimensional view of an object, and the primitive artist uses this fact to construct, not an object, but the mental form of the object, the "cubic result," which arises out of the interaction between viewer and visual sensation.[35] "The cubic" (*das Kubische*) is Einstein's designation in *Negro Sculpture* for the mind's synthesis of the memories of separate perspectives on an object into a single momentary experience of a three-dimensional object.

In an African sculpture, the artist creates this mental synthesis for the viewer (see fig. 6). The "deformation" of African sculpture is thus not a distortion but a creation of the formal structure through which objects should be viewed. An African sculpture constructs this structure of seeing by providing a synthesis of different perspectives on the object in one single view: "The three-dimensionally situated pieces must be depicted simultaneously, i.e., scattered space must be integrated into a single field of vision."[36] In order for form to become visible in a sculpture, every aspect of the sculpture must be shaped and "deformed" so that depth is absorbed into a single view. The appearance of the object from the rear and the sides must be integrated into the frontal view of the object. Such a sculpture will be weighted toward one side because this side will

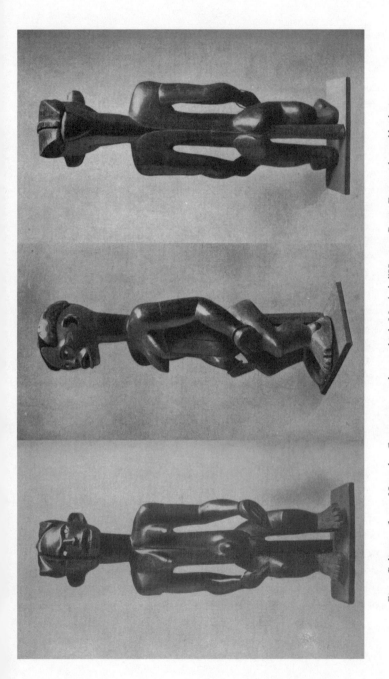

Fig. 6. Reliquary figure, Ngumba, Cameroon, wood, 68 cm high. Musée de l'Homme, Paris. Front, side, and back views, reproduced from Carl Einstein, Negerplastik (Leipzig: Verlag der weißen Bücher, 1920).

incorporate the totality of three-dimensional space into a single view of the object.[37] This single view provides the viewer with the form of the object, that is, the object as it exists in consciousness in one moment. The sculpture does not present an object but a way of seeing objects, and the form of a sculpture consists of the specific rules of seeing through which the sculpture depicts an object.

Einstein's understanding that the form of African sculpture is a synthesis of the possible perspectives on the object into a single view coincides with his analysis of the creation of form in cubist painting. Whereas cubism integrates the different views of the object into a single two-dimensional surface, the African sculpture integrates these views into a single frontal view of the sculpture.[38] In both cases, the essential issue is the presentation, in a single moment, of the object as a psychic "form" or "*Gestalt*."[39] The presentation of the different perspectives of a three-dimensional object in a single view is analogous to the mind's synthesis of latent memories into a single object. In both cases, the object cannot be defined unless it is presented as a single moment in which all of the psychic forces that go into forming the object are presented in their precise relation to one another.[40] By incorporating all of these forces into a fixed construction, the work of art reenacts the creation of form in the psyche.[41] If perception is understood as the translation of sensory and psychic data into psychic forms, art performs a retranslation of psychic forms into an aesthetic form.

AESTHETIC FORM AND RELIGIOUS TRANSCENDENCE

If art is to create an aesthetic equivalent for a psychic totality, it must maintain a purity of form: "this analogy has artistic value when it is perceived unconditionally and without relation to anything extraneous."[42] For only a closed form can fully determine the viewer's vision.[43] If the viewer is allowed to construct the object on her or his own, then the object is no longer a work of art that constructs a way of seeing. It is merely an object, whose structure conforms to a previously established perspective. A closed form on the other hand imposes a total perspective from which the form gains meaning. This form can only be understood to the extent that the viewer shares the perspective that creates it. The closed form determines all aspects of the object for consciousness, and alternative perspectives, which would be "impious," are ruled out by the construction of aesthetic form.[44]

Because this form sums up both the structure of the object and the structure of consciousness in one single moment, the work of art's formal construction of an object is simultaneously a determination of the form of consciousness: "For form is that complete identity between vision and specific realization in which they correspond to each other in their structure and do not relate to each other as a concept to a particular case."[45] The formation of the object and the construction of the subject are combined in artistic form into a single process. By presenting an exemplary form for consciousness, primitive art functions to determine the individual's mode of seeing. Rather than seeing African sculpture as a reproduction of objects, Einstein considers it to be an attempt to create both objects and consciousness by determining the way in which the individual combines different perspectives on the object so as to create a unified impression.

Through participation in the totality of the work of art, the viewer is subordinated to a particular communal construction of reality. The essential difference between form in the psyche and form in a work of art is that while the latter is a collective determination the former risks being a private fantasy. To prevent such a creation of a private, idiosyncratic reality, the aesthetic determination of form must integrate each individual construction of reality into a collective vision.

The work of art takes on a disciplinary function in which aesthetic form turns perception into a group event by compelling individual perception to adhere to a collective pattern. Rather than being free to develop idiosyncratic modes of seeing, the individual is compelled by art to adhere to the perceptual norms of a wider community. The closed form is the work of art's depiction of the communal totality into which the viewer is to be integrated.

Yet because this totality is not a self-sufficient whole but a mediation of conflicting forces, totality cannot be objective or scientific but must be culturally specific. At the same time, the aesthetic construction of a cultural totality is a metaphysical event because it is not an event like all others but *the* event that structures all other experience. Art for Einstein attains a mythic status, and the integration of the viewer of an African sculpture into a closed form is consequently a religious event: "It does not mean anything, it does not symbolize anything; it is the god that guards the closed mythic reality into which it integrates the adorer, transforming him into something mythic and negating his human existence."[46] The absolute power of the god creates a totalizing religious view of the world that presents itself in a closed form. By integrating the viewer into the totality implied by this form, the African sculpture integrates him or her into a timeless mythic reality. The different views, separated in time, that make up our experience of three-dimensional space are combined in African sculpture into one fixed structure. Aesthetic experience thereby transcends normal experience by creating the forms that govern the creation of normal experience. This determination of individual experience becomes the key characteristic of a religious art. Einstein describes African art as timeless because it condenses time into a single defining moment that determines the entire process of time outside of the work of art.[47] Mythic reality is not a backward or pathological fantasy world but the foundation of human perception, functioning to determine the structures through which humans experience the world.

By defining the religious quality of art in terms of the psychology of perception, Einstein suggests a connection between formal aesthetic autonomy and religious transcendence: "Formal and religious closure correspond to each other."[48] The aesthetic character of religious forms that Einstein uncovers leads him to argue for the fundamentally religious purpose of all art. Because aesthetic forms can only become collective ones to the extent that they create the transcendent parameters by which experience is organized, even twentieth-century European art is charged with the task of creating collective myths. Though Einstein emphasizes the creative character of cubism in *Twentieth-Century Art*, this artistic creativity is still linked to the task of giving human meaning to reality.[49]

Einstein's arguments in *Negro Sculpture* already provide the building blocks for his theory that art is the creation of a collective.

On the one hand, he argues that the sacred status of the work of art is African art's basic presupposition—the work of art is or contains the god.[50] This religious significance accorded to art depends upon the community of viewers having an implicit consensus as to how to view objects. The stronger this implicit identification of the viewer with the artist, the less the artist needs to present naturalistic cues to help the viewer create a common basis and the more the artist can rely on a closed form.[51] This closed form can only create a totality if it appears within an appropriate community context that will accept the sacred quality of the form. Yet this collective construction of reality is not a given; it must itself be created in the closed forms of art. Religious transcendence, and with it a collective understanding of reality, is not founded on the belief of the viewer but is the result of aesthetic experience. The power of the sacred object does not simply derive from the religious context of belief that creates it but from the formal consistency of its structure: "For imitation is out of the question; whom could a god imitate, to whom could it be subordinated? A consistent realism of transcendent form is the result. . . . The work of art is real due to its closed form."[52] Just as the creation of the object and of consciousness occur in a single, mutually defining process, so the creation of form in art and of a community consensus determine each other in a single process.

MYTHIC TOTALITY

Because the phenomena of the psyche depend on their relation to memories, Einstein's model of consciousness is very similar to the understanding implicit in Freud's work.[53] But while Freud understood his work to be natural science, Einstein's account of the difference between natural and psychic phenomena demonstrates the impossibility of using a positivist framework to adequately study psychic phenomena.

Freud's method is marked by a constant tension between a natural scientific outlook that separates the subject from the object and a specifically psychological attempt to discover the forces through which the subject at hand perceives the world and functions within it. To the extent that Freud pursues a psychological method as opposed to a natural scientific one, he does not reject divergences between the neurotic's sense of reality and an "objective" reality as mistakes or fantasies. Rather, Freud attempts to understand the neurotic's specific reality in terms of the forces of desire and necessity that affect the individual psyche. Since the neurotic's construction of an idiosyncratic reality is a function of the memories and traumas of his or her past, the neurotic provides the categories that Freud uses to analyze this reality. Psychoanalysis occurs as a reenactment or mimesis of the patient's psychic traumas, and the particular form that these traumas take in the psyche is itself a mimesis of the constellation of forces acting on the psyche.

When Freud discovers that the psychological constructions of the neurotic often correspond to the cultural constructions of primitive cultures, he interprets this coincidence as a sign of the backwardness of primitive culture. For Freud, the neurotic's and the primitive's projection of psychic structures onto an outside reality so as to create a unity of subject and object is not a normal process but a pathological one.

This view stems from his assumption that the primitive condition of totality has been left behind with the onset of the modern age. Freud's depiction of the situation of the scientist, "that the world is unknown and that means must therefore be sought for getting to know it," corresponds to Georg Lukács's depiction in *Theory of the Novel* of a modern "transcendental homelessness."[54] Both Freud and Lukács assume that the modern world is irretrievably separated from a primitive totality, and in doing so they betray an adherence to an idea of progress that prevents an appreciation of the value of primitive thought for the modern world.

Freud considers the primitive worldview to be inferior to a scientific one because it overestimates the power of the mind and psyche. Nevertheless, his description of a primitive confusion between mind and outside world can also be read as a model for Einstein's sense of totality in which individual and world form a unity:

> When we, no less than primitive man, project something into external reality, what is happening must surely be this: we are

recognizing the existence of two states—one in which something is directly given to the senses and to consciousness (that
is, is *present* to them), and alongside it another, in which the
same thing is *latent* but capable of re-appearing. In short, we
are recognizing the co-existence of perception and memory,
or, putting it more generally, the existence of *unconscious* mental processes alongside the *conscious* ones. It might be said that
in the last analysis the "spirit" of persons or things comes
down to their capacity to be remembered and imagined after
perception of them has ceased.[55]

Totality can make sense for the modern world because the spirit of
a person or thing as a primitive understands it must coincide in the
modern world with the significance that person or thing has in the
consciousness of an individual, even when that person or thing is
not immediately present. Psychological factors come into play to
determine the character of this spirit. Because spirit is the latent aspect of consciousness, it must also be for Freud a determining element of consciousness, just as latent memories rather than manifest
ones are the fundamental determiners of the structures of the human psyche. The construction of spirit through memory provides
the organizing template through which external reality is perceived
by the individual in both traditional and modern societies.

If perception is thus shaped by memory, then the construction of
spirit in myth is also the point at which a culture constitutes a latent
dimension that influences individual perception by invoking the
spirit of the thing. Rather than assuming a fixed opposition between subject and object, ideal and real, myth conceives of reality as
a flux of forces in which human desires must contend with natural
forces in order to determine the final content of reality as a set of objects. Ideal and real are never to be found in isolation but are always
merged in the construction of reality out of the meeting of perception and memory, of new event and old conflicts. In this way, the
aesthetically organized structures of myth provide the overarching
context within which our perception of the world can take place.

Within this epistemology, myth retains a specific function in human society that distinguishes it from science and history. The con-

structions of myth do not function to solve technical problems as science does, nor do they serve as a guide to primal scenes in the prehistory of culture. Instead, myth provides a collective depiction of the conflict between human desires and natural forces that structures the latent memories of the individuals in a particular culture. To provide this structure to consciousness, myth must delineate the fundamental values by which a culture must constantly define its character in opposition to nature. It is only after this mythic construction has been accomplished that scientific knowledge can develop. Science does not replace but presupposes myth as the totalizing foundation upon which the problems of science can gain meaning.

From this mythic perspective, the sickness of the neurotic is a result of the alienation of people from objects in modern society. Because a rationalistic society separates an outer world of objects from an inner subjective world, the subjective forces that always play a part in constructing objects are not recognized in this society's cultural constructions of reality. The creation of psychic forms must still occur in a rationalistic society because this is the only way in which an individual consciousness can perceive. But since the creation of forms in the psyche is not accomplished in works of art that provide a communal determination of the form of objects for consciousness, the individual must construct these forms according to his or her own idiosyncratic interpretation of the psychic meaning of objects. In such a society the construction of experience is no longer a collective process, and there is no collective place in the world for the psychic forces that play an essential part in the construction of objects in an individual consciousness. Because the individual is left to accept the natural scientific interpretation of objects, which ignores psychic processes, the consequent repression of these processes leads to their return in the form of an individual psychic occupation of the object world, that is, the neuroses that cannot be understood by the rest of the society.

In the realm of sculpture, the repression of the psychic role in constructing objects manifests itself as a belief in the possibility that objects can be represented objectively. According to Einstein, European sculpture from the Renaissance until the beginning of the twentieth century ignores cubic space and uses a "painterly" (*ma-lerisch*) technique to create sculptures.[56] "Painterly" sculpture does not consider the problem of space to be an issue. Instead, this type of sculpture simply assumes that, since it is working with a three-dimensional mass, the spatial determination of the sculpture is produced automatically.[57] But because the ability to perceive depends upon a psychological synthesis that creates a form, the existence of a three-dimensional mass is insufficient for the perception of space.[58] A mass cannot be perceived in one view, and European sculpture depends upon the viewer of the sculpture to create a formal synthesis on his or her own. The viewer, and not the artist, constructs the object for consciousness: "The optical naturalism of Western art is not the imitation of the natural world outside; the nature that is passively imitated is the standpoint of the viewer. This is how to understand the genetic, exceedingly relative character of most of our art. Such art adapted itself to the viewer (frontality, distanced image) and the creation of the final optical form was entrusted increasingly to an actively participating viewer."[59]

Einstein considers a sculpture that reproduces an object without depicting its form for consciousness to be "tautological" because it merely reproduces an object that has already been constructed according to a previously determined form. On the one hand, such an imitation of an object merely repeats an old form. On the other hand, it will be left up to the viewer to determine the form by which he or she regards the object. The viewer is left to choose an already familiar form in order to create a mental construction of the object. Consequently, the construction of the object is completely independent of the work of art and tends to reproduce old ways of seeing that may or may not correspond to a current organization of psychic forces.

Although the final optical form given to the viewer is not determined by the artist but by the viewer, the creation of objects in a rationalistic culture still depends upon a subjective appropriation. The denial of the psychological element of object construction is a self-deception that leaves European sculpture unable to provide the viewer with an artistic determination of form. In this situation, each individual observer must appropriate the object on his or her

own without the guidance that an artistic and thus collective determination of form might provide. As Einstein will emphasize later
in *The Fabrication of Fictions* (*Die Fabrikation der Fiktionen*), a hermetic aestheticist art is the result of a neurotic reaction to the absence of communal constructions of reality. Instead of creating collective forms, twentieth-century European art often retreats into
an idiosyncratic construction of reality analogous to that of the
neurotic.

In contrast to the modern alienation that creates both representational art and hermetic aestheticist art, both a natural scientific and
a neurotic reality, Einstein's model of totality presents art as an essential mediator between individual and communal constructions
of reality. A primitive sculpture provides a community of viewers
with the form (*Gestalt*) that an object assumes in the mind. This determination of perception through artistic form creates a collective
experience of perception rather than allowing each individual (or
separate artist) to construct an idiosyncratic view of the world.
Thus, though primitive art is organized according to the qualities
and forms of the individual consciousness, the goal of artistic form
is the creation of a community consciousness. Even in a universal
culture that does not recognize the role of art in the creation of
community, a society's stability depends upon local culture having
the ability to create a set of aesthetic forms that structure experience.

To the extent that art is a social event, its formal organization is
not completely idiosyncratic to an individual. Rather, the structures of seeing developed in art create the basis for communication
by serving to mediate between the individual's perception and that
of the community. Accordingly, in "Totality" Einstein already
speaks not of the perception of the individual but of the "eyes of the
collective": "In order for the eyes of the collective to achieve order,
laws of seeing are necessary that appraise the material of physiological seeing in order to endow it with a human meaning."[60] Since an
object can only exist by assuming a specific function in the psyche,
human interaction is only possible to the extent that the objects of
perception are collectively endowed with a human meaning. The
creation of objects must occur collectively for a community to exist,

and the work of art is the point of contact between the latent, unconscious memories of the psyche and the organization of the community.

If community consensus and closed form are two moments that
make up a single totality, then both African and twentieth-century
European art share the same basic function of constructing the fundamental aesthetic basis for community experience. Since both
must link aesthetic form to community, there is no essential difference between the parameters of African and European art. Einstein's later critique of the hermeticism of European aestheticism is
not a critique of his own earlier conception of the role of art but of
the inability of many twentieth-century European artists to effec-
tively integrate collective experience into the work of art so as to
construct a collective rather than an individual determination of
reality.[61]

The basic conflict in Einstein's ideas noted by commentators
stems from the fact that in his discussions of African art and cubism
he attempts to distinguish between the two on one crucial point.
While he considers African art to be based ultimately on a presupposed religious transcendence that is a repetition of old structures,
he reads cubism in the 1926 edition of *Twentieth-Century Art* as a
creation and establishment of the new. Yet Einstein is unable to
maintain this distinction for long. While he emphasizes the creative
aspect of aesthetic intuition in 1926, he explicitly connects creativity
to the "making human" of reality in 1931. In the 1926 edition of
Twentieth-Century Art, Einstein writes: "Creative freedom is integrated into the intuition, and its conventional determination,
which reduces it complacently to a servile means, is shattered."[62] In
the 1931 edition, Einstein has revised this passage to read: "In art intuition becomes a productive moment into which creative freedom
is integrated, and in this way intuition becomes human."[63] Einstein's thought shifts from an emphasis on the shattering of older
forms in 1926 to a desire to mobilize creativity for the purpose of
mediating between reality and consciousness in 1931. The change

signals his declining interest in pure innovation and his increasing concern for the practical goals of creativity.[64] As a consequence, the 1931 edition also emphasizes twentieth-century art's mythic function: "One notes the return of a mythic stance; the tautological in terms of memory is finally overcome, and the creative moment is thereby strengthened."[65]

Einstein's theoretical and artistic work is marked by the contradiction between his attempt to differentiate between religious transcendence and the creation of the new on the one hand and his attempt to unify primitive and twentieth-century European art, that is, religious art and "new" art, on the other hand. This contradiction leads to Einstein's shifting characterizations of twentieth-century art, which Kiefer reads as an alternation between subjectivist and materialist phases in his development.[66] From the beginning of his career Einstein refuses to accept the twentieth-century innovations of European art as idiosyncratic constructions of individual artists. Instead, he attempts to link these innovations to the construction of a binding community reality. By linking art to the construction of community, he confines the freedom of art to a specifically religious project. At the same time, he does not argue for a return to the mythic structures of the past, but for the creation of new mythic forms for the present. Recognizing that religious art's function is to construct community by imposing a closed form, he argues that the construction of community in contemporary society must be grounded in an aesthetically rather than a dogmatically based mythology. His attempt to relate this "postprimitive" to a "preprimitive" while at the same time maintaining some type of distinction between the two determines the contradictions in his theories of art and myth.[67]

Though he was not able to resolve many of the issues he posed, Einstein's claim that the essence of twentieth-century art was the "return of a mythic stance" is unambiguous in its demonstration that this art is not new in terms of the mechanisms by which it operates. These same aesthetic mechanisms also operate within a traditionally based mythic art. The newness of art is not a function of its modernity versus a former primitivity but rather of its constant need, both in a "modern" and a "traditional" context, to renew its

forms in order to adequately relate to a present reality. Rather than
a reified religious dogma, myth is for Einstein a malleable aesthetic
structure that is constantly being recreated to fit psychic exigencies. While myth operates with the same formal and aesthetic processes as twentieth-century art in order to maintain legitimacy,
twentieth-century art is not completely free, but must operate according to the same necessities that determine the structure of
myth. Einstein's explanations of African sculpture and cubism
point toward the inseparability of aesthetic plausibility and religious transcendence in both forms of art.

This binding quality that Einstein sees as the essential characteristic of both African and twentieth-century European art can only
arise out of a closed structure to the extent that this structure imitates psychic processes. The sacred status of the work of art creates
an authoritative distance between the work and the viewer in which
the viewer accepts the construction of consciousness created by the
work of art. At the same time, the aesthetic status of the sacred object maintains a connection between the form of the object and the
specific psychic experience of the viewer. A religious form is not arbitrary, but must be constructed as an aesthetic mimesis of psychic
processes. Such an aesthetic-religious form can only be understood
by the viewer to the extent that it is a summation of latent structures
in the viewer's psyche. The figures and images of myth are a result of
artistic constructions that attempt to imitate psychic forms: "The
object is now the last peripheral experience and is only valid within
the process of subjective creation. One creates forms that are constructed according to psychic processes, and thanks to this fact we
grasp them. Gradually, mythic figures grow out of this freedom of
imagination and construction, and what could be more real than
myth and imagination that emerge out of regions that are psychi-
cally more immediate than objects?"[68]

There are thus two processes that define the work of art's collective and religious status. On the one hand, the religious work of art
constructs the viewer's perception of the world and obliges the
viewer to accept the religious totality upon which the collective understanding of reality is based. On the other hand, the work of art's
construction of reality is not arbitrarily based on a blind belief, but

is a mimesis of the psychic forces that are consciously or unconsciously active in the viewer's mind. These two processes are primarily aesthetic. The religious quality that these aesthetic processes attain is a function of their success in creating a collective affirmation of their power. The more successful the work of art, the more readily it will be accepted as a necessity and not as a mere construction.

Whereas in "Totality" and *Negro Sculpture* Einstein concentrates on the power of art to impose ways of seeing onto a collective, his arguments in *Twentieth-Century Art* increasingly suggest that there is also a mimetic component to the construction of collective visions.[69] Though the notion of forces is already implicit in his earlier ideas, Einstein argues explicitly in *Twentieth-Century Art* that the collective character of art is based on art's ability to reenact the play of forces that determine the life of the psyche.[70] Because art must mediate between the individual consciousness and the community, it is subject to the same forces that Freud reveals as the two determiners of psychic life: individual desires and social necessities.

This parallel between the form of art and the form of consciousness functions on two levels. First, art mediates between individual and community by imposing on the individual a collective fixation of the form of objects. The work of art thereby becomes the site where the unconscious visions of individuals can be subjected to a group determination of these visions' validity. Second, art mediates between desires and necessities by imitating the psyche's construction of a totality of latent memory and new object. This aesthetic mimesis is not an imitation of objects. Objects themselves are already the result of an aesthetic process, and an imitation of objects would be merely an imitation of the results of a previous aesthetic construction of the rules of perception. Instead, the specific organization of objects in an aesthetic totality is determined by the opposing *forces* acting upon the psyche.

These forces present themselves to the psyche as a conflict between inner desires and outer necessities. As Einstein writes in *Twentieth-Century Art*, the form of an object depends upon the psyche's interpretation of an individual sensation in terms of its own practical desires: "Vision is directed toward actions and determined by purposes, and in this way extraneous conceptions, feelings, and memories blend in with this seeing. Our vision is determined above all by practical motives."[71] Since the form of objects depends upon the individual's practical goals and desires, an aesthetic determination of the form of objects is simultaneously a determination of the relation of an object to the goals of the subject. Since the object itself only exists as a function of these goals, the consolidation of physical sensations into a form, in addition to constructing the forms of consciousness, presents the forces of desire and necessity that determine an individual's psychology. Painting and sculpture function as reenactments of the formation of objects in the psyche. Form both creates an artistic and thus creative determination of the object and is a mimesis of the forces of the psyche: "One now constructs forms that correspond to unmediated psychic processes, and their structure is determined by these processes."[72]

Though in his early work Einstein primarily emphasizes the creative aspect of totality when he describes its construction of objects and the psyche, his discussion of "intensities" in "Totality" relates totality to a mimesis of forces. Rather than imitating a previous and perhaps outdated construction of objects, the task of art in this early essay is to imitate the current forces that act upon experience to create psychic totality. Art's construction of ways of seeing is not an imitation of objects but of the play of forces that create psychic forms. As a mimesis of the forces acting on the psyche, one artistic totality can be differentiated from another by the specific constellation of forces (or in Einstein's terms, the "intensities") that, in their interaction, result in the creation of objects.[73]

A particular painting or sculpture presents the psychic result of the conflict of the forces of desire and necessity that dominate mental life. Art thereby makes manifest the latent structures of experience that arise out of the exigencies of the present time and place. The structures of seeing created by art are not arbitrarily constructed; they are a mimesis of the constellation of forces already latent in memory but not previously presented.[74] This fixation of a present constellation of forces into an aesthetic form creates a communal reality without relying on a set of prior beliefs nor on the fixed archetypes of a collective unconscious.

European sculpture's denial of its responsibility to create forms not only leaves the individual on his or her own to construct the memory structures of consciousness, but also impairs a culture's ability to reconstruct each new historical moment. Since it does not create new forms, it cannot rethink and thus criticize old ways of seeing. Representational art simply reproduces old structures of perception and becomes profoundly conservative.

In contrast to this repetition of the old, art for Einstein must criticize and revise old structures by reconstructing the forms of objects according to the current forces acting upon consciousness: "Seeing, one transforms humans and the world. Intuition and seeing change and exhaust each other, and optical dissatisfaction forces a change, regardless of whether an inherited intuition collapses; for it is not a matter of reproduction but production. In this way painting or sculpture necessarily becomes a critique of intuition and one's legacy."[75] The critique of traditional structures that Einstein sees in cubism is essential to a reconstruction of forms. Consequently, even though Einstein does not explicitly emphasize it, in his conception African sculpture must maintain the same critical attitude toward tradition that cubism does. The construction of objects and the mimesis of forces occur in a single process of creation that lies at the basis of myth: "With the construction of new objects the turn to myth was completed."[76]

The constant critique that is part of primitive culture is not obvious, however, because such a culture is also characterized by a strong sense of the sacred. But because the sacred is in fact constructed through aesthetic forms, it is also constantly undergoing a process of reappropriation and critique. This process is carried out as much in the reception as in the production of myth. For one of myth's defining characteristics is its embeddedness within an oral tradition that ensures that the reception of the myth is as important as the creation for its final determination. The decisions of the recipients about whether to transmit or to ignore a particular aesthetic construct is the final step in the creation of myth, integrating communal experience into the mythic form.

3. Primitivism in Prose

7

NARRATIVE FORM
AND EXPERIENCE
IN CARL EINSTEIN'S
PROSE THEORY

If Carl Einstein's theory of visual art links everyday vision to the collective creation in art of a totality for consciousness, the same project determines his theory of prose. But while painting and sculpture present totality in a single moment, prose works with narrative sequences. The stories presented in prose activate memories of past events in the psyche of the reader or listener and fit them into a particular narrative form that creates an interpretation of these past events. In the same way that African sculptures create a communal perception of *objects*, stories create a communal perception of *events*, providing a template for the perception of past events and a model for understanding future ones.

Because Einstein's prose theory considers totality to be a fundamental structure of human consciousness rather than a characteristic of specific, undeveloped cultures, his vision of prose differs markedly from that of Georg Lukács in his *Theory of the Novel*. Though they wrote in the same period about the idea of totality and its relation to epic forms, their approaches mark out two opposing directions for considering nineteenth- and twentieth-century European prose. While Lukács considers totality to be a historico-philosophical category whose parameters have changed in the history of the West, Einstein considers it from the point of view of the psychology of perception and understands its mechanisms to be constants in human history. As a result, the differences in genre and structure that Lukács understands to be the result of a historical development become, in Einstein's account, distinctions between competing forms.

In Lukács's evolutionary account of prose forms, the Homeric epic, the Greek tragedy, and the realist novel are three stations in a development away from the organic totality of a harmonious community that is no longer possible in the modern world.[1] Like the art historians who classified the abstract forms of African sculpture as a crude first step in the evolutionary development toward realism, Lukács contrasts the "childlikeness" of the Homeric epic to the "virile maturity" of the novel.[2] His distinction is based on the idea that the Homeric epic exists in a lost world dominated by an organic totality whose harmony, once shattered, can never be recovered. In the epic, life and essence are one. Only with the advent of tragedy "did men become aware that life as it was . . . had lost the immanence of the essence."[3]

Rather than existing in an organic totality, the novel for Lukács presupposes the death of God and a consequent split between essence and life. Since material reality is no longer suffused by essence, totality is no longer a given, but must be constructed by the individual subject in the confrontation with reality. The novel is consequently constructed as the individual's attempt to construct a totality that can no longer be presumed: "Art, the visionary reality of the world made to our measure, has thus become independent: it is no longer a copy, for all the models have gone; it is a created totality, for the natural unity of the metaphysical spheres has been destroyed forever."[4] The individual subject becomes the source of the ideas that construct a totality, and the outside world has become empty matter, devoid of spirit and thus a foreign terrain for the subject rather than a transcendental home. "The epic individual, the hero of the novel, is the product of estrangement from the outside world."[5] The task of the novel is to use formal structure to forge a unity of subject and object that is centered around the life of the individual: "The central character of a biography is significant only by his relationship to a world of ideals that stands above him: but this world, in turn, is realised only through its existence within that individual and his lived experience."[6] Totality is based in the individual and can only refer to a transcendent reality by developing an individual subject's ideas.

By understanding organic totality as a state of harmony between life and essence and then setting totality in the irretrievable past, Lukács assumes that it is possible to conceive of a material reality that exists without a totality that pre-forms it. But as Einstein demonstrates, every subject and all material reality presuppose a prior totality. For totality is *never* a given, but always an aesthetic event that must constantly be reconstructed for a culture to survive. For Einstein, in constructing plots narrative form fills an inherent lack in human experience: "Without the novel humanity would be incomplete, for it is in need of epic vision."[7] An epic vision that forms experience into a narrative unity creates the temporal totality within which an individual lives. Yet this totality is not an objective one and cannot come from pure perception. Instead, it arises out of the forms that narrative provides when it depicts experience according to specific patterns.

Because immediate experience in every consciousness needs an aesthetic organization of impressions to become intelligible, narrative must create this organizational structure to enable our experience of time. The crucial element of the narrative is consequently not the representation of an individual's consciousness, but the presentation of exemplary actions, and Einstein conceives of the novel as a unity of subject and object in the plot of the story.[8] The totality constructed in narrative cannot be a product of the subject in its confrontation with the world, as Lukács contends. Rather, totality transcends both subject and object, preceding them as the frame that allows both to constitute each other.

If totality is indispensable for perception then the modern situation is not fundamentally different from an ancient one. From Einstein's perspective, the evolutionary progression from epic to tragedy to novel in Lukács's account becomes a typology of various competing forms. As Erich Auerbach would later point out, the Homeric epic and Old Testament myth, though dating from approximately the same period of human history, demonstrate two opposing approaches to representation. In Homer, the naive fascination with the material world and the absence of psychology contrast sharply with the metaphysical reach and psychological depth of Old Testament myths: "Far from seeking, like Homer, merely to make us forget our own reality for a few hours, it [the Biblical narrative] seeks to overcome our reality: we are to fit our own life into its world, feel ourselves to be elements in its structure of universal history."⁹ Auerbach's distinction between Homeric epic and Old Testament myth adheres to the same logic as Nietzsche's distinction between Apollinian and Dionysian art. In both accounts, the two forms of art are not stages in an evolution but expressions of two opposing art forces with two different functions. While the former serves as a diversion and a form of entertainment, the latter is constitutive for the structure of consciousness. Though they can be conceptually distinguished from each other, both art forces exist in every work of art to varying degrees.

Rather than attempting to create Apollinian illusions, Einstein's prose theory seeks to recreate Dionysian myth. The return of mythic structures is not a regression, however, but a rediscovery of art's role in creating the mythic totality that is necessary for the construction of human subjectivity. Lukács's prose theory cannot account for the mythic character of twentieth-century European prose because it presumes a definitive break between the traditional and the modern world. A return to mythic forms can only be a regression for Lukács. By contrast, Einstein develops a prose theory that can consider the novel, not as the final stage of a civilizational development, but as merely one of many possible options for organizing narrative experience. A particular style is established not as part of the universal progress of art but because a cultural decision was made that has specific consequences for the resulting structures of consciousness.

Einstein is able to consider different forms and styles of prose outside of a narrative of civilizational progress because he believes that the consciousness of temporal experience can only constitute itself within the totality provided by narrative structures. Temporal experience is never simply given, but must always be constructed out of the never-ending flow of impressions that continually replace each other.¹⁰ For this flow to gain coherence, its continual movement must be perceived in terms of repetitions in the flow that appear according to recognizable patterns. The patterns of recurrence are not inherent to consciousness, but must be provided by the narratives that make one's experiences become intelligible as a cohesive whole rather than a jumble of disparate impressions. Totality is essential for the coherence of consciousness because consciousness by itself lacks the patterns necessary for turning the flood of impressions it receives into intelligible experiences.

Like the flow of experience, narrative exists as a temporal sequence that is in constant forward movement. Because temporal experience gains meaning through recurrence, patterns of repetition are also indispensable for structuring separate events into a comprehensible plot of a story. Repetition is not a product of stagnation but a reaction against constant movement. Because a particular experience immediately moves irretrievably into the past, its meaning will be ephemeral unless it is repeated. The creation of meaning depends upon a plot that in repeating an experience points to it and emphasizes it. Repetition is thus a way of limiting the constantly changing character of reality and is the result of a concentration of forces around an experience. Without this privileging of particular events and experiences, consciousness would be incapable of constituting itself.

FATEFUL NARRATIVES

Narrative in Einstein's prose theory functions in the same way that latent memories function for Freud. Both are prerequisites for the construction of subjective experiences. Events in narrative and in memory are reenacted through patterns of repetition that result from the concentration of psychic forces around a particular event. The more powerful these forces are, the more insistent and compulsive the repetition becomes. Yet for both Einstein and Freud, the fact that the forces of desire and necessity that create repetition have a psychic character does not mean that they do not have a basis in an outside reality. Both consider psychic forces to be the translation into consciousness of the outside forces that determine the patterns of human experience.

These outside forces are for Einstein the ultimate source of form in narrative: "The Greeks created *ananke*, *athe*, in order to constrain themselves to form. Balzac found greed and Flaubert slow death, that remaining-the-same or becoming-small which invisibly surrounds us. They discovered inescapable forces; only these create form."[11] Form here is neither arbitrary nor a result of human endeavor, but a product of a mimesis of "inescapable forces." These forces determine the patterns of repetition that result in narrative. Binding narratives attain their force through their traumatic quality as experiences illuminating the forces that limit our desires and goals. Normal experience occurs as a reenactment, a repetition, of these binding, "traumatic" narratives, and repetition itself is the translation into time of outside forces.[12]

To create a mimesis of these forces, prose cannot present subjective individual nor arbitrary narratives. It must recount stories that are both "typical" and fateful.[13] The crucial concept for Einstein's theory of prose is, thus, not the freedom or dominance of the subject but the fatefulness of actions.[14] Because for humans the form of time does not lie in its measurable progression but in their consciousness of time as fate, events in a story appear *as if* they were simultaneous: "Events in a conventional fable are given to us as if they were simultaneous; it is only that language is incapable of recounting them in a single breath."[15] This "as if" simultaneity does not conceive of the action of a story as a momentary structure but refers instead to the fateful character of the events.[16] Fatefulness takes a particular narrative sequence and makes it "seem" simultaneous by emphasizing its binding character. By linking a particular action to a particular set of consequences, fate creates a story in which each event is essential and cannot be arbitrary. Though the story is expressed in language that unfolds as a series rather than in an image, the building blocks of the story, action and consequence, only gain significance through the idea that a specific action is both irreversible and leads to a limited number of consequences. The resulting fatefulness of actions creates a mythic understanding of action and consequence that is not based on rational deductions but on the perception of patterns of experience whose fixity attests to time's existence both as a one-way flow and as an unfolding that adheres to repetitive patterns.

The fate that the action depicts is not only beyond the control of the characters of the story but also the will of the author, who is "trapped" within the story because the plot must depict a fate that cannot be arbitrarily constructed: "The epic poet forms the events, and his virtue demands that he only cultivate himself as far as the plot allows. He is trapped within his book."[17] To create such a non-arbitrary plot, the author must avoid extraneous explanations and descriptions that detract from the purity of the action.[18] Instead, each element in the plot must follow from the preceding elements in such a way that the development of the action follows an inner logic. Consequently, Einstein rejects both "psychological" novels, which attempt to artificially justify events through human psychology, and anecdotes, whose motives and endings could be changed without affecting the character of the story.[19] Rather than psychological novels and arbitrary anecdotes, Einstein attempts to create stories whose plots are determined by fateful forces.

Einstein's primary example of such a prose is the parable, a story that has been reduced to the essential elements of the action that determine its form.[20] Because the goal of such narrative is to depict narrative structures rather than to provide a "realistic" portrayal of empirical reality, the author is free to develop its plot according to the demands of psychic forces. These forces turn the parable into a spiritual narrative to the extent that the parable can present the structure of our mental existence.[21] By exercising a structuring power over normal experience, narrative forms guarantee the stability of mental processes and thereby fulfill a religious function. The essence of this metaphysical character does not lie in religious dogma, however, but in the ability of certain aesthetic forms to provide a foundational structure for consciousness. Consequently, the aesthetic success of a narrative goes hand in hand with its spiritual power. A work of art for Einstein cannot simply exist as an aesthetic object; it must attain a religious significance through its capacity to structure human experience in the same way as myth.[22]

By the same token, religious forms have an aesthetic component that is essential to their spiritual significance, and Einstein describes religious art in terms of its formal aesthetic characteristics: "Certain psychic structures emerge from religion and attained in the church plastic form and structure. Ordered elements exist here that are imagination from the very beginning, however, not in the sense of illusion (fantasy), but of a psychic reality with function and power."²³ Einstein develops a distinction between a purely fantastic imaginative construction and a binding one that can form the basis of a mythic reality. Religious forms are not simply fantasy, but have a psychic significance that determines the patterns by which mundane reality progresses.

Thus, in his discussion of Catholicism in "On Paul Claudel," Einstein is drawn to those elements of Catholicism that create narrative forms that become binding for a collective. The issue for Einstein is not so much the particular tenets of the Catholic religion but the specifically *primitive* aesthetic forms active in the stories around which Catholicism is based. His interest in Catholicism should not be taken as a sign of his religious beliefs but of his attempt to understand religion's power as a function of its use of aesthetic forms for creating sacred experience.²⁴ Rather than presenting a defense of religion, Einstein investigates how art mediates individual experience in the parables of Catholicism. Einstein does not treat these stories as explanations of religious dogma but as autonomous aesthetic forms that become binding for the listener because of their formal structure.

Parables become binding through the exemplary character of their stories rather than through blind faith. To become exemplary, a parable's meaning must arise out of its capacity to reenact experience according to forces active in the psyche. To the extent that the parable provides an adequate mimesis of these forces, its action becomes exemplary and, when juxtaposed to mundane experience, exercises a structuring power that transforms empirical reality itself into parable: "Above all, and this is important, Claudel portrays that person in whom the things of the world turn into a parable and how this person is himself a parable. This is important; for it guarantees sharp boundaries between fictional regions, a staircase of parables [*ein Stufenbau von Gleichnissen*]."²⁵ The parable's analogical relation to the events that make up experience provides a model around which mundane experience is organized, and every experience becomes another repetition in the "staircase of parables."

To the extent that a particular parable is able to provide patterns and an overarching totality for experience, it acquires a sacred quality, and the constructed totality is understood in Catholicism as a divine unity: "The writer is left with the concentrated richness of the parables, through which each thing is related to the human and the human, as a finite being, is in turn integrated into the perfection of god."[26] By constantly referring each experience to a parabolic model of experience, the parable creates a connection between each individual experience and the totality, which in Christianity is referred to as the perfection of God. The continual relation of mundane experience to a psychic totality is the primary function of both art and religion for Einstein.[27]

To provide an example of a parable that exercises a controlling power over a community, Einstein presents the idea of original sin as an aesthetic construction based on a dramatic contradiction: "Within original sin there exists a dialectical, even dramatic conflict which is capable of binding a group."[28] The drama of original sin is not guaranteed by a dogma but through a narrative structure that presents both the original sin and all subsequent actions as expressions of freedom and as demonstrations of the necessity of fate and death. This "dramatic conflict" between freedom and fate, which lies at the basis of original sin, provides in compressed form the structure by which one interprets one's own individual experience as a series of voluntary acts with fateful consequences.[29]

Yet at the same time as Einstein develops this connection between aesthetic and religious forms, he also recognizes that this conception of aesthetic form threatens to devalue experience in favor of art, making art into the continual repetition of eternal structures. He attempts to avoid this result by connecting the creation of structure in works of art to the creation of structure inherent to all perception of reality. Here, Einstein distinguishes between a mythic religious art and a dogmatic religious art.

In the example of original sin, Einstein notes that by concentrating on the eternal Claudel risks overlooking the aesthetic importance of the narrative and the drama for the creation of the eternal: "However, we do not wish to conceal the danger that, in the face of the incomparable and eternal, the temporal (and thus the plot and the drama) can be considered a detour or an excuse."[30] Instead of relying on the plot of the narrative, the creator of a parable might be tempted to consider the parable as secondary to the dogma and the temporal as secondary to the eternal. This attitude results in the creation of works of art that do not have an inherently sacred character. Instead, they deteriorate into "a vast repetition of the dogma; these things were repeated often and without example. These dramas are paraphrases, or even overburdened allegories of the dogma."[31] Rather than basing religion on the presupposition of faith in a dogma, Einstein constructs a model of religion in which faith is the result of an aesthetic experience of the parable, and the eternal is not a pure form but is always linked to bodily experience.

MIRACLE AND SACRIFICE

To link the eternal to materiality, Einstein defines religion as an ecstatic aesthetic experience based on the miracle, and Nietzsche's *Birth of Tragedy* provides the model for Einstein's consideration of the homology between artistic and religious forms of ecstasy.[32] For both Nietzsche and Einstein, meaning occurs in the moment of the miracle, which transforms life in order to make it into a function of the eternal: "Through the miracle life becomes a function of the eternal, which can confirm itself in life only through antinomy. Belief is the precondition of this act, and consequently life and not the eternal becomes paradoxical for the believer. Temporal action only attains meaning in the moment of the miracle, in order to recognize God and the eternal."[33] The miracle does not merely present the eternal but, more importantly, demonstrates the eternal aspect of temporal life and thereby gives form to the temporal. For the miracle to function it does not need to break the rules of normal experience but to create the rules of experience as corollaries to the sacred experience. Thus, the prerequisite for the miracle is the belief in a spiritual reality. Unless the recipient accepts the significance of the spiritual construction for material reality, the miracle will not be able to set up a relation between the spiritual and the material.

At the same time, the belief in a spiritual reality is also a consequence of the experience of the miracle. In religion, the relation between miracle and normal experience corresponds to the relation between fantastic and real that Einstein thematizes in his novel, *Bebuquin*. On the one hand, sensual reality depends on the miracle for its structure. On the other hand, the miracle must forge a link to a sensual reality to gain legitimacy.

Because the miracle must relate the spiritual to the sensual, it cannot be separated from a bodily experience, and Einstein develops an understanding of the miracle as a sacrifice. In its inherent disdain for the material world in favor of a higher goal, sacrifice gives spiritual form to the world: "Claudel is not concerned with things, but with their principles, which are embodied in humans, yet, not entirely—principles exceed the human. In order to be king, the king must sacrifice himself, and in the same way the saint gives himself over to the miracle."[34] Material being must be sacrificed in order to create form and the miraculous as functions of the eternal. But the sacrifice of material reality only gains significance to the extent that the value of material life is affirmed through this sacrifice. Sacrifice must not be a rejection of the material in favor of the form but rather a realization of the ways in which form permeates the material. Accordingly, death must retain a fateful and defining significance for life.

Einstein demonstrates the aesthetic functioning of the miracle as sacrifice in Christianity by citing the parabolical significance of the life of Christ as an example of a sacrificial death: "The pre-condition for the drama is not some teaching, however, but the dramatically predetermined parable, the myth. Christianity possesses in a certain sense only one: the life of Christ."[35] The defining element of this life is not any fixed dogma but the sacrifice that connects the mysterium, a religious form, to the tragic, an aesthetic form. Insofar as tragedy arises out of a sacrifice of the material in favor of the metaphysical, Einstein understands religion to be a product of mythic sacrifice.

The mediator of the metaphysical, Christ in this case, despairs of the absence of the metaphysical in the material world. His willingness to sacrifice himself is a rejection of a material world in which the spiritual is not present. This sacrifice is consequently an affirmation of faith in the importance of the metaphysical. Since the miracle is a presentation of the eternal within the temporal, the sacrifice creates the miracle by providing an example of a rejection of an exclusively material reality, that is, one that does not participate in the spiritual.

Consequently, the mediator of the spiritual exists within a state of despair that leads to the sacrifice of a material reality devoid of spiritual content.[36] The result of the sacrifice is a miracle that does not exist for the mediator, but only for the community that the mediator creates by invoking the eternal aspect of material life: "The tragic is valid in the mysterium only insofar as the mediator of the metaphysical dies; for the miracle does not occur for him but for the others. The mediator is left with despair, and he carries out within himself the sacrifice."[37] Though the mediator dies, this death, as a sacrifice, enables the creation and continued existence of a mythic tragedy that holds the community together, not through a blind faith, but through dramatic (aesthetic) forces: "It is important that belief presupposes despair—in this way it becomes an immediate force, a dramatic force, not opinion. Belief without action, without sacrifice is almost like a theory and is in any case just a pretentious assertion."[38]

As an aesthetic experience, the tragedy of the sacrifice is a *sensual* affirmation of the primacy of the spiritual in spite of the power of the material. Because of its sensuality, the sacrifice is not directed toward an otherworldly reality but toward the community, for which the sacrifice becomes an exemplary act: "Since the miracle is the projection of an inner eternity, a sensual creation, it must necessarily always relate to others, even if only as an example."[39] By linking ecstatic aesthetic experience to the idea of sacrifice, Einstein envisions the "corporeal" miracle, which he seeks to attain in his prose.

In its linking of materiality to spirituality, the sacrifice does not create an abstractly transcendent reality. Rather, by implicitly establishing a hierarchy of values sacrifice provides a concrete example of how materiality is to be overcome in a particular culture. But in outlining the material structure of transcendence for a culture, sacrifice also provides the basic schema by which consciousness constitutes reality. By analyzing the structures of sacrifice that motivate a culture's narratives, one can deduce the parameters of the overarching totality within which consciousness in that culture constructs meaning. Sacrifice illuminates the metaphysical structure of our lives.

8

FROM FANTASY TO SACRIFICE IN *BEBUQUIN OR THE DILETTANTES OF WONDER*

Originating out of a search for the new, Carl Einstein's *Bebuquin or The Dilettantes of Wonder* stages an expressionist reenactment of the primitive. Though the novel's prose was conceived and written as a revolt against nineteenth-century realist forms of narration, this reaction did not lead to further progress toward an intensified modernization. Rather, Einstein's prose enacted a critique of progress and demonstrated a new interest in tradition. Einstein's rejection of an aesthetics of representation and realist description resulted in narrative forms whose logic resembles that of "primitive" prose forms such as myth, parable, and legend. This return occurred in spite of his own self-understanding as a creator of the "new." In fact, it was perhaps this conscious attempt to create the new that allowed Einstein to reenact the old and to "become" primitive rather than to create a romantic idealization of a past or exotic culture.

As we have seen, the interpretation of the relation between the real and the fantastic is crucial to the development of a primitivist aesthetic. While a scientific perspective affirms the validity of the distinction between real and ideal, a primitivist aesthetic does not. Rather, it combines the two in order to mediate the exigencies of an outside reality with the desires and goals of the individual psyche. Einstein worked to formulate such a mediation between the real and the ideal on the level of prose by dissolving the boundary between the real and the fantastic.

Tzvetan Todorov describes this dissolution as the primary characteristic of twentieth-century prose as opposed to a nineteenth-century prose in which the distinction is constantly being tested but is always maintained. In differentiating the nineteenth-century literature of the fantastic from twentieth-century prose, he emphasizes the latter's "normalization" of the supernatural. His primary example is the work of Kafka: "The fantastic started from a perfectly natural situation to reach its climax in the supernatural. 'The Metamorphosis' starts from a supernatural event, and during the course of the narrative gives it an increasingly natural atmosphere—until at the end, the story has gone as far as possible from the supernatural."[1] This merging of the natural with the supernatural is also the primary characteristic of myth. As Erich Auerbach points out, "the sublime influence of God here [in the Old Testament] reaches so deeply into the everyday that the two realms of the sublime and the everyday are not only actually unseparated but basically inseparable."[2] In the same way that for Auerbach the sublime becomes inseparable from the everyday and for Einstein the miracle in a religious work of art creates meaning for temporal existence, for Todorov "the fantastic becomes the rule, not the exception" in the twentieth-century text.[3] Because Einstein attempted to create a prose that could establish the organizing structure for experience, his writing begins to reproduce mythic structures that testify to both the metaphysical aspect of expressionist prose and the aesthetic character of myth.

THE MERGING OF SUBJECT AND OBJECT

Bebuquin or The Dilettantes of Wonder creates mythic forms by attempting to dissolve the distinction between reality and fantasy. The broad rejection of realist imitations of empirical reality leads Einstein into his theoretical investigations of the possibilities of fantasy in prose.[4] Thematically, the plot of the story revolves around an attempt to determine how to create a fantasy that still retains binding force for reality. The plot structure of the novel adheres to the schema of an age-old genre—the story of a hero engaged in a quest.[5] In this case, the hero, Giorgio Bebuquin, searches for a "corporeal miracle"—a fusion of the real and the fantastic. This thematic goal is reflected on a formal level in the structure of the story, in which events do not resemble events in empirical reality but instead function as conceptual, psychic events. The fantastic elements of the text describe the psychic processes that constantly accompany a subject's relation to the outside world. Though Bebuquin's search for the corporeal miracle has its parallel in the text's formal attempt to integrate fantasy with reality, the fulfillment of both the thematic and the formal goals of the novel only occurs at the end, when these two goals not only reflect each other but become a single unified experience. Reality becomes a function of the imagination at the point when the content expresses itself purely in terms of form.

In its attempt to approach this goal, the novel begins by breaking down the distinction between subject and object through the following synesthetic presentation of light as a mediator between objects and subjective impressions: "The shards of a yellow glass lantern rattled against the voice of a woman: 'Do you want to see your mother's spirit?' The unsteady light dripped onto the delicately marked pate of a young man, who turned away anxiously in order to prevent any considerations regarding the composition of his person."[6] In this passage, light acts as a mediator between the different figures and objects described, emphasizing the impossibility of a direct perception of the reality of objects by a subject. Light is not neutral but suffuses objects with a particular subjective perspective that mediates between the viewer and the perceived object. Instead of being described as an objective natural scientific force, light functions as an emotional force that illuminates objects in such a way as to shape them according to the subjective impressions of the viewer. The light reflects from the woman's voice as the "shards" of a lamp that drop incessantly upon Bebuquin's head. The discomfort of the "rattling shards" of light dripping onto Bebuquin's head reflects his fear that the woman's offer to show him the spirit of his mother could lead to questions about his identity.

Following the model proposed by Nietzsche in "On Truth and Lie in an Extra-Moral Sense," Einstein's text demonstrates that perception is metaphorical and mediated through the categories of the subject.[7] Many of the fantastic passages in *Bebuquin* are constructed to highlight the mediating factors that determine a subject's perception of things. While light in the passage just quoted was suffused with Bebuquin's fear, in a later scene it functions according to the patterns of Bebuquin's desire: "The moons of the arc-lamps became obscene, their rays fingering the décolletées of the ladies; they listened to Bebuquin's soft, dry voice telling of his last love" (20). In this passage, the "obscenity" of the light is a result of the subjective desires that guide Bebuquin's male perspective on the scene. By the end of the scene there is a clear relation between the movement of light and his sexual desires: "A diamond above Euphemia's décolletée caught the unused morning light and concentrated it. Giorgio was frightened by her brightness, screamed 'damn' and went to visit her apartment" (22). Such fantastic elements of the story, which highlight the subject's role in perception, cannot be distinguished from the realist elements. Rather, the story is told as a description of psychic experience in which real objects can only be perceived through a psychic construction that merges the outer with the inner world in order to create meaning for the subject.

In the plot of the story, both Bebuquin and Nebuchadnezzar Böhm seek a form of perception that would relate objects to the consciousness of the subject. They are opposed to a positivist view in which an object is trapped in a logic of cause and effect that has nothing to do with the subject. But while Bebuquin tries to find a subjective creation that still maintains a link to a corporeal reality, Böhm, considering the world of objects to be "a question of power, a matter of naming and self-hypnosis" (5), denies that objects have any independent reality outside of the will of the subject.[8]

Böhm exemplifies E. B. Tylor's negative image of the deluded primitive, who "mistakes" thoughts for objects.[9] Because objects must always exist for the mind as thoughts, Böhm presumes that objects function purely in terms of the concepts and desires of the subject: "The concept strives toward things, but I want exactly the opposite. I direct my attention toward enjoyment" (11). Concentrating on subjective pleasure as opposed to real objects, Böhm creates a second kind of fantasy in the story that is not a form of mediation between subject and object but a creation of a completely new fantastic reality in which the subject maintains absolute domination.

Böhm's creation of an alternative fantastic reality brings him into violent conflict with empirical reality. This conceptual conflict is depicted in the first chapter of the story as an event that, like the opening sentence of the novel, takes place as a reflection of light:

> Nebuchadnezzar bent his head over Euphemia's massive bosom. A mirror hung above him. He saw how her breasts sparkled and split themselves into multifarious and strange forms in the finely polished precious stone plates in his head, forms that no reality thus far had been able to give him. The engraved silver refracted and refined the glitter of the forms. Nebuchadnezzar stared into the mirror with greedy joy over how he was able to divide up reality, how his soul was the silver and jewels, his eye the mirror.
>
> "Bebuquin," he screamed and collapsed; for he was still incapable of enduring the soul of things. (5–6)

The reflection of Euphemia's breasts in the mirror creates a new reality that is determined by the patterns of chased silver and gems on Böhm's head. In contrast to Bebuquin's bald head, which was vulnerable to the effects of the "shards" of light, Böhm's head reflects the light so he can create his own idiosyncratic image of reality. By concentrating on this projected reality, Böhm's conception of objects as products of the subject comes into conflict with the view that objects belong to an outside reality governed by laws of cause and effect. Because his subjective reality rejects the validity of the forces of an outside empirical reality, he can no longer exist in the empirical world and dies. His collapse is a result of his rejection of the empirical world and the limits that it places on the freedom of the subject.

By the end of the paragraph, Böhm constructs a new logic out of the forms of the chase-work on his head: "This multiplied his power, he believed himself to be in another, perpetually new world with new pleasures" (6). There is a conflict between a view of the world in which objects are empirically given to consciousness and one in which consciousness constructs its own fantasy objects. Böhm resolves this conflict by taking the projection of the world provided by his silver head as the valid one and by rejecting, not only the empirical world of cause and effect, but also the reality of pain that results from the limitations that reality places on his existence: "He no longer felt his bodily form through his sense of touch. It was almost forgotten, was writhing in pain, for the visible world was not in accord with it" (6). This virtual "forgetting" of limitations on his fantasies allows him, within the logic of the story, to continue to exist in the story after his death.

In contrast to Bebuquin's susceptibility to outside forces and his use of fantasy to mediate between the subject and outside reality, Böhm's form of fantasy creates a whole new fantastic reality that conforms completely to his wishes. His "posthumous" existence in the story is his demonstration that natural laws are not conceptually binding for the psyche and that limiting thought to natural laws would reduce the possibilities for human experience. As an immortal figure, he is a walking advertisement for the nonreal: "I assure you, I, for example, am alive only because I suggest myself to myself; in reality I'm dead. You know of course that I've been entombed. But I promised myself that I would walk around as an advertisement for the unreal until some idiot experiences me as a miracle" (18). The idiosyncrasy of Böhm's reality corresponds to Einstein's vision of the hermetic aestheticist artist, whose aesthetic constructions never attain a communal meaning, but instead remain part of a private, and thus pathological, mythology.

SACRIFICE AS CORPOREAL MIRACLE

Both Böhm and Bebuquin reject the view of reality provided by a positivist worldview and search for the miraculous. Indeed, Böhm bluntly states at the outset: "I seek the miracle" (5). His understanding of the miracle is a constructivist one, which not only abandons empirical objects but the entire mimetic attitude to the world. Consequently, he contents himself with absurd flights of fantasy in which he flies through the air or transforms the bar into a giant bird that also takes flight (24, 35–36). Bebuquin, holding onto a mimetic impulse, maintains a desire for limitations on the nonreal: "'We don't sacrifice anything anymore,' Bebuquin screamed into the street. 'The sublime is disappearing. You criticize the miracle, the miracle only makes sense when it is corporeal [*leibhaftig*], but you have destroyed all forces that go beyond the human'" (17). Searching for a fusion of the miraculous with physical reality, Bebuquin declares that the affirmation of the metaphysical can only occur as a recognition of powers that are beyond human control.

Bebuquin's attempt at a mimesis of such powers is depicted in the novel as a search for limits on subjective freedom that could create a binding narrative or myth. According to Bebuquin, Böhm's rejection of both the validity of physical laws and the finality and necessity of death leaves him oblivious to the limitations that material reality places upon human existence. It is not the unwillingness to let go of empirical reality but the elimination of outside necessities that is, for Einstein, the work of a "dilettante." In its belief in a complete artistic freedom, Böhm's dilettantism ignores the constraints that create the work of art's connection to both psychic and natural forces. In so doing, the dilettante leaves the realm of concrete actions and lives in a mad fantasy world.[10] Against such a dilettantism, Einstein, along with the character Bebuquin, searches out those elements of reality that place limits on the freedom of the subject.[11]

Bebuquin's simultaneous affirmation of the metaphysical and the physical world is the thematic expression of the novel's formal attempt to merge the fantastic and the real, construction and mimesis. Whereas Böhm rejects the limitations of the latter in favor of the freedom of the former, Bebuquin (on the thematic level) and the novel as a whole (on the formal level) attempt to merge bodily constraints with miraculous effects. This quest culminates in Bebuquin's affirmation of sacrifice. But in the course of this quest, he must struggle against the temptation to accept Böhm's offer to liberate him from the limitations that the body places on consciousness. Thus, the major events of the novel—the birth of the child, Emil; Böhm's death and continued postmortem existence; Euphemia's unwillingness to break her neck in the circus; Bebuquin's attempt to bury Böhm; and Bebuquin's death at the end—all involve the relation of the subject to mortality.

Böhm understands death to be the liberation of the subject from the constraints of the body, suggesting to Bebuquin that "metamorphosis comes perhaps with death" (39). However, Bebuquin responds with the idea that death is not freedom but limitation. In his view, death is not a new beginning but rather "is entangled with life, and every day of struggle and growth is a day of death" (41). This view of life as inextricably linked to death allows Bebuquin to reject Böhm's escape into death yet still retain death as a possible source of metaphysical experience. As in Einstein's prose theory, Bebuquin links the metaphysical to an intense preoccupation with the limitations of the physical. He does not consider death as an alternative realm but as the element of fate that gives form to life.

In this conception, the subject/object distinction is replaced by the conflict between the imagination and the power of death. For Bebuquin, the miracle must negate death without abandoning the laws of nature and the body. As a consequence, the miracle he seeks must maintain an aesthetic form in which the human imagination (the constructive aspect of art) is mediated with death as the limitation of the body (the mimetic aspect of art):

> Death, father of humor, if only a miracle that I see with my eyes would destroy you;
> your enemy is the fantastic which stands outside of all rules;
> but art forces it to stand, and, exhausted, it takes form.
> I name you, death, the father of intensity, the Lord of form. (42)

For Bebuquin, the force of death can only exist for consciousness if death is conceived as a final determining experience for all life, and the integration of a consciousness of death into life can only occur when works of art "relinquish themselves mimetically to reification, their principle of death."[12] By conceiving of art as the mediator of death to human consciousness, Bebuquin defines art as the site for a mediation of the metaphysical with the physical.[13]

As with Freud's similar reinterpretation of the subject/object distinction as a conflict between inner wishes and external forces, for Einstein rational thought must give way to aesthetic experience as the mediator between these two opposing forces. The conflict between subjective desires and objective forces shapes both aesthetic form for Einstein and magic for Freud, resulting in "corporeal" miracles. In the shaping of aesthetic form, fantasy is constructed according to subjective desire and objective forces. The resulting form is a mediation of inner wishes with external constraints, and art in Einstein's view is consequently very close to myth to the extent that both attempt to create a spiritual mediation between the poles of a contradiction in reality.[14]

The similarity between Einstein's view of the task of art and Freud's understanding of the mechanisms of magic suggests an essential link between art and sacred ritual for Einstein. His novel investigates this connection when Bebuquin attempts to bury Böhm and thereby recover the significance of the body for consciousness. The burial is both an aesthetic and a sacred act. Yet this act, meant to exorcise Böhm's flippant irreality, gradually itself turns into an act of absurdity. After digging a grave, Bebuquin's actions quickly become a caricature of a funeral:

> He continued to dig, then placed himself as a monument behind the pit, repeating the following epitaph several times:
>   "Weep tenderly and remain bowed!"
> And folded his hands across his breast.
>   The sun rose and sparkled upon him, who stood as crucified.
>   Gradually this pose shifted into a well-regulated free-style gymnastics. (49)

The eulogy is already ironic, and the image of crucifixion becomes absurd in its exaggeration, even without the passage into gymnastics.

Kiefer reads this passage as an ironic reference to turn-of-the-century "body culture" movements and cites Nietzsche's criticism of "the whole Christian system of *training* in penance and salvation."[15] However, the novel's veiled reference to Nietzsche suggests that for Einstein the death of Christ is to be read, as in Nietzsche's argument, both as a defense of Christ himself and an attack on the Christian church.[16] Nietzsche praises the person of Christ for his ability to merge the divine and the mundane in his death but criticizes the institution of Christianity for reintroducing a separation between the two in the doctrine of the resurrection. This distinction between death as a separation and death as a merging of the metaphysical with the physical defines the conflict between Böhm and Bebuquin and determines the significance of Bebuquin's gymnastics at the funeral.

Though the gymnastics "training" can be read as a caricature of the empty rituals of an institutionalized Christianity, the alternative that Bebuquin presents at the end of the story is another kind of training whose discipline is directed at the body and its metamorphosis. In describing this understanding of training, Einstein writes in 1929: "It is precisely this exercise, this ecstatic *training* which has been pushed by Masson to perfection."[17] This ecstatic training is directed at one's own body and its death: "The pious man is the well-practiced suicider, he is a dilettante when anything resounds in his ears other than the word in which the world died."[18] The only valid word is the one with which the self and the world die. This word is directed at materiality but only in order to eliminate it.

This double movement defines the aesthetic of the novel. On the one hand, the word is made flesh, and the aesthetic experiments of the novel are based on this materialization of the word. Abstract phrases and concepts are all taken literally to create the events of the story. For example, Böhm's death and afterlife is a literal rendering of his discursive insistence on the primacy of fantasy; he demonstrates the freedom of fantasy by turning the bar into a bird and flying through the air with it; and Bebuquin's insistence on the integration of death into life takes bodily form in the image of the neighbor who has been "dead through his own will," living "only apparently" and thereby "deceiving death" (43). The absurdity of the literal, bodily rendering of an abstract idea destroys the idea and its abstraction. On the other hand, this continual destruction of ideas in the novel does not lead it to abandon the spiritual realm. Rather, it conceives of the metaphysical, not as a conceptual entity, but a gesture that is created through a moment of sacrifice in which the material world is consciously negated. The metaphysical force of the word does not lie in its content but in its formal negation of the body, much like the gymnast's negation of the limitations of the body in favor of aesthetic form.

The materialization of the metaphysical that dominates the events of the novel culminates in the last chapter. There, words lose their substantive meaning in favor of a gestural one, and the body increases in significance only to be negated in a last linguistic act. There is no dialogue in the last chapter, speech becoming subsumed within Bebuquin's increasing attention to his own body during his last three nights. On the first night, the narrator does not recount what Bebuquin says, but rather only describes his ability and inability to speak: "He was unable to speak. After an hour he spoke with self-control" (50). Language is not described as a content—dialogue—but as a bodily gesture. On the second night, this gesture begins to take on its own content of ecstatic excitement: "He speaks excitedly and senses dark birds fluttering around him" (50). Finally, language ceases and becomes subjugated to the domination of the body: "Then his jaws become rigid" (50). On the third and last night, the narrator describes Bebuquin as a series of uncontrollable gestures: "Bebuquin fell asleep peacefully, in his sleep his hands shot up a few times; gradually his face lay convulsed, the skin folded and wrinkled around the whole skull. His eyelids jerked open for a few seconds, he stretched his fingers and toes, spreading them out, then he contracted tightly and trembled vigorously. Toward morning he awoke, was unable to speak and could not eat unassisted" (50). While the last three nights describe Bebuquin's diminishing ability to speak and an accompanying determination of his actions by involuntary gestures, in the next sentence, which ends the novel, Bebuquin confronts the dominance of his body and commits with one final word the suicide in which word and gesture are one:

> He looked only once coolly inside and spoke
> Out. (50)

This final word, both describing and enacting Bebuquin's death as well as the end of the story, functions at once as action and as expression.[19] It links gesture and speech in a death that is not a bridge to another world but a concentration on, yet a negation of, the physical world. The power of materiality at the end of the story limits Bebuquin's options until the only means left to oppose materiality is through his sacrifice of materiality itself in suicide. This suicide results in a corresponding affirmation of spirituality itself, though not of any of the particular religious forms parodied throughout the novel. Rather than affirming a universal religion, Bebuquin insists on the connection between the metaphysical and a particular material context. By abandoning the content of speech and reducing the word to its function as a negation of the body, the final "Out" links the physical to the metaphysical in a sacrificial gesture, whose movement defines the novel's metaphysical project and underlines its primitivist impulse.

9

EXPRESSIONIST MYTH AND AFRICAN LEGEND

In 1925 Carl Einstein published *Afrikanische Legenden*, a collection of African stories that he gathered and translated into German from French transcriptions. One of these stories, "The Wanderer of the Plain" ("Der Gaukler der Ebene"), originated as a southeast African legend of the Thonga people that had been collected and translated into French by Henri Junod in 1898.[1] Though Einstein's version cannot be designated as a true myth or legend belonging to an oral tradition passed down through several generations, it is a German expressionist attempt to imitate a mythic performance and reenact it in literature.[2] Einstein carries out this project by continuing the process initiated by Junod of transcribing and translating orally transmitted African tales into European languages, thus attempting to reproduce the structure of a traditional oral tale. The result is that the story demonstrates the essential characteristics of his ideal prose: a firm connection between action and consequence leading to a "simultaneity" of events and a fatefulness of the plot, a parabolic structure composed of a "staircase" of parables, and an emphasis on the importance of sacrifice for defining and maintaining a community.

"The Wanderer of the Plain" leads a double life because of its translation out of an African context and into a German one. On the one hand, this translation demonstrates the centrality of cultural context in determining the meaning of the story. The actions and decisions of the figures in the story only make sense in terms of the specific marriage rituals normally observed by the Thonga people, and Einstein's decision to exclude this context from his presentation of the story prevents the story from being the mediator of any cultural exchange. Rather, Einstein's omission of information about the cultural context (which was available to him in the same volume from which he obtained the French version of the story) creates a sense of alienation in the German reader. Rather than being a tool of cultural exchange, the story mediates a feeling of the strange and exotic.

On the other hand, this African story provides the parameters for reinterpreting European culture in terms of a primitive perspective in which the story of Enlightenment becomes a version of the myth of Oedipus—a story about the persistence of generational conflict rather than the overthrowing of tradition. The similarity of "The Wanderer of the Plain" to the myth of Oedipus provides a bridge between southeast Africa and Germany, revealing the primitive dimension of European culture. In reintroducing the Oedipal myth by way of Africa, Einstein's translation attempts to demonstrate that the structures of kinship are still defining ones for a "modern" context and that the cross-cultural conflicts of "modern" society are also central for "primitive" contexts. He thereby dissolves the distinction between "civilized" and "primitive" cultures in order to illuminate the contradictions that lie at the heart of every culture.

KINSHIP AND AFFINITY

The story begins with a son's decision to search for a wife in another country rather than accept a "local" wife chosen by his parents. The son seeks independence from his parents in his decisions about marriage, and this framing story considers the consequences of his choices. This primary conflict between parents and children is interwoven with a conflict between disparate cultures. The conflict between the parents and the son is tied to the foreign bride's decision to bring her country's buffalo with her to her new land. This decision gives rise to another story within the original framing story that repeats the conflict between parents and children and local and foreign culture while at the same time adding a spiritual dimension through the figure of the buffalo. The interweaving of a family conflict with an intercultural conflict indicates that the fundamental problem in both stories is a tension between the kinship and familial bonds enforced by the parents on the one hand and the affinity bonds pursued by the children on the other.[3]

The son's journey to a distant land to find a wife is initially described as his refusal of his parents' authority: "'We want to choose a pretty wife for you whose parents are good people.' But he refused. 'No,' he said, 'don't go to this trouble. I don't like the girls around here. When I must marry, I will seek myself for the one that I desire.' 'Do as you will,' the parents said to him. 'If you are unhappy later, it will not be our fault.'"[4] From the beginning of the story the conflict between parents and children is constructed as a conflict between the principle of kinship (the parents would like to choose a local bride) and the idea of affinity (the son intends to marry the girl that he desires). By seeking a foreign bride, the son attempts to use personal affinities, as expressed by his desires, to transcend the confines of his culture.

Once he finds a wife, the son's handling of the marriage further diminishes the role of kinship rituals and intensifies his rejection of the kinship principle. Though he duly pays the bride-price, which he has brought with him, the son does not have his parents come to claim the wife as is customary. He explains to the parents of the bride that his own parents might offend the people of the bride's village by insulting them.[5] By circumventing the traditional rituals in which the parents of the bride and groom exchange gifts and interact with each other in a joint ritual and celebration, the son abandons the mechanisms by which the two disparate cultures might begin to find some common ground and thereby establish that the marriage is anchored within relations of kinship.[6] Instead, the paying of the bride-price becomes an economic transaction rather than the establishment of a social bond, a pure exchange rather than a ritual.[7]

The rebellion against kinship bonds is repeated by the bride when she leaves with her new husband to go to his village. Before leaving, the parents offer the bride any girl in the village to bring with her as a maidservant, a typical practice amongst the Thonga.[8] She refuses and insists instead on bringing the village's buffalo: "'give me the country's buffalo, our buffalo, the Wanderer of the Plain. It will serve me.' 'What?,' they said, 'you know that our life depends on it. Here it is well fed and well taken care of. What will you do with it in another country? It will be hungry, it will die, and we will all die with it.'"[9] But the bride insists, and the parents let her take the buffalo. The bride's refusal of a girl in favor of the buffalo is another departure from the accepted norm. The wife not only neglects the cultural specificity of the buffalo by taking it to a foreign country but she also reduces the buffalo to her servant. Rather than concentrating on caring for the buffalo as the villagers insist is necessary, she uses it to gather wood, bring water, and plow the fields. Her attempt to simply use the buffalo for its powers, feeding it only in exchange for its services, ultimately undermines the ritual role her village accords to the buffalo. Like the husband, she replaces a set of ritual gifts and sacrifices with a relationship of exchange.

By interpreting gift and sacrifice as exchange, both the husband and the wife attempt to replace bonds of kinship with bonds of affinity as the regulators of social relations. While kinship bonds are based on limitations and sacrifice, the affinity bonds are an expression of freedom and the interaction of like with like. The couple's endeavors recall Horkheimer and Adorno's account of the strategy of Homer's Odysseus in that they use their cunning to turn the irrationality of sacrifice into the rationality of exchange.[10] But unlike Odysseus the couple's cunning turns against them, and the final result of the underemphasis of kinship bonds is a disastrous suicide.

THE BUFFALO AS MEDIATOR

To make the contradiction between kinship and affinity tangible, Einstein's story employs an intermediary figure—the buffalo—that becomes the site of conflict. The conflict between kinship and affinity is conducted as a battle between varying interpretations of the animal's meaning. Like the coyote of American Indian myths described by Lévi-Strauss, the buffalo functions as a mediator.[11] Just as Lévi-Strauss describes how the mediator serves to embody, but never truly resolve, an unbridgeable contradiction, so the buffalo is not able to defuse the contradiction between cultures that lies at the root of each story.[12] Rather, the changing perspectives on the mediator of the story's participants define the irreconcilability of the contradictions.

In "The Wanderer of the Plain" the buffalo functions as a mediator between the two opposing cultures. It is at first only visible to the wife and the people of her native village, and it then acts as the "force" that aids the wife in doing all of her chores after she moves with it to her husband's village. It does not exist for the husband and his village. Their failure to perceive the buffalo results in a failure to feed it as well—there is no bowl for the buffalo in the wife's new home, and it has nothing to eat. But when the wife insists on feeding it by having it steal from the villagers' fields, the villagers begin to be able to perceive it as well. However, their perception differs markedly from that of the wife. The villagers react to the intrusion on their fields by setting up a watch, and when the buffalo steals from the husband's fields he himself kills the buffalo with his spear (in Einstein's version; in Junod's version the husband uses a gun). The villagers celebrate by cutting up the buffalo and eating it.

The wife reacts by attempting to ward off this materialist understanding of the buffalo as a source of food. She takes the head and uses it to attempt to resurrect the buffalo by means of a magical spell. The conflict between the spiritual and the materialist view of the buffalo is staged during her attempts at resurrection. Her incantation designates the buffalo as both father and the movement of death:

> O my father, Wanderer of the Plain.
> They said to me, Wanderer of the Plain,
> You roam through deep darkness,
> You meander in all directions, Wanderer of the Plain.
> You are the young plant that grows out of the ruins,
>   that dies before its time,
> Consumed by the gnawing worm.
> You fell flowers and fruits in your path,
>   Wanderer of the Plain.[13]

These verses invoke the buffalo as something beyond death, as the force of death itself, which cuts short the life of flowers and plants but also allows new life to begin, growing "out of the ruins." Death can only be overcome by recognizing its power, and the resurrection of the buffalo depends upon the Dionysian invocation of death as the prelude to regeneration: "When she finished her incantations, the head moved. The limbs returned. The buffalo began to feel itself returning to life." But then her husband arrives and calls to the wife, and as a result "the head of the buffalo falls to the ground, dead, impaled as before."[14] The buffalo returns to the state of dead matter, that is, the form in which it is seen by the husband. The wife repeats her invocation of the spirit of death two more times but is interrupted at the same point each time, first by her husband again and then by her mother-in-law. After the third failed attempt, the buffalo can no longer be resurrected, and the wife returns to her village to announce its death.

The double aspect of the buffalo is a result of the wife's efforts to invoke it as a material mask for a spiritual reality. This goal coincides with the metaphysical goal of twentieth-century European writers and artists. For example, the wife's incantations closely resemble Antonin Artaud's invocation of a metaphysical language of the theater: "To make a metaphysics out of spoken language is to make language express what it does not usually express. It is to use it in a new, exceptional, and unaccustomed way, to restore its possibilities for physical shock, to divide it and distribute it actively in space, to use intonations in an absolutely concrete manner and to restore their power to hurt as well as really to manifest something, to turn against language and its basely utilitarian—one might almost say alimentary—sources, against its origins as a trapped animal, and finally, to consider language as *Incantation*."[15] In contrast to the husband and mother-in-law, the wife seeks to banish the "alimentary" aspect of the buffalo as "trapped animal" by means of her incantation. As Lévi-Strauss points out with respect to religious art, the buffalo is structured as a split representation in which the material aspect is only a function of the metaphysical aspect, which is in turn indispensable to the foundation of a social order.[16] By invoking the buffalo as the physical mask for a spiritual reality, the wife also seeks to carve out a space for the buffalo within the social world, a space that the husband and mother-in-law fail to recognize.

As the husband's and mother-in-law's interruptions demonstrate, the wife cannot resurrect the buffalo alone within a foreign social context. She needs the support of her native village to keep the buffalo alive as a spiritual force, and the competing views of the buffalo not only define a conflict between a materialist and a spiritual understanding of its reality but also illustrate a conflict between two cultures, only one of which recognizes the buffalo's spiritual significance. The resulting divergence of perspectives is never resolved in the story. Instead, the buffalo remains a split figure, understood differently by the two cultures, as the exchange between the husband and the people of the wife's village illustrates:

> They were all there when the husband, who had followed his wife, entered the village. He leaned his spear against a tree trunk and sat down. Everyone greeted him and said: 'Welcome, murderer, welcome. You have killed us all.' He did not understand at all and asked them how they could call him a murderer, 'I killed a buffalo, that is all.'
>
> 'Yes, but this buffalo was your wife's servant, it brought back water for her, it cut wood for her, it worked in the fields.'
>
> The husband was surprised and said: 'Why did you not let me know? I would not have killed it.'
>
> 'You see,' they added, 'our life depended on it.'
>
> Then they all began to cut their throats, the young woman first. She cried:
>
> 'Oh my father, the Wanderer of the Plain.'"[17]

While the buffalo is no more than an animal for the husband, the wife and her village consider it, again referred to as the father, to have an additional spiritual aspect upon which their lives depend. The husband remains as uncomprehending of the mass suicide as the reader or listener of the story, and this inability to understand a different culture and its means of perceiving the world is as absolute at the end of the story as the significance of the buffalo is to the survival of the wife's village. Without the buffalo, the village has no collective, that is, metaphysical, basis for perceiving the world. Even the children are killed, for "they would in any case go insane."[18]

EINSTEIN AS EDITOR

It is at this point that Einstein's version of the story ends. In the version that was originally recounted by Junod the husband returns home, where his parents reproach him for having lost his bride-price by marrying outside of his country: "You see? Did we not tell you that you would run into misfortune? When we offered to choose for you an appropriate and obedient woman, you wanted to do as you pleased, and you lost your fortune."[19] The disparity between cultures becomes the justification for adhering to family customs. Though Einstein tried to delete this moralizing conclusion to the story, this perspective nevertheless motivates the entire story. For the reproach that the parents direct toward the son is a repetition of a reproach already directed against the wife by her parents: "You see, we were right. You refused all the gifts that we offered and only wanted the buffalo. You have killed us all."[20] In both cases, the child is reproached for having acted not just against the parents' wishes but against the very principle of kinship. The ideas of independence and exchange that replace it are depicted in the end, not as signs of rationality, but of a childish selfishness and irresponsibility.

Einstein attempted to excise the moralizing tone of the ending because he believed that the point of the story is not to communicate a moral. It is to give tangible form to a contradiction between the children's "reasonable" adherence to free choice and affinity as guides for action directed at material improvements and the parents' insistence on the demands of kinship and cultural specificity. The function of the story is not to teach a lesson but to present a contradiction.[21] This presentation does not follow the rules of realism but rather a hidden logic that exists behind reality. As Nietzsche insists in *The Birth of Tragedy*, the primal contradiction at the heart of the world cannot be perceived directly in the myth. Rather, it must express itself through the mask of appearances.

All of the concerns and perspectives that impact upon the contradiction at the heart of Einstein's story have been merged into the single figure of the buffalo in the same way that the different possible views of a three-dimensional object have been merged into a single view in an African sculpture. In both cases, the resulting work of art makes a set of intangible relations into something tangible that can be collectively viewed and discussed.

Einstein's deletion of the moralizing ending does more than place the emphasis on contradiction and increase the disturbing nature of the story. It also serves to separate the story from the African context in which it originated. The moral is the link between the story's reality and the listener's reality. In breaking this link, Einstein increases the distance between the story and an outside context. Though this makes it easier to refunctionalize the story and integrate it into an alternative, German context, it also increases the "alienation effect" of the story, which is further intensified by Einstein's one other editorial alteration. As noted earlier, he transforms the gun in Junod's version into a lance. As Kiefer has pointed out, this change is an attempt to evoke an African milieu, an exoticizing move that maintains the reader's distance from the story's reality.[22]

These changes, which increase the distance between the German reader and the original African context, turn the story itself into the same type of cultural artifact as the buffalo within the story. Like the buffalo, the story can either be the mediator of a spiritual relation to the world or a type of "dead" language without this spiritual dimension. By removing it from its proper context, Einstein risks eliminating its spiritual power. Once this power disappears, the story can no longer serve as a mediator of cross-cultural interaction but only as a gauge of cross-cultural conflict, changing in meaning and function as it is transported from one culture to the other. Einstein's method thus places him in the same position as the son in the story who in his decision to marry remains oblivious to the gravity of cultural differences. In both cases, the naive attempt to bridge cultural differences as if they did not exist only leads to an exacerbation of those differences.

The disparity of cultures is, in both the story itself and in Einstein's unintentional reenactment of the story, accompanied by a congruence between the structure of the framing story and the story within. The story of the wife and the buffalo reenacts the story of the son and the wife, and Einstein's translation efforts reenact both stories within the cross-cultural nexus of Germany and Africa. His conscious efforts to maintain a separation between Africa and Germany become, unconsciously, the mechanism by which his own actions mimic the plot of the story.

Yet just as the tragic ending of "The Wanderer of the Plain" projects the negative image of a possible reconciliation between cultures through a sharing of rituals, Einstein's editorial decisions also point out the terms of a possible cultural reconciliation between Thonga and Germany. For the introduction of the lance into "The Wanderer of the Plain" can be seen as a way of demonstrating a parallel in the story with a possible framing story from the European literary context. The lance, by recalling the lance with which Oedipus kills his father, can also relate Einstein's story to the Oedipal myth of generational conflict. Because the buffalo functions as the "father" for the wife and her village, the son's killing of the buffalo places him in the same patricidal role as Oedipus. In the African version of the Oedipal story, the question of technology connoted by the gun is subsumed under the question of generational conflict. In Einstein's German version, the lance helps to integrate the African story into a European mythic context.

OEDIPAL VARIATIONS

Einstein's primitivist perspective entails a philosophy of history in which the distinction between "modern" and "traditional" loses its world-historical character and becomes a specific case of a wider phenomenon. He delineates a constant conflict between two opposing perspectives that can express themselves in any society, from ancient to contemporary times, and in various cultures of the world. From this primitivist point of view the conflict between "modern" and "traditional" perspectives is another specific instance of the generational conflict that defines the structure of every community, and the Enlightenment is merely an extended period of time in which the perspective of children has been dominant over that of parents within intellectual circles.

In "The Wanderer of the Plain" the conflict between parents and children is intertwined with the question of marriage. Similarly, Nietzsche refers to the connection between generational conflict and gender in the opening passage of *The Birth of Tragedy* by introducing the opposition between Apollo and Dionysus as both a generational and a gender conflict: "We shall have gained much for the science of aesthetics, once we perceive not merely by logical inference, but with the immediate certainty of vision [*logischen Einsicht, sondern zur unmittelbaren Sicherheit der Anschauung*], that the continuous development of art is bound up with the *Apollinian* and *Dionysian* duality [*Duplicität*]—just as procreation depends on the duality of the sexes [*wie die Generation von der Zweiheit der Geschlechter*], involving perpetual strife with only periodically intervening reconciliations."[23] The opposition of logic to "vision" (or "intuition" [*Anschauung*]) becomes not only a duplicity of Apollinian and Dionysian but a duality of the exemplary image as well. While the "*Zweiheit der Geschlechter*" seems at first glance to mean "duality of the sexes" and has been duly translated by Kaufmann in this way, there is an ambiguity in the German word *Geschlechter* in which it could just as easily mean "generations," designating here the duality between parents and children. The immediately succeeding phrase, which emphasizes the continual conflict between the two *Geschlechter*, supports this latter interpretation.

The continual cycle of individuation and dissolution of each generation creates the conflict that drives human history, and this generational conflict lies at the foundation of the contradiction between logic and intuition and Apollo and Dionysus. The children in Greek tragedy, Oedipus and Pentheus, for example, as well as the children of "The Wanderer of the Plain," attempt to use their rational faculties to differentiate themselves from their parents according to an Apollinian principle of individuation. The parents in Greek tragedy, Cadmus and Agave, as well as the parents of "The Wanderer of the Plain," pay homage to Dionysus and recognize the limitations of human aspirations and the inevitability of death and dissolution. This continual conflict between the parents and children guarantees the recurrence of generational conflict within human experience. It bases the question of origins in the repetition of certain conflicts within the psyche of each successive generation and thus within each individual subject.

Yet the gender distinction in Nietzsche's word *Geschlechter* is not dispelled by the generational conflict. The ambiguity in Nietzsche's phrasing presents a duplicity between gender and generations in which both issues are linked together in the question of human origins. Human generation depends as much upon the duality of gender as the conflict between the generations. As Lévi-Strauss writes, the Oedipus myth "has to do with the inability, for a culture which holds the belief that mankind is autochthonous (see, for instance, Pausanias, VIII, xxix, 4: plants provide a *model* for humans), to find a satisfactory transition between this theory and the knowledge that human beings are actually born from the union of man and woman. Although the problem obviously cannot be solved, the Oedipus myth provides a kind of logical tool which relates the original problem—born from one or born from two?—to the derivative problem: born from different or born from same?"[24] One of the primary issues of the Oedipal myth is that a human comes from two rather than one. This fact, which provides the starting point for definitions of kinship, is the key determinant of human social structure, creating the system of dichotomies and contradictions that lie at the center of both the incest taboo and marriage rituals.

In his reading of the Oedipal myth, Lévi-Strauss notes a basic contradiction between an underrating and an overrating of kinship bonds: "the overrating of blood relations is to the underrating of blood relations as the attempt to escape autochthony is to the impossibility to succeed in it."[25] It would be perhaps more accurate to define the conflict as one between an emphasis on kinship and an attempt to escape kinship through affinity. In the case of the Oedipus myth, the marriage to the mother is not so much an overrating of blood relations as part of an attempt to escape from blood relations—Oedipus acts as if blood relations did not exist and did not matter. If blood relations did not matter, then the principle of affinity would inevitably lead to incest. For as Freud notes, each of us has a natural tendency toward incest: "While the poet, as he unravels the past, brings to light the guilt of Oedipus, he is at the same time compelling us to recognize our own inner minds, in which those same impulses, though suppressed, are still to be found."[26] The revelation of Oedipus's incest presents a realization of both the pervasiveness of such inner impulses and the consequent continuing significance of kinship.

The children's underrating of kinship bonds in "The Wanderer of the Plain" is made possible by the escape the principle of affinity offers them. This opposition between kinship and affinity is in turn repeated in the opposition between a local (autochthonous) culture and a foreign culture in which the children's attempt to escape a local culture, both in "The Wanderer of the Plain" and in the case of Oedipus, ultimately ends in disaster. The generational struggle is intertwined with a cross-cultural conflict, which indicates that there is a fundamental contradiction between the principles of kinship and affinity, in which kinship is related to autochthony and affinity is related to mobility.

Yet the principle of affinity is not simply an enemy but rather also lies at the center of kinship dynamics because of the fact of gender: humans come from two rather than one, and every marriage involves a linking of two families. Marriage rituals thus become the nexus at which the local and the foreign meet and interact. The task of marriage is to integrate the foreign with the local by means of kinship rituals that recognize the power of affinity but force it to make the sacrifices necessary for maintaining generational ties.

According to Lévi-Strauss, the myth of Oedipus comprises not just the classical Greek versions but all the known versions that have been documented in different cultures throughout the world.[27] According to this perspective, not only "The Wanderer of the Plain" but also the history of the Enlightenment can be read as variations of the Oedipal myth. As Nietzsche points out, the gender/generational conflict embodied in the myth is intertwined with the question of enlightenment. Oedipus not only rejects generational ties by leaving his homeland and killing his father but is also, like the Enlightenment thinker who rejects tradition, the solver of riddles. Yet in contrast to the myth of Enlightenment, the Oedipal myth itself does not end with a solution but with an irresolvable contradiction that links knowledge with suffering: "the man who solves the riddle of nature—that Sphinx of two species—also must break the most sacred natural orders by murdering his father and marrying his mother. Indeed, the myth seems to wish to whisper to us that wisdom, and particularly Dionysian wisdom, is an unnatural abomination; that he who by means of his knowledge plunges nature into the abyss of destruction must also suffer the dissolution of nature in his own person. 'The edge of wisdom turns against the wise: wisdom is a crime against nature.'"[28] The mediation of Thonga with Germany through "The Wanderer of the Plain" can only occur if the images in this Oedipal myth of the contradictions between knowledge and suffering, generation and gender, kinship and affinity, local and foreign are still of crucial importance for modern culture and its construction of reality.

THE PERSISTENCE OF THE PRIMITIVE

"The Wanderer of the Plain" ends in the same way as Einstein's *Bebuquin*, with a final sacrifice of the protagonist. Suicide merges a physical with a spiritual reality by subordinating physical well-being to a higher goal. The mastery of the body is the sole means of invoking a metaphysical reality in both stories. The final suicide is in each case simultaneously a bodily and a miraculous event. By eliminating any doctrine that might accompany the stories, Einstein depends upon the aesthetic effect to create a mythic art. This effect depends upon audience reception.

This reception is the final step in the creation of myth, and "The Wanderer of the Plain" demonstrates the essential characteristics of mythic prose for Einstein: the integration of necessity into the story by means of the relation between action and consequence; the mediation to the audience of a basic contradiction that structures the audience's experience; and the affirmation of a spiritual reality through the sacrifice of materiality. If these elements of Einstein's prose theory are also the characteristics of myth, then myth is primarily an aesthetic event with aesthetic rules. It does not depend for its power upon a religious dogma nor a prior system of belief nor a set of rituals. Instead, it depends upon the ability of its images and structures to mimic the essential forces that define the experience of the audience.

The "truth" of a story depends on its ability to reenact and make tangible a contradiction that dominates the experience of the readers and listeners. As Lévi-Strauss writes concerning the Oedipus myth: "Although experience contradicts theory, social life validates cosmology by its similarity of structure. Hence cosmology is true."[29] Mythic stories such as "The Wanderer of the Plain" become a means for gauging the continuing significance of kinship bonds and the extent to which its contradictions still resonate within an audience. The "truth" of such stories does not lie in any particular moral or teaching, but rather in their ability to recapitulate to a collective audience a contradiction that shapes its experience.

Both Levi-Strauss's interpretation of the function of intermediary terms and Einstein's use of such terms recall Nietzsche's understanding of the tragic myth. For Nietzsche, the tragic myth expresses a Dionysian truth—the primal contradiction at the heart of the world, the contradiction between individuation and dissolution, between life and death—with Apollinian means. The myth attempts to mediate to the audience in an Apollinian image the experience of Dionysian contradiction. When understood simply as life versus death, this contradiction is too abstract to have any meaning. The myth makes this contradiction concrete by creating an image that expresses the opposition and its irresolvability. In doing so, the myth itself acts as an intermediary, making the primal contradiction palpable for consciousness and imposing the "stamp of the eternal" onto the mundane experience of the spectator. In the process, both the eternal and the temporal are transformed. The eternal is revealed in its bodily aspect, and temporal experience becomes both social and spiritual. The contradictory structure of the sacred is a consequence both of its merging of the concrete with the eternal and of the transitory character of this merging.

The myth is not merely a representation of the primal contradiction but a performance of it. The figures on the stage are only a mask for the Dionysian truth behind the appearances. But the mask is essential. As Lévi-Strauss has pointed out in his discussion of the art of face painting: "Decoration is actually *created* for the face; but in another sense the face is predestined to be decorated, since it is only by means of decoration that the face receives its social dignity and mystical significance. Decoration is conceived for the face, but the face itself exists only through decoration. In the final analysis, the dualism is that of the actor and his role, and the concept of *mask* gives us the key to its interpretation."[30]

Einstein demonstrates his adherence to a similar aesthetic in "The Wanderer of the Plain." To gain an intuition of this aesthetic, one must regard an African Dan mask, for instance, not as a presentation of what one sees with one's eyes but of what one sees with

eyes closed, in the mind's eye. Primitivist artists such as Kandinsky, in an attempt to reinvest art with a spiritual meaning, attempted to construct paintings according to this same logic.

If the modern project can be characterized as an attempt to escape the irresolvable contradictions of myth, the primitivist project has consisted of a return to those contradictions and their irresolvability. The contradictions of Einstein's work are mythic rather than modern ones. Whereas the prose of the modern era has attempted to come up with solutions, primitivist prose has attempted to reformulate problems in such a way that no solutions are possible. If such problems engender a sense of alienation, this is only a measure of our Enlightenment estrangement from a primitive perspective. But if such contradictions nevertheless command our fascination, this can only be due to the persistence of the primitive in our mind's eye.

Notes

INTRODUCTION

1. Homer, *Odyssey* 12.166–200.

2. Franz Kafka, "The Silence of the Sirens," in *The Complete Stories*, ed. Nahum N. Glatzer, trans. Willa and Edwin Muir (New York: Schocken, 1971), 430.

3. Kafka, "Silence of the Sirens," 431.

4. Kafka, "Silence of the Sirens," 432.

5. Max Horkheimer and Theodor Adorno, *Dialectic of Enlightenment*, trans. John Cumming (New York: Continuum, 1972), 34, 58–59.

6. Kafka, "Silence of the Sirens," 431.

7. Horkheimer and Adorno, *Dialectic*, 35–36.

8. Horkheimer and Adorno, *Dialectic*, 62–67.

9. Kafka, "Silence of the Sirens," 432.

10. Discussions of the ambivalence of expressionism include Silvio Vietta and Hans-Georg Kemper, *Expressionismus* (Munich: Fink, 1975), 21–24, who describe a "'dialectic' of subject dissociation and renewal of humanity" (22); and Thomas Anz, "Gesellschaftliche Modernisierung, literarische Moderne und philosophische Postmoderne: Fünf Thesen" in *Die Modernität des Expressionismus*, ed. Thomas Anz and Michael Stark (Stuttgart: Metzler, 1994), 2–3, who notes the ambivalent position of both literary expressionism and postmodern philosophy with respect to processes of modernization. See also Jill Lloyd, *German Expressionism: Primitivism and Modernity* (New Haven: Yale University Press, 1992), vi–ix.

11. Since the mid-1980s a growing body of work has investigated the primitivist character of modernism. In art history the most important texts to date include Robert Goldwater's classic study, *Primitivism in Modern Art* (New York: Random House, 1938; Vintage Books, 1967); the catalog of the exhibition at the Museum of Modern Art in New York edited by William Rubin, *"Primitivism" in 20th Century Art: Affinity of the Tribal and the Modern* (New York: Museum of Modern Art, 1984); and such recent books as Karla Bilang, *Bild und Gegenbild: Das Ursprüngliche in der Kunst des 20. Jahrhunderts* (Stuttgart: W. Kohlhammer, 1989); Lloyd, *German Expressionism*; Colin Rhodes, *Primitivism and Modern Art* (London: Thames and Hudson, 1994); and Peg Weiss, *Kandinsky and Old Russia: The Artist As Ethnographer and Shaman* (New Haven: Yale University Press, 1995).

Other recent works on primitivism include Elazar Barkan and Ronald Bush, eds., *Prehistories of the Future: The Primitivist Project and the Culture of Modernism* (Stanford: Stanford University Press, 1995); Frances S. Connelly, *The Sleep of Reason: Primitivism in Modern European Art and Aesthetics, 1725–1907* (University Park PA: Pennsylvania State University Press, 1995); Sally Price, *Primitive Art in Civilized Places* (Chicago: University of Chicago Press, 1989); Michael D. Hall and Eugene W. Metcalf Jr., eds., *The Artist Outsider: Creativity and the Boundaries of Culture* (Washington DC: Smithsonian Institution Press, 1994); Michael Taussig, *Mimesis and Alterity: A Particular History of the Senses* (New York: Routledge, 1993); Marianna Torgovnick, *Gone Primitive: Savage Intellects, Modern Lives* (Chicago: University of Chicago Press, 1990); Marianna Torgovnick, *Primitive Passions: Men, Women, and the Quest for Ecstasy* (New York: Alfred A. Knopf, 1997); and C. Stanley Urban and S. Thomas Urban in collaboration with Jeff Urban, *Anti-Primitivism and the Decline of the West: The Social Cost of Cultural Ignorance*, 2 vols. (Lewiston NY: Edwin Mellen Press, 1993).

With regard to German literature, Regina Baltz-Balzberg provides an overview of broadly defined primitivist tendencies in the early twentieth century in order to demonstrate the "primitivity of modernism." See Regina Baltz-Balzberg, *Primitivität der Moderne: 1895–1925 am Beispiel des Theaters* (Königstein im Taunus: Hain, 1983), 7. Meanwhile, August K. Weidmann makes a similar argument about the pervasiveness of "'primalizing' tendencies" in German literature and art in the early twentieth century to show, however, that modernist primitivism "knowingly or unawares, paved the way for Hitler" (*The German Quest for Primal Origins in Art, Culture, and Politics 1900–1933: "Die Flucht in Urzustände"* [Lewiston NY: Edwin Mellen Press, 1995], 4).

12. See, for example, Vietta and Kemper, *Expressionismus*, 18–19.

13. See Peter Bürger, *Theory of the Avant-Garde*, trans. Michael Shaw (Minneapolis: University of Minnesota Press, 1984), 47–50.

14. Franz Marc, "Two Pictures," in *The Blaue Reiter Almanac*, ed. Wassily Kandinsky and Franz Marc (1912; reprint, New York: Viking, Da Capo Paperback, 1974), 65–67. This was a documentary edition edited by Klaus Lankheit.

15. *Nouveau Larousse illustré* (Paris: Librairie Larousse, 1897–1904), s.v. "primitif," 32. Cited in William Rubin, "Modernist Primitivism: An Introduction," in *"Primitivism" in 20th Century Art*, 2.

16. For an analysis of such exoticism in Max Pechstein and Emil Nolde, see Lloyd, *German Expressionism*, 161–234, and Russell Berman, "German

Primitivism/Primitive Germany: The Case of Emil Nolde," in *Fascism, Aesthetics, and Culture*, ed. Richard J. Golsan (Hanover NH: University Press of New England, 1992), 56–66.

17. For a description of Kafka's anarchist interests see Michael Löwy, " 'Theologia Negativa' and 'Utopia negativa': Franz Kafka," chap. 5 in *Redemption and Utopia: Jewish Libertarian Thought in Central Europe: A Study in Elective Affinity* (Stanford: Stanford University Press, 1992), 72, 82–83.

18. For an extended analysis of the different political tendencies within a "charismatic modernism," see Russell Berman, *The Rise of the Modern German Novel: Crisis and Charisma* (Cambridge: Harvard University Press, 1986).

19. My use of the word *primitive* is an attempt to redeem it from a modern, evolutionary perspective and emphasize the possible proximity between the primitive and the primitivist. If recent research has been successful in demonstrating the primitivist character of modernism, this very success has also resulted in such a broad definition of primitivism that it now encompasses not just an interest in the art of Africa, the Americas, and Oceania, but also the art of the insane and of children, "back to nature" movements, exoticism, African-American art and culture, "outsider" art, and a general interest in violence and sexual freedom. The result is that the specificity of that which is "primitive" rather than "primitivist" in modernism has been obscured and even denied. See, for example, Connelly, *Sleep of Reason*, 5–6; and William Rubin, "Modernist Primitivism," 1 n. 1, 5–6. As Thomas McEvilley comments, "Rubin and Varnedoe make it clear that they are concerned not with the primitive but with the primitivist–which is to say they ask only half the question." See Thomas McEvilley, William Rubin, and Kirk Varnedoe, "Doctor Lawyer Indian Chief: '*Primitivism*' in *20th Century Art* at the Museum of Modern Art," in *Discourses: Conversations in Postmodern Art and Culture*, ed. Russell Ferguson, William Olander, Marcia Tucker, and Karen Fiss (New York: New Museum of Contemporary Art; Cambridge: MIT Press, 1990; reprint of a debate in *Artforum* in 1984–1985), 342. For Rubin's response, see McEvilley, Rubin, and Varnedoe, "Doctor Lawyer Indian Chief," 356.

20. See Sibylle Penkert, *Carl Einstein: Beiträge zu einer Monographie* (Göttingen: Vandenhoeck & Ruprecht, 1969); and Bernd Witte, *Walter Benjamin: An Intellectual Biography* (1985), trans. James Rolleston (Detroit: Wayne State University Press, 1991). For details on the circumstances of Benjamin's death, see Ingrid Scheurmann, "New Documents on Walter Benjamin's Death," in *For Walter Benjamin*, ed. Ingrid and Konrad Scheur-

mann, trans. Timothy Nevill (Bonn: Arbeitskreis selbständiger Kultur-Institute, 1993), 265–97.

21. Rainer Rochlitz, *The Disenchantment of Art: The Philosophy of Walter Benjamin*, trans. Jane Marie Todd (New York: Guilford Press, 1996), 214. See also Richard Wolin, *Walter Benjamin: An Aesthetics of Redemption*, 2d ed. (Berkeley: University of California Press, 1994), 224–25.

22. John McCole notes the following with regard to Benjamin's wavering between two approaches to aura and to tradition: "Benjamin's work celebrates and mourns, by turns, the liquidation of tradition." See McCole, *Walter Benjamin and the Antinomies of Tradition* (Ithaca: Cornell University Press, 1993), 8.

23. Benjamin, "On Some Motifs in Baudelaire," in *Illuminations*, trans. Harry Zohn (New York: Schocken, 1968), 159. See also Benjamin, "The Storyteller," in *Illuminations*, 102.

24. Benjamin, "The Storyteller," 84.

25. Benjamin, "The Storyteller," 83.

26. Benjamin, "Surrealism" in *Reflections*, trans. Edmund Jephcott (New York: Schocken, 1986), 179. In his attempt to develop a theory of mimesis that would be a kind of "sensuous knowledge in our time" (44), Michael Taussig reads Benjamin as a primitivist (*Mimesis and Alterity*, 19–20). Yet because Benjamin attempts to merge "primitive" structures into a "modern" situation, for example, in his idea of "profane illumination," Taussig's own conception of sensuous knowledge becomes a fusion "where science and art coalesce to create a defetishizing/reenchanting modernist magical technology of embodied knowing" (24). In contrast to Taussig, my discussion of Nietzsche in chapter 1 demonstrates that one of the primary characteristics of primitivism is its insistence on the separateness of the two spheres of science and art.

27. Benjamin, "On Some Motifs," 163.

28. Benjamin, "The Work of Art in the Age of Mechanical Reproduction," in *Illuminations*, 230–41. For a discussion of Benjamin's progressivism, see Russell Berman, "The Aestheticization of Politics: Walter Benjamin on Fascism and the Avant-garde," chap. 2 in *Modern Culture and Critical Theory: Art, Politics, and the Legacy of the Frankfurt School* (Madison: University of Wisconsin Press, 1989), 34–36.

29. Benjamin, "On Some Motifs," 188.

30. Benjamin, "On Some Motifs," 102.

31. Winfried Menninghaus, *Schwellenkunde: Walter Benjamins Passage des Mythos* (Frankfurt am Main: Suhrkamp, 1986), 91, my translation. Men-

ninghaus also describes Benjamin's vision of myth as being determined by his utopian goal of liberation from the domination of nature (73–75, 80–81).

32. Benjamin, "The Storyteller," 102.

33. Benjamin, "On Some Motifs," 159.

34. Benjamin, "The Storyteller," 87.

35. See Helmut Pfotenhauer, *Ästhetische Erfahrung und gesellschaftliches System: Untersuchungen zu Methodenproblemen einer materialistischen Literaturanalyse am Spätwerk Walter Benjamins* (Stuttgart: J. B. Metzler, 1975), 75–76.

36. Carl Einstein, "Probleme heutiger Malerei," lecture given at the Berliner Staatliche Kunstbibliothek on February 16, 1931, in Carl Einstein, *Werke*, vol. 3, *1929–1940*, ed. Marion Schmid and Liliane Meffre (Berlin: Medusa, 1985), 576. This and all subsequent translations of passages unavailable in English are my own. Compare, for example, Georg Simmel, "The Metropolis and Mental Life," in *The Sociology of Georg Simmel*, trans. and ed. Kurt H. Wolff (New York: Free Press, 1950), 409–24, which describes the shock effects of the modern city but sees them as unique to modern urban society. Simmel was one of Einstein's professors when he was studying in Berlin (Penkert, *Carl Einstein: Beiträge*, 44–45).

37. Benjamin, "The Storyteller," 87.

38. Einstein, *Werke*, 3:578.

39. Einstein, *Werke*, 3:581.

40. Klaus H. Kiefer, *Diskurswandel im Werk Carl Einsteins: Ein Beitrag zur Theorie und Geschichte der europäischen Avantgarde* (Tübingen: Max Niemeyer Verlag, 1994), 519.

41. Walter Benjamin, "The Work of Art," 241.

42. See Renate Reschke, "Barbaren, Kult und Katastrophen: Nietzsche bei Benjamin. Unzusammenhängendes im Zusammenhang lesen," in *Aber ein Sturm weht vom Paradiese her: Texte zu Walter Benjamin*, ed. Michael Opitz and Erdmut Wizisla (Leipzig: Reclam, 1992), 322–23; and Willi Bolle, *Physiognomik der modernen Metropole: Geschichtsdarstellung bei Walter Benjamin* (Cologne: Böhlau, 1994), 211, 214–22.

43. "In order for the eyes of the collective to be able to achieve a structure, laws of seeing are necessary that evaluate the material of physiological vision in order to grant it a human meaning" (Einstein, "Totalität," in *Werke*, vol. 1, *1908–1918*, ed. Rolf-Peter Baacke with Jens Kwasny [Berlin: Medusa, 1980], 223).

44. Benjamin, "On Some Motifs," 159.

45. Einstein, *Negerplastik*, in *Werke* 1:251.

46. Bürger, *Theory of the Avant-Garde*, 51–54.

47. I follow here Peter Uwe Hohendahl's argument that "[w]hat these different [modernist] models ultimately share is the valorization of the aesthetic sphere, the instistence [*sic*] that art is not only autonomous but can and will eventually change history" ("The Loss of Reality: Gottfried Benn's Early Prose" in *Modernity and the Text: Revisions of German Modernism*, ed. Andreas Huyssen and David Bathrick [New York: Columbia University Press, 1989], 93–94).

48. See, for example, Vietta and Kemper, *Expressionismus*, 134–42, and Seth Taylor, *Left-Wing Nietzscheans: The Politics of German Expressionism 1910–1920* (Berlin: Walter de Gruyter, 1990), 16–59.

49. Friedrich Nietzsche, *The Birth of Tragedy*, in *The Birth of Tragedy and the Case of Wagner*, trans. Walter Kaufmann (1872; reprint, New York: Random House, 1967), 95–96.

50. Manfred Frank distinguishes between myth and ritual in order to derive the sacred quality of the former from the reality of the latter. See Frank, *Gott im Exil: Vorlesungen über die neue Mythologie* (Frankfurt am Main: Suhrkamp, 1988), 35–37. In contrast to Frank, Freud reads both myth and ritual as manifestations of the play of psychic forces, thereby providing a psychological rather than a "material" explanation of both myth and ritual.

51. This idea of mimesis is similar to the one developed later by Theodor W. Adorno in *Aesthetic Theory*, ed. Gretel Adorno and Rolf Tiedemann, trans. Robert Hullot-Kentor (Minneapolis: University of Minnesota Press, 1997), 111–13, except that Adorno both avoids a comparison of art and myth that would seek to bring the two together (98–99) and sees human rationality rather than nature as the source of suffering in human experience (Adorno, *Ästhetische Theorie*, ed. Gretel Adorno and Rolf Tiedemann [Frankfurt am Main: Suhrkamp, 1973], 170–73). By assuming that all suffering is a result of the concept and projecting a possible preconceptual state of reconciliation into nature, Adorno overlooks the suffering that accompanies the relation between man and nature (108–10). For Nietzsche, rationality is the source of suffering only to the extent that it obscures man's subjugation to nature.

52. Einstein, *Werke*, 3:579.

53. Demonstrating his view that the essential issue in primitivism is not the exotic but the "elementary," Einstein criticizes the artists Erich Heckel and Ernst Ludwig Kirchner because their primitivism does not attain the "elementary" aspects that Einstein seeks. See Einstein, "Ausstellung der Sezession in Berlin," *Merker* 4 (1913), reprinted in Einstein, *Werke*, 1:189.

54. Edmund Husserl developed a similar derivation of mythic cate-

gories out of phenomenological necessities. See Guido D. Neri, "Earth and Sky: An Analysis of Husserl's 1934 Manuscript on 'The Spatiality of Nature,'" *Telos* 92 (summer 1992): 63–84. Einstein's work can be read as an attempt to base aesthetics in everyday life by using phenomenological categories such as those developed by Husserl. Though he never defined his work in this way, Einstein developed a phenomenological aesthetic that integrates the forces of everyday life into an aesthetic form. This form in turn structures our perception of the world. While his arguments about the proximity of the modern and the mythic are similar to arguments made by Horkheimer and Adorno in *Dialectic of Enlightenment*, the crucial difference is that the latter were always suspicious of both mythic and phenomenological approaches to reality. See Russell Berman, "Cultural Criticism and Cultural Studies: Reconsidering the Frankfurt School," chap. 1 in *Cultural Studies of Modern Germany: History, Representation, and Nationhood* (Madison: University of Wisconsin Press, 1993), 24–25.

55. Einstein, *Werke*, 3:579.

56. Kurt Pinthus, "Before," in *Menschheitsdämmerung: Dawn of Humanity: A Document of Expressionism with Biographies and Bibliographies*, ed. Kurt Pinthus, trans. Joanna M. Ratych, Ralph Ley, and Robert C. Conard (1920; reprint, Columbia SC: Camden House, 1994), 34–35.

57. Horkheimer and Adorno, *Dialectic*, 9.

58. Horkheimer and Adorno, *Dialectic*, 10.

59. See, for example, Einstein, *Die Fabrikation der Fiktionen*, ed. Sibylle Penkert (Reinbek bei Hamburg: Rowohlt, 1973).

1. THE PRIMITIVE AND THE CIVILIZED IN
BIRTH OF TRAGEDY

1. Goldwater, *Primitivism in Modern Art*, 15–50. For a discussion of the prejudices of nineteenth- and early-twentieth-century anthropologists regarding the "primitive," see Urban and Urban, *Anti-Primitivism*, vol. 1, *The Primitive and the Supernatural*, 3–7. See Connelly, *The Sleep of Reason*, 11–34, for a description of the eighteenth- and nineteenth-century view of "'primitive' art as the inverse of classicism."

2. See, for example, Tzvetan Todorov's description of Columbus's differentiation between the "primitives" of the Americas and the "civilized" cultures of the Far East in Todorov, *The Conquest of America: The Question of the Other*, trans. Richard Howard (New York: Harper and Row, 1984), 22, 31–36.

3. *Oxford English Dictionary*, 2d ed., s.v. "primitive," 483. In French:

"Qui est à son origine, à ses debuts"; see *Trésor de la Langue Française: Dictionnaire de la langue du XIXe et du XXe siècle (1789–1869)* (Paris: Gallimard, 1988), s.v. "primitif," 1193.

4. OED, s.v. "primitive," 483–84.

5. OED, s.v. "primitively." For the French etymology, see Walther v. Wartburg, *Französisch Etymologisches Wörterbuch*, vol. 1 (Basel: R. G. Zbinden, 1959), s.v. "primitif," 380–81.

6. Jean-Jacques Rousseau, "Discourse on the Origin and Foundations of Inequality" (1754), in *The First and Second Discourses*, trans. Roger D. and Judith R. Masters (New York: St. Martin's Press, 1964), 92.

7. OED, s.v. "primitive," definition A. I.2.a.

8. The first such use of the word that the OED documents is from 1779. Forrest, *Voy. N. Guinea*, 273, cited in OED, s.v. "primitive," 485.

9. Hans Schulz and Otto Basler, *Deutsches Fremdwörterbuch* (Berlin: Walter de Gruyter, 1942), s.v. "primitiv."

10. "*ur-* C 1 wird seit der 2. Hälfte des 18. jhs. etwas in *ur-* C 4 c umgedeutet; vgl. *ursprung* 5. 'da ein ding in seinem ursprunge am meisten das ist, was es sein soll, unverändert, unvermischt von und mit anderem, so ist mit *u[rsprünglich]* auch zuweilen der begriff der reinheit, unverdorbenheit, vorzüglichkeit verbunden' (CAMPE). der wandel der bed. vollzieht sich fast unmerklich, theilweise unter einwirkung fremder wörter" (Jacob Grimm and Wilhelm Grimm, *Grimm Deutsches Wörterbuch*, s.v. "ursprünglich").

11. "wo die urzeit des völkerlebens gemeint ist, das land des urzsprungs und der jugend des menschengeschlechts" (*Grimm*, s.v. "ursprünglich").

12. Nietzsche, *Birth of Tragedy*, 36. Cited hereafter as BT followed by the page number. Nietzsche, *Die Geburt der Tragödie*, in *Sämtliche Werke: Kritische Studienausgabe in 15 Bänden*, ed. Giorgio Colli and Mazzino Montinari (Berlin: Walter de Gruyter, 1967–1977), 1:28–29. Cited hereafter as GT followed by the page number.

13. See in particular, Torgovnick, *Gone Primitive* and Lloyd, *German Expressionism*.

14. See Paul de Man, "Genesis and Genealogy (Nietzsche)," chap. 4 in *Allegories of Reading: Figural Language in Rousseau, Nietzsche, Rilke, and Proust* (New Haven: Yale University Press, 1979), 93; Frank, *Gott im Exil*, 43–46; and Sloterdijk, *Thinker on Stage: Nietzsche's Materialism*, trans. Jamie Owen Daniel (1986; Minneapolis: University of Minnesota Press, 1989), 29.

15. Marianna Torgovnick argues, for instance, that "the primitive is the sign and symbol of desires the West has sought to repress - desires for direct correspondences between bodies and things, direct correspondences be-

tween experience and language, direct correspondences between individual beings and the collective life force. It is the sign and symbol of desire for a full and sated sense of the universe" (Torgovnick, *Primitive Passions*, 8).

16. Nietzsche, "On Truth and Lies in a Nonmoral Sense," in *Philosophy and Truth: Selections from Nietzsche's Notebooks of the early 1870's*, trans. and ed. Daniel Breazeale (Atlantic Highlands, NJ: Humanities Press, 1979), 87. Nietzsche "Ueber Wahrheit und Lüge im aussermoralischen Sinne," in *Sämtliche Werke*, 1:885–86.

17. Jürgen Habermas, "The Entwinement of Myth and Enlightenment: Horkheimer and Adorno," in *The Philosophical Discourse of Modernity*, trans. Frederick Lawrence (1985; reprint, Cambridge: MIT Press, 1987), 124.

18. Habermas, "Entwinement of Myth," 127.

19. Arthur C. Danto, *Nietzsche As Philosopher* (1965; New York: Columbia University Press, 1980), 38.

20. Danto, *Nietzsche As Philosopher*, 59–60. See also Walter Kaufmann, *Nietzsche: Philosopher, Psychologist, Antichrist* (Princeton: Princeton University Press, 1974), 391–98. For a critique of Kaufmann's attempt to reconcile Nietzsche with Socratic optimism, see Julian Young, *Nietzsche's Philosophy of Art* (Cambridge: Cambridge University Press, 1992), 27–29.

21. Danto, *Nietzsche As Philosopher*, 39.

22. Javier Ibáñez-Noé, "Nietzsche: Nihilism and Culture," in *Nietzsche-Studien: Internationales Jahrbuch für die Nietzsche-Forschung*, vol. 25, ed. Ernst Behler, Eckhard Heftrich, Wolfgang Müller-Lauter, Jörg Salaquarda, and Josef Simon (Berlin: Walter de Gruyter, 1996), 15–20. Alexander Nehamas, *Nietzsche: Life As Literature* (Cambridge: Harvard University Press, 1985), 42–43. Allan Megill, *Prophets of Extremity: Nietzsche, Heidegger, Foucault, Derrida* (Berkeley: University of California Press, 1985), 37, 57, 355. The quotations are from Danto, *Nietzsche As Philosopher*, 61.

23. Danto, *Nietzsche As Philosopher*, 30.

24. Stanley Corngold, "The Subject of Nietzsche: Danto, Nehamas, Staten," *Nietzsche in American Literature and Thought*, ed. Manfred Pütz (Columbia SC: Camden House, 1995), 266–67.

25. de Man, *Allegories of Reading*, 100.

26. de Man, *Allegories of Reading*, 101.

27. de Man, *Allegories of Reading*, 101. Similarly, John Sallis, *Crossings: Nietzsche and the Space of Tragedy* (Chicago: University of Chicago Press, 1991), 71, interprets Nietzsche's constant references to "the primal unity" as denying its independent existence by reading it as a "vacuous opposite" of cognizable appearances.

28. Megill, *Prophets of Extremity*, 76.

29. Megill, *Prophets of Extremity*, 53.

30. Megill, *Prophets of Extremity*, 83.

31. de Man, *Allegories of Reading*, 96. Sallis, *Crossings*, 52.

32. Nietzsche, *Sämtliche Werke*, 7:203. Quoted in Sallis, *Crossings*, 67.

33. Sallis, *Crossings*, 66.

34. Nietzsche, *Gesammelte Werke* (Munich: Musarion Verlag, 1920), 3:239. Cited in de Man, *Allegories of Reading*, 100.

35. de Man, *Allegories of Reading*, 100.

36. Adorno would later refer to this dimension as "nonidentity." See Adorno, *Aesthetic Theory*, 108; Adorno, *Ästhetische Theorie*, 114.

37. Nietzsche, *The Will to Power*, trans. Walter Kaufmann and R. J. Hollingdale (New York: Random House, 1967), 302. Nietzsche, *Sämtliche Werke*, 12:580. Thomas Böning reads this passage as denying the significance of the primal unity to Nietzsche's understanding of the Dionysian by arguing that the rejection of the thing-in-itself is also a rejection of the primal unity. See Böning, *Metaphysik, Kunst und Sprache beim frühen Nietzsche* (Berlin: Walter de Gruyter, 1988), 208–23.

38. For a discussion of this idea of forces in Nietzsche's thought, see Gilles Deleuze, *Nietzsche and Philosophy*, trans. Hugh Tomlinson (1962; reprint, New York: Columbia University Press, 1983), 39–42. For an alternative application of Deleuze's ideas to *The Birth of Tragedy*, see Keith M. May, *Nietzsche and the Spirit of Tragedy* (New York: St. Martin's Press, 1990), 1–26.

39. Nietzsche, "On Truth and Lies," 86–87. Nietzsche, "Ueber Wahrheit und Lüge," 884.

40. Compare Rainer Nägele, *Theater, Theory, Speculation: Walter Benjamin and the Scenes of Modernity* (Baltimore: Johns Hopkins University Press, 1991), 115, who contends that Nietzsche sets up an opposition between aesthetics and morality.

41. Danto, *Nietzsche As Philosopher*, 37–38, 60–61.

42. Though Nietzsche refers to Socrates as the "prototype of the theoretical optimist" (BT 97, GT 100), he still emphasizes that while the Socratic perspective is based on the ideas that truth is comprehensible and progress of human knowledge is possible, Socrates himself was not completely convinced by this perspective. Nietzsche refers, for example, to the "artistic Socrates," who at the end of his life looked to art rather than science as his true calling (BT 92–93, GT 95–96).

43. As Reinhart Maurer has pointed out, Nietzsche emphasizes the importance of the death of Christ in *The Antichrist* in order to defend Christ against the Christian church. See Maurer, "Thesen über Nietzsche als

Theologen und Fundamentalkritiker," in *Nietzsche-Studien: Internationales Jahrbuch für die Nietzsche-Forschung*, vol. 23, ed. Ernst Behler, Eckhard Heftrich, and Wolfgang Müller-Lauter (Berlin: Walter de Gruyter, 1994), 105–6.

44. Megill, *Prophets of Extremity*, 102.

2. THE DIONYSIAN AESTHETICS OF MYTH

1. Alfred Baeumler, "Bachofen, der Mythologe der Romantik," introduction to *Der Mythus von Orient und Okzident*, by J. J. Bachofen (Munich: C. H. Beck'sche Verlagsbuchhandlung, 1926; reprint, 1956), ccxliv.

2. Baeumler, "Bachofen," ccxlix, my translation.

3. Baeumler, "Nietzsche" (1930), in *Studien zur deutschen Geistesgeschichte* (Berlin: Junker und Dünnhaupt Verlag, 1937), 258. Marianna Torgovnick's view of the primitive is similar to Baeumler's in that she also relies on Bachofen's work rather Nietzsche's. In contrast to Baeumler, however, she fails to see how Bachofen and Nietzsche differ in their approaches to the primitive and claims that "Bachofen's theories also informed Friedrich Nietzsche's attention to the battle of Apollonian and Dionysian forces in Greek drama" (Torgovnick, *Primitive Passions*, 38–39).

4. de Man, *Allegories of Reading*, 93. See also Rainer Nägele's interpretation in which he writes: "For both Nietzsche and Benjamin, the aesthetic sphere is determined by the category of *Schein* (appearance)" (*Theater, Theory, Speculation*, 110).

5. de Man, *Allegories of Reading*, 94–95.

6. de Man, *Allegories of Reading*, 98.

7. de Man, *Allegories of Reading*, 98.

8. Young, *Nietzsche's Philosophy of Art*, 1992), 35–37.

9. In Kaufmann's translation, the last sentence reads "depth of his [*sic*] being," which is obviously incorrect as a rendering of "aus dem Abgrunde des Seins."

10. Frank, *Gott im Exil*, 46, my translation.

11. de Man, *Allegories of Reading*, 98.

12. Young, *Nietzsche's Philosophy of Art*, 49.

3. THE PRIMITIVE AND THE BARBARIC

1. Walter Benjamin, *The Origin of the German Tragic Drama*, trans. John Osborne (1928; reprint, London: New Left Books, 1977), 103, translation modified. The original German for the Nietzsche quotation is as fol-

lows: "Wo die Kunst dergestalt die Mitte des Daseins bezieht, daß sie den Menschen zu ihrer Erscheinung macht, anstatt gerade ihn als ihren Grund-nicht als ihren Schöpfer, sondern sein Dasein als den ewigen Vorwurf ih-rer Bildungen-zu erkennen, entfällt die nüchterne Besinnung überhaupt." See Walter Benjamin, *Ursprung des deutschen Trauerspiels* in *Gesammelte Schriften*, 3 vols., ed. Rolf Tiedemann and Hermann Schweppenhäuser (1974; paperback edition, Frankfurt am Main: Suhrkamp, 1980), 1:281–82. For a discussion of this passage and the relation between Benjamin's and Nietzsche's aesthetics, see Nägele, *Theater, Theory, Speculation*, 110–18. For a critique of Nietzsche's aestheticism similar to Benjamin's, see Gert Sauter-meister, "Zur Grundlegung des Ästhetizismus bei Nietzsche: Dialektik, Metaphysik und Politik in der 'Geburt der Tragödie,'" *Naturalismus/Äs-thetizismus*, ed. Christa Bürger, Peter Bürger, and Jochen Schulte-Sasse (Frankfurt am Main: Suhrkamp, 1979), 234ff.

2. "It was not in law but in tragedy that the head of the genius first emerged above the cloud of guilt, for in tragedy the hold of demonic fate is broken. Not, however, in the replacement of the inscrutable pagan concate-nation of guilt and atonement by the purity of man, absolved and recon-ciled with the pure god. It is rather that in tragedy pagan man realizes that he is better than his gods, but his realization strikes him dumb, and it re-mains unarticulated" (Benjamin, *Origin*, 109–10).

3. "Tragic poetry is based on the idea of sacrifice. But in respect of its vic-tim, the hero, the tragic sacrifice differs from any other kind, being at once a first and a final sacrifice. A final sacrifice in the sense of the atoning sacrifice to gods who are upholding an ancient right; a first sacrifice in the sense of the representative action, in which new aspects of the life of the nation be-come manifest. These are different from the old, fatal obligations in that they do not refer back to a command from above, but to the life of the hero himself" (Benjamin, *Origin*, 106–7). Rainer Nägele notes regarding this passage that "Benjamin's emphasis is not on the new *order* but on the explo-sive and subversive force against the old mythical order" (*Theater, Theory, Speculation*, 38).

4. Habermas, "Entwinement of Myth," 124.

5. "We men of today feel precisely the opposite: the richer a man feels within himself, the more polyphonic his subjectivity is, the more power-fully is he impressed by the uniformity of nature; with Goethe, we all rec-ognize in nature the great means of composure for the modern soul, we lis-ten to the beat of the pendulum of this mightiest of clocks with a longing for rest, for becoming settled and still, as though we could imbibe this uni-formity into ourselves and thereby at last come to an enjoyment of our-

selves" (Nietzsche, *Human, All Too Human: A Book for Free Spirits*, trans. R. J. Hollingdale [Cambridge: Cambridge University Press, 1986], 63–64; Nietzsche, *Sämtliche Werke*, 2:113).

6. Friedrich Kaulbach, in his essay on Nietzsche and nature, understands "great nature" (*die große Natur*) as a positive concept in which man frees himself from subjective limitations. See Kaulbach, "Nietzsches Interpretation der Natur," *Nietzsche Studien* 10/11 (1981–1982): 461. However, in the following quotation from the unpublished manuscripts later collected under the title *Der Wille zur Macht*, Nietzsche demonstrates his contempt for the civilized forgetting of self in "great nature": "So humans also go into great nature, not in order to find themselves, but in order to lose and forget themselves in it. 'Being outside oneself' as the wish of all the weak and those discontented with themselves" (*Sämtliche Werke*, 10:291, my translation).

7. "Man is the *rule*, nature is *irregularity*—this proposition contains the fundamental conviction which dominates rude, religiously productive primitive cultures [*Urculturen*]" (Nietzsche, *Human, All Too Human*, 63; Nietzsche, *Sämtliche Werke*, 2:112).

8. Nietzsche, *Human, All Too Human*, 65. Nietzsche, *Sämtliche Werke*, 2:115.

9. I follow Kaulbach ("Nietzsche's Interpretation," 453) in noting the relation between a natural existence and moral discipline. Even in much later texts such as *Beyond Good and Evil*, Nietzsche adheres to this schema in which he defends the mythically mediated regulation of human behavior inherent in the primitive conception of nature. Opposing Rousseau's idea of what it means to live "naturally," Nietzsche insists that living in nature means living with rules: "The essential and invaluable element in every morality is that it is a protracted constraint. . . . But the strange fact is that all there is or has been on earth of freedom, subtlety, boldness, dance and masterly certainty, whether in thinking itself, or in ruling, or in speaking and persuasion, in the arts as in morals, has evolved by virtue of the 'tyranny of such arbitrary laws'; and, in all seriousness, there is no small probability that precisely this is 'nature' and 'natural'—and *not* that *laisser aller!*" (*Beyond Good and Evil: Prelude to a Philosophy of the Future*, trans. R. J. Hollingdale [London: Penguin, 1990], 110–11; Nietzsche, *Sämtliche Werke*, 5:108).

10. "If we think back to rude, primitive conditions of peoples, or if we look closely at present-day savages, we find them determined in the strongest way by the *law*, by *tradition* [*Herkommen*]" (Nietzsche, *Human, All Too Human*, 64; Nietzsche, *Sämtliche Werke*, 2:113).

11. "In brief, the religious cult rests on the ideas of sorcery as between

man and man; and the sorcerer is older than the priest. But it *likewise* rests on other and nobler ideas; it presupposes relations of sympathy between man and man, the existence of goodwill, gratitude, the hearing of petitions, treaties between enemies, the bestowal of pledges, the claim to protection of property" (Nietzsche, *Human, All Too Human*, 65; Nietzsche, *Sämtliche Werke*, 2:115–16).

12. Danto, *Nietzsche As Philosopher*, 59–60.

13. Sloterdijk, *Thinker on Stage*, 27.

14. Sloterdijk, *Thinker on Stage*, 29.

15. de Man, *Allegories of Reading*, 100; Sloterdijk, *Thinker on Stage*, 24.

16. Sloterdijk, *Thinker on Stage*, 30; Sloterdijk, *Thinker on Stage*, 55–56.

17. In making this argument, Nietzsche prefigures Max Horkheimer's and Theodor Adorno's tracing of Nazi barbarism to Enlightenment ideologies in *Dialectic of Enlightenment*. The crucial difference between their accounts, however, is that while Nietzsche defends myth by differentiating it from rationality, Horkheimer and Adorno posit a dialectic of myth and enlightenment in order to indict reason for regressing back to what they view as the barbarism of myth. On the connection between rationality and barbarism, see also Zygmunt Baumann, *Modernity and the Holocaust* (Ithaca: Cornell University Press, 1989).

18. For accounts of Gauguin's primitivism, see Kirk Varnedoe, "Gauguin" in *"Primitivism" in 20th-Century Art*, 179–209; Gill Perry, "Primitivism and the 'Modern,' " in *Primitivism, Cubism, Abstraction: The Early Twentieth Century*, by Charles Harrison, Francis Frascina, and Gill Perry (New Haven: Yale University Press, Open University, 1993), 8–34; Connelly, *The Sleep of Reason*, 55–77; and Nancy Perloff, "Gauguin's French Baggage: Decadence and Colonialism in Tahiti," in *Prehistories of the Future*, 226–69.

4. THE PRIMITIVE DIMENSION IN *TOTEM AND TABOO*

1. Sigmund Freud, "Über einige Übereinstimmungen im Seelenleben der Wilden und der Neurotiker," *Imago* 1, no. 1 (1912), 17–33. For details of the publishing history, see Freud, *Totem and Taboo: Some Points of Agreement between the Mental Lives of Savages and Neurotics*, in *The Standard Edition of the Complete Psychological Works of Sigmund Freud*, trans. and ed. James Strachey, 24 vols. (London, 1953–1974), 13: x–xii.

2. Hal Foster, " 'Primitive' Scenes," *Critical Inquiry* 20, no. 1 (autumn 1993): 71–72. Freud, *Standard Edition*, 13:1.

3. Analyses of different cultures that placed them in an evolutionary lad-

der from primitive to civilized were by no means uniformly racist as Foster suggests concerning Freud. Edward B. Tylor notes, for instance: "For the present purpose it appears both possible and desirable to eliminate considerations of hereditary varieties or races of man, and to treat mankind as homogeneous in nature, though placed in different grades of civilization. The details of the enquiry will, I think, prove that stages of culture may be compared without taking into account how far tribes who use the same implement, follow the same custom, or believe the same myth, may differ in their bodily configuration and the colour of their skin and hair" (*Primitive Culture: Researches into the Development of Mythology, Philosophy, Religion, Art, and Custom*, 2 vols. [London: John Murray, 1871], 1:6–7).

4. Tylor, *Primitive Culture*, 1:116. Cited in Freud, *Standard Edition*, 13:79.

5. Freud, *Standard Edition*, 13:85.

6. Freud, *Standard Edition*, 13:83.

7. Freud, *Standard Edition*, 13:91.

8. Freud, *Standard Edition*, 13:160–61.

9. Freud, *Standard Edition*, 13:161.

10. Freud, *Standard Edition*, 13:141–42.

11. Freud, *Standard Edition*, 13:98.

12. Freud, *Standard Edition*, 13:98.

13. Freud, *Standard Edition*, 13:xiv.

14. Freud, *Standard Edition*, 13:92.

15. James George Frazer, *The Golden Bough*, vol. 1, part 1, *The Magic Art and the Evolution of Kings* (New York: Macmillan, 1935), 420. Cited in Freud, *Standard Edition*, 13:83.

16. Frazer, *Golden Bough*, 421.

17. Freud, *Standard Edition*, 13:88.

18. Freud, *Standard Edition*, 13:93.

19. Frazer, *Golden Bough*, 420.

20. Freud, *Standard Edition*, 13:87.

21. Harold Bloom, "Reading Freud: Transference, Taboo, and Truth," in *Centre and Labyrinth: Essays in Honour of Northrop Frye*, ed. Eleanor Cook, Chaviva Hoffek, Jay MacPherson, Patricia Parker, and Julian Patrick (Toronto: University of Toronto Press, 1983), 310.

22. A. L. Kroeber, "Totem and Taboo: An Ethnologic Psychoanalysis" (1920), in *Sigmund Freud: Critical Assessments*, ed. Laurence Spurling, vol. 3, *The Psychoanalysis of Culture* (London: Routledge, 1989), 37–38.

23. Claude Lévi-Strauss, *The Elementary Structures of Kinship*, ed. and trans. Rodney Needham (London: Eyre & Spottiswoode, 1969), 491.

24. Freud, *Standard Edition*, 13:141–43, 13:161.
25. Freud, *Standard Edition*, 13:90.
26. Freud, *Standard Edition*, 13:90.

5. ABSTRACT ART AND THE PRIMITIVE SPIRIT

1. Goldwater, *Primitivism in Modern Art* (1967), 15–16. He also mentions Carl Einstein as the "first and most influential" of those writers who were able to appreciate primitive art (35–36).

2. Rubin, "Modernist Primitivism," 17–18.

3. Patricia Leighten, "The White Peril and *L'art nègre*: Picasso, Primitivism, and Anticolonialism," *Art Bulletin* 72 (1990): 609–30.

4. Hal Foster, *Recodings* (Seattle: Bay Press, 1985), 185.

5. Torgovnick, *Gone Primitive*, 136. See also James Clifford, "Histories of the Tribal and the Modern," chap. 9 in *The Predicament of Culture* (Cambridge: Harvard University Press, 1988), 191–202.

6. McEvilley, Rubin, and Varnedoe, "Doctor Lawyer Indian Chief," 372. Though McEvilley uses this distinction to argue against the integration, in *"Primitivism" in 20th Century Art*, of primitive art into a Western vision of aesthetic appreciation, the distinction can also be useful for understanding modernist primitivism as an attempt to move away from a "Western" view of aesthetic activity and toward a primitive understanding.

7. Lloyd, *German Expressionism*, 109. On Nolde, see also Berman, "German Primitivism/Primitive Germany," 56–66; Donald E. Gordon, "German Expressionism," in *"Primitivism" in 20th Century Art*, 379–83; and Bilang, *Bild und Gegenbild*, 98–102. Connelly extends this thesis to modernist primitivism in general in *The Sleep of Reason*, 34, 111–14. See also Perry, "Primitivism and the 'Modern,' " 62–82. But as Gordon and Bilang have shown, apart from Nolde, other *Brücke* artists such as Pechstein (Bilang, *Bild und Gegenbild*, 92–98) and Karl Schmidt-Rottluff (Bilang, *Bild und Gegenbild*, 87–92, and Gordon, "German Expressionism," 384–85, 393–95) were able to glean formal techniques from primitive art, which they integrated into their own art, thus escaping the exoticizing attitude that Lloyd describes. In particular, Karl Schmidt-Rottluff distinguished himself from the other *Brücke* artists by the extent to which he was able to integrate a primitive aesthetic into his art such that "the African model was transformed into a form that was his very own, belonging to the essence of his art" (Bilang, *Bild und Gegenbild*, 88). Schmidt-Rottluff's particular mode of primitivism is also of interest because, as Gordon has shown ("German Expressionism," 393–95), he based much of his work during World War II

on photographs of African sculptures from Carl Einstein's 1915 book *Negro Sculpture* (*Negerplastik*), which points out the formal innovations of African art.

8. Lloyd, *German Expressionism*, vii.

9. Foster, "'Primitive' Scenes," 76.

10. Torgovnick, *Primitive Passions*, 219.

11. Torgovnick, *Primitive Passions*, 15–16.

12. In her conclusion she alternates between these two evaluations of the primitive as "oceanic" (Torgovnick, *Primitive Passions*, 213–19).

13. Weiss, *Kandinsky and Old Russia*, 27.

14. See Weiss, *Kandinsky and Old Russia*, 33–69.

15. Weiss, *Kandinsky and Old Russia*, 81–92, 153–67.

16. See Bilang, *Bild und Gegenbild*, 103–13, for an overview of primitivist influences and tendencies amongst artists connected with *Der Blaue Reiter*. For a description of the integration of primitive art into the almanac *Der Blaue Reiter*, see Weiss, *Kandinsky and Old Russia*, 92–99.

17. See Weiss, *Kandinsky and Old Russia*, 1–32; Carol McKay, "Kandinsky's Ethnography: Scientific Field Work and Aesthetic Reflection," *Art History* 17, no. 2 (1994): 182–208; and Carol McKay, "Modernist Primitivism? The Case of Kandinsky," *Oxford Art Journal* 16, no. 2 (1993): 21–36, for discussions of Kandinsky's ethnographic work on folk culture in the Russian Empire and its relation to his early interest in folk motifs.

18. *Arrival of the Merchants*, tempera and gouache on canvas, 1905, private collection, Germany; Vivian Endicott Barnett, *Kandinsky Watercolours: Catalogue Raisonné*, vol. 1, *1900–1921* (Ithaca: Cornell University Press, 1992), no. 191. *Motley Life*, tempera and gouache on canvas, 1907, Städtische Galerie, Munich; Barnett, *Kandinsky Watercolours*, no. 219. For a detailed account of Kandinsky's reliance on the images and information he obtained in his ethnographic work to develop the motifs in these and other paintings of this period, see Weiss, *Kandinsky and Old Russia*, 37–52.

19. *Composition II*, oil on canvas, 1910, destroyed during World War II; Hans K. Roethel and Jean K. Benjamin, *Kandinsky: Catalogue Raisonné of the Oil-Paintings*, 2 vols. (Ithaca: Cornell University Press, 1982–84), vol. 1, no. 334 (this text hereafter referred to as RB followed by the volume and catalog number). In the following I will refer to *Sketch for Composition II*, oil on canvas, 1910, The Solomon R. Guggenheim Museum, New York; RB, 1, no. 326. See Hans K. Roethel in collaboration with Jean K. Benjamin, *Kandinsky* (New York: Hudson Hills Press, 1979), 66, 72; and Weiss, *Kandinsky and Old Russia*, 52, for descriptions of Kandinsky's thoughts about the development toward *Composition II*, which were published in the Russian

edition of his *Reminiscences* (English translation in Wassily Kandinsky, *Kandinsky: Complete Writings on Art*, ed. Kenneth C. Lindsay and Peter Vergo, 2 vols. [Boston: G. K. Hall, 1982], 2:890. This text hereafter cited as Lindsay and Vergo, *Kandinsky*). Weiss, *Kandinsky and Old Russia*, 52–55, uses Kandinsky's comments as the starting point for a demonstration of the abundance of Zyrian folk motifs in *Composition II*.

20. *The Last Supper*, glass-painting, 1910, Städtische Galerie, Munich; RB, I, no. 372. *Christ on the Cross*, oil on cardboard, 1911, Herbert Campendonk, RB, I, no. 406. *Saint Vladimir*, glass painting, 1911, Städtische Galerie, Munich, RB, I, no. 411. See Weiss, *Kandinsky and Old Russia*, 56–63, for a description of motifs taken from Zyrian folk culture present in the *All Saints' Day* paintings and *Saint Vladimir*. Rose-Carol Washton Long, *Kandinsky: The Development of an Abstract Style* (New York: Oxford University Press, 1980), 75–87, provides a detailed explanation of Kandinsky's borrowing of motifs such as the golden trumpet, the walled city, and the horse and rider from Bavarian glass paintings and Russian *lubki* broadsheets.

21. "In his own paintings on glass he took over the peasant delight in color and the naive mode of expression, and adapted them to his own artistic sensibility; but he was unquestionably also influenced by reminiscences of Russian prints. He also took over the techniques: he uses silver or quicksilver coatings, and occasionally even his composition is similar to that of Murnau glass paintings, for instance, in *Sancta Francisca* which Kandinsky in 1911 gave his janitor in Munich for Christmas" (Will Grohmann, *Kandinsky: Life and Work* [New York: Harry N. Abrams, 1958], 112). See also Long, *Kandinsky*, 81, and Bilang, *Bild und Gegenbild*, 107, for discussions of the influence of Bavarian glass painting on Kandinsky's development toward abstraction.

22. For the glass paintings: *St. George II*, glass painting, 1911, Städtische Galerie, Munich, RB, I, no. 414. *All Saints I*, glass painting, 1911, Städtische Galerie, Munich, RB, I, no. 412. *Glass-Painting with Sun* (also known as *Kleine Freuden*), glass painting, 1910, Städtische Galerie, Munich, RB, I, no. 370. Grohmann, *Kandinsky*, 108–12.

For the oil paintings: *St. George I*, oil on canvas, 1910, private collection, Zurich, RB, I, no. 362. *St. George II*, oil on canvas, 1911, Russian Museum, Leningrad, RB, I, no. 382. *St. George III*, oil on canvas, 1911, Städtische Galerie, Munich, RB, I, no. 391. *All Saints II*, oil on canvas, 1911, Städtische Galerie, Munich, RB, I, no. 409. *Small Pleasures*, oil on canvas, 1913, The Solomon R. Guggenheim Museum, New York, RB, I, no. 466.

23. "Because Kandinsky was determined to use painting as a major 'weapon' in the creation of a new utopian realm, he tried to develop a

method which avoided 'materialistic' representation but which could still reach a wide audience. His messianic impulse led him to use hidden apocalyptic images to give his paintings cosmic significance" (Long, *Kandinsky*, 12).

24. See Long, *Kandinsky*, 108–12, for an analysis of the Christian religious motifs presented in *Composition I* and *Composition II*. See Weiss, *Kandinsky and Old Russia*, 52–56, for a description of the Zyrian folk motifs in these paintings. Philippe Sers, *Kandinsky. Philosophie de l'Abstraction: L'Image Métaphysique* (Geneva: Skira, 1995), 132, sees these two compositions as further developments of the folk images from *Arrival of the Merchants* and *Motley Life*.

25. *Composition V*, oil on canvas, 1911, private collection, Switzerland, RB, I, no. 400. *Sound of Trumpets (Large Resurrection)*, watercolor, Indian ink, and pencil on thin cardboard, 1910–11, Städtische Galerie, Munich, Barnett, *Kandinsky Watercolours*, no. 259. *All Saints II*, oil on canvas, 1911, Städtische Galerie, Munich, RB, I, no. 409.

Rose-Carol Washton Long writes that Kandinsky "took as a starting point the stylized motifs found in folk art–Russian *lubki*, 'Gothic' fifteenth-century woodcuts, and Bavarian glass paintings–but he then transformed these motifs by veiling and stripping them to hide the images. In this way, he dematerialized the object and created a sense of mystery which not only mirrored the chaos of his age but also suggested the struggle involved in trying to understand hidden truths. If his paintings were too easily understood they would not be suitable equivalents for the intimation of the higher world." See Long, "Kandinsky's Vision," in *The Life of Vasilii Kandinsky in Russian Art: A Study of "On the Spiritual in Art,"* ed. John E. Bowlt and Rose-Carol Washton Long (Newtonville MA: Oriental Research Partners, 1980), 53–54. See also Long, *Kandinsky*, 113–16; and Sers, *Kandinsky*, 134. Though he comes to different conclusions about the specific allusions hidden in Kandinsky's images, Hans-Martin Dziersk's approach is similar to Long's in that he also seeks to demonstrate the veiled references in Kandinsky's images. See Dziersk, *Abstraktion und Zeitlosigkeit: Wassily Kandinsky und die Tradition der Malerei* (Ostfildern, Germany: Tertium, 1995), 11, 23–25.

26. Weiss, *Kandinsky and Old Russia*, 99–100.

27. Weiss, *Kandinsky and Old Russia*, 102–5. She also demonstrates that Kandinsky considered *Composition V* to be a tool for cultural healing, one "rooted in Kandinsky's concept of the therapeutic power of art and in his sense of mission as cultural 'shaman' " (Weiss, *Kandinsky and Old Russia*, 106).

28. Jelena Hahl-Koch, *Kandinsky* (New York: Rizzoli, 1993), 163. She refers to *Fragment of Composition II*, oil on cardboard, 1910, private collection, RB, 1, no. 325, and *Improvisation 10*, oil on canvas, 1910, Galerie Ernst Beyeler, Basel, RB, 1, no. 337.

29. Sixten Ringbom, *The Sounding Cosmos: A Study in the Spiritualism of Kandinsky and the Genesis of Abstract Painting* (Abo, Finland: Abo Akademi, 1970), 159.

30. Lindsay and Vergo, *Kandinsky*, 1:128.

31. Lindsay and Vergo, *Kandinsky*, 1:212.

32. Richard Sheppard, "Kandinsky's *oeuvre* 1900–14: The *Avant-garde* As Rear-guard," *Word & Image* 11, no. 1 (1990): 49.

33. Wassily Kandinsky, letter to Gabriele Münter, Nuremberg, January 19, 1912, Gabriele Münter- und Johannes Eichner-Stiftung, Munich, quoted in Hahl-Koch, *Kandinsky*, 170.

34. Lindsay and Vergo, *Kandinsky*, 1:197. Reading this passage as a rejection of "pure abstraction" and playing down the implied emphasis on the spiritual as the crucial determinant of the value of a work of art, Peg Weiss argues that Kandinsky's theory of abstraction develops out of his own experience working in the decorative arts and with craft techniques. See Weiss, *Kandinsky in Munich: The Formative Jugendstil Years* (Princeton: Princeton University Press, 1979), 116–26. But she also points out that Kandinsky's theories on abstraction in *On the Spiritual in Art* are based upon his differentiation of abstraction from the "merely ornamental" (Weiss, *Kandinsky in Munich*, 135).

35. Lindsay and Vergo, *Kandinsky*, 1:212.

36. Lindsay and Vergo, *Kandinsky*, 1:238.

37. Lindsay and Vergo, *Kandinsky*, 1:213.

38. Lindsay and Vergo, *Kandinsky*, 1:212.

39. August Macke writes: "The African considers his idol the comprehensible form for an incomprehensible idea, the personification of an abstract concept. For us the painting is the comprehensible form for the obscure, incomprehensible conception of a deceased person, of an animal, of a plant, of the whole magic of nature, of the rhythmical" ("The Masks," *Blaue Reiter Almanac*, 88).

40. *"This 'What?' is that content which only art can contain, and to which only art can give clear expression through the means available to it"* (Lindsay and Vergo, *Kandinsky*, 1:138).

41. Lindsay and Vergo, *Kandinsky*, 1:143.

42. In addition to Ringbom's comprehensive analysis, see also Armin Zweite, "Free the Line for the Inner Sound: Kandinsky's Renewal of Art in

208

the Context of His Time," in *Kandinsky: Watercolors and Drawings*, ed. Vivian Endicott Barnett and Armin Zweite (Munich: Prestel, 1992), 9–32.

43. Ringbom, *Sounding Cosmos*, 111.

44. For a more complete description of this view of the relation between abstraction and transcendence, see Carl Einstein, *Negerplastik* in *Werke*, 1:253–54.

45. Ringbom, *Sounding Cosmos*, 87.

46. Lindsay and Vergo, *Kandinsky*, 1:214 (emphasis in original).

47. "Clashing discords, loss of equilibrium, 'principles' overthrown, unexpected drumbeats, great questionings, apparently purposeless strivings, stress and longing (apparently torn apart), chains and fetters broken (which had united many), opposites and contradictions–this is our *harmony. Composition on the basis of this harmony is the juxtaposition of coloristic and linear forms that have an independent existence as such, derived from internal necessity, which create within the common life arising from this source a whole that is called a picture*" (Lindsay and Vergo, *Kandinsky*, 1:193).

48. See Magdalena Dabrowski, *Kandinsky Compositions* (New York: Museum of Modern Art, 1995), 19–22; and Ringbom, *Sounding Cosmos*, 88–91.

49. Lindsay and Vergo, *Kandinsky*, 1:200.

50. Lindsay and Vergo, *Kandinsky*, 1:246.

51. Lindsay and Vergo, *Kandinsky*, 1:182–83.

52. Lindsay and Vergo, *Kandinsky*, 1:201.

53. Ringbom, *Sounding Cosmos*, 130.

54. I oppose here the view of Michel Henry, who accepts the idea that an inner tone constitutes the "ontological reality of this color or that form" and can have a universal significance independent of context. Henry, "Montrer l'Invisible: Sur Kandinsky et la peinture abstraite," in *Montrer l'Invisible: Figuration et invention du reél dans la peinture*, ed. Jean-Pierre Sylvestre (Dijon: Editions universitaires de Dijon, 1993), 36.

55. Carl Einstein, *Die Kunst des 20. Jahrhunderts* (Berlin: Propyläen, 1931), 207.

56. Einstein, *Kunst*, 206. This critique forms part of Einstein's own understanding of form as a mediator between art and psychic experience.

57. Letters to Gabriele Münter of November 8 and December 3, 1910, Gabriele Münter- und Johannes Eichner-Stiftung, Munich, quoted in Hahl-Koch, *Kandinsky*, 174.

58. Einstein, *Kunst*, 23.

59. "L'élément pur de l'art matérialise le contenu intérieur, le *pur et*

éternel Artistique, de même que les objets du monde matérialisent un principe unique commun" (Sers, *Kandinsky*, 200).

60. Sers, *Kandinsky*, 198–99. For an elaborate description and critique of Kandinsky's "essentialism," see Mark A. Cheetham, *The Rhetoric of Purity: Essentialist Theory and the Advent of Abstract Painting* (Cambridge: Cambridge University Press, 1991), 65–101.

61. Lindsay and Vergo, *Kandinsky*, 1:175.

62. Einstein, *Kunst*, 207.

63. Cheetham, *Rhetoric of Purity*, 68–69.

64. *Division-Unity*, mixed media on canvas, 1934, Seibu Museum of Art, Tokyo, RB, 2, no. 1044. *Animated Stability*, mixed media on canvas, 1937, Miyagi Museum of Art, Sendai, Japan, RB, 2, no. 1084. *Dusk*, oil on cardboard, 1943, The Solomon R. Guggenheim Museum, New York, RB, 2, no. 1157. *Circle and Square*, mixed media on cardboard, 1943, private collection, Paris, RB, 2, no. 1153. Zweite, "Free the Line," 30, uses the subjective element in Kandinsky's later works to distinguish them from the "Constructivist" work of artists such as Mondrian and Malevich.

65. Cheetham, *Rhetoric of Purity*, 79, 169 n. 34; Sers, *Kandinsky*, 196–99.

66. Sheppard notes how this view of nature underlies Kandinsky's *Sounds*: "Indeed, in the second half of *Sounds*, we find an almost dadaist sense that a redemptive power of renewal is at work *within* Nature and the material world" ("Kandinsky's *oeuvre*," 59). Sheppard notes a contradiction between this view of nature and the "gnostic split between spirit and matter" of Kandinsky's theories.

6. CONSTRUCTION AND MIMESIS

1. Though published in 1915, most of the work for this book was probably completed in the first half of 1914. See Jean-Louis Paudrat, "From Africa," in *"Primitivism" in 20th Century Art*, 151.

2. Einstein, *Negerplastik*, in *Werke*, 1:245. For a description of the development of Einstein's philosophy of history, see Kiefer, *Diskurswandel*, 332–37.

3. I diverge here from Heidemarie Oehm's reading in which she argues that for Einstein the primitive identity between subject and object is a paradise from which humanity has regressed in its history. See Oehm, *Die Kunsttheorie Carl Einsteins* (Munich: Fink, 1976), 32. Joachim Schultz demonstrates Einstein's distance from a romanticizing praise of everything African by contrasting Einstein's work with that of Blaise Cendrars. See Schultz, "Carl Einstein, Blaise Cendrars and Andere. Zum Primitivismus

in der europäischen Literatur der Avantgarde zwischen 1900 und 1940," in *Carl-Einstein-Kolloquium 1986*, ed. Klaus H. Kiefer (Frankfurt am Main: Peter Lang, 1988), 49–65. Klaus H. Kiefer also describes Einstein's avoidance of exoticism in "Carl Einsteins Negerplastik: Kubismus und Kolonialismus-Kritik," in *Literatur und Kolonialismus I*, ed. Wolfgang Bader and János Riesz (Frankfurt am Main: Peter Lang, 1983), 235. See also Kiefer, *Diskurswandel*, 146–64.

4. Einstein, *Negerplastik* in *Werke*, 1:246.

5. Einstein, *Negerplastik* in *Werke*, 1:246.

6. Einstein, *Negerplastik* in *Werke*, 1:246.

7. Kiefer discusses this connection in "Carl Einstein's Negerplastik," 243, and *Diskurswandel*, 311–13. See also Rhys W. Williams, "Primitivism in the Works of Carl Einstein, Carl Sternheim and Gottfried Benn," in *Journal of European Studies* 13, part 4, no. 52 (December 1983): 251. For a more general discussion of the relation between Einstein's ideas on African art and his reception of cubism, see Klaus H. Kiefer, "Fonctions de l'art africain dans l'oeuvre de Carl Einstein," in *Images de l'Africain de l'Antiquité au XXe Siècle*, ed. Daniel Droixhe and Klaus H. Kiefer (Frankfurt am Main: Peter Lang, 1987), 152–54; and Jens Kwasny, " 'Als die Augen sich Katastrophen noch erschauten': Über Kubismus und Poesie aus der Sichtweise Carl Einsteins," in *Kubismus: Künstler, Themen, Werke 1907–1920* (Cologne: Josef-Haubrich-Kunsthalle, 1982), 119–25.

8. Einstein based his conception of art on the theories of Heinrich Wölfflin (with whom Einstein studied in Berlin), Adolf von Hildebrand, and Conrad Fiedler. For a discussion of their influence on Einstein's thought, see Kiefer, "Carl Einstein's Negerplastik," 236–37, and *Diskurswandel*, 118–27, 299–302. For a discussion of Fiedler and Einstein, see Penkert, *Carl Einstein: Beiträge*, 46–47; and Hansjörg Diener, *Dichtung als Verwandlung: Eine Studie über das Verhältnis von Kunsttheorie und Dichtung im Werk Carl Einsteins* (Zürich: LEU-Verlag, 1987), 18–20. On Hildebrand's and Fiedler's influence on Einstein, see Andreas Michel, *Europe and the Problem of the Other: The Critique of Modernity in the Writings of Carl Einstein and Victor Segalen* (Ph.D. diss., University of Minnesota, 1991), 54–78.

9. Carl Einstein, *Afrikanische Plastik* (Berlin: Wasmuth Verlag, 1921), reprinted in *Werke*, vol. 2, *1919–1928*, ed. Marion Schmid with Henriette Beese and Jens Kwasny (Berlin: Medusa, 1981), 62–144.

10. See Kiefer, "Carl Einsteins Negerplastik," 241. For a comprehensive account of the development of Einstein's interest in African art and the circumstances leading to his writing of *Negerplastik*, see Paudrat, "From Africa," 151–52; and Kiefer, *Diskurswandel*, 155–66.

11. Georges Didi-Huberman, "L'anachronisme fabrique l'histoire: sur l'inactualité de Carl Einstein," *Etudes Germaniques* 53:1 (January–March 1998): 52. Didi-Huberman sets himself in opposition to commentators who have posited a break in Einstein's work between a subjective and a materialist phase. Oehm first posited this break in *Die Kunsttheorie Carl Einsteins*, but this idea has also been taken up by many subsequent studies of Einstein's work. See, for example, Ines Franke-Gremmelspacher, *"Notwendigkeit der Kunst"?: Zu den späten Schriften Carl Einsteins* (Stuttgart: Hans-Dieter Heinz Akademischer Verlag, 1989), 17–20; Jochen Schulte-Sasse, "Carl Einstein; or, The Postmodern Transformation of Modernism," in *Modernity and the Text*, 36–59; and Neil Donahue, "Analysis and Construction: The Aesthetics of Carl Einstein," chap. 5 in *Forms of Disruption: Abstraction in Modern German Prose* (Ann Arbor: University of Michigan Press, 1993), 101–26.

12. As Lucien Stéphan has pointed out, *Negro Sculpture* and *African Sculpture* are successive and complementary works because the former's legitimation of African art through reference to modernist art is the necessary precondition for the latter's attempt to delineate a field of research devoted exclusively to African art. See Stéphan, "Théorie de la sculpture et arts nègres chez Carl Einstein," *Etudes Germaniques* 53, no. 1 (January–March 1998): 205–6. For an account of Einstein's research into African art and culture, see Kiefer, *Diskurswandel*, 187–88, 193–97.

13. Reprinted in Carl Einstein, *Werke*, 2:240–63 and 2:298–312, respectively.

14. "Masque de danse rituelle Ekoi," in *Documents* 5 (1929): 285; reprinted in Einstein, *Werke*, vol. 3, *1929–1940*, ed. Marion Schmid and Liliane Meffre (Vienna: Medusa, 1985), 505. "Masques Bapindi" in *Documents* 1 (1930): 48; reprinted in Einstein, *Werke*, 3:506. "Art des nomades de l'asie centrale," exhibition catalog (Paris: Galerie de la Nrf, March 16–April 10, 1931); reprinted in Einstein, *Werke*, 3:557–62. "Preface," *Exhibition of Bronze Statuettes B.C. (Hittite, Etruscan, Egyptian, Greek)* (New York: Stora Art Galleries, 1933); reprinted in Einstein, *Werke*, 3:543–56.

15. Einstein, *Werke*, 3:544.

16. Bürger, *Theory of the Avant-Garde*, 51.

17. Einstein, *Werke*, 3:544.

18. As Franke-Gremmelspacher points out, this essay also includes passages taken directly from *Georges Braque*. See Franke-Gremmelspacher, *"Notwendigkeit der Kunst,"* 34. The simultaneous use of ideas from *Georges Braque* and *Die Fabrikation der Fiktionen* suggests that the critique of modernist aestheticism in Einstein's late work is not so much a radical material-

ist departure from an earlier subjectivist aesthetic as a continuation of his primitivist concerns.

19. Einstein, "Totalität I-V," in *Werke*, 1:229. This essay was originally published with the titles "Anmerkungen" (for "Totalität I-II") in *Die Aktion* 4 (1914): 277–79; "Totalität" (for "Totalität III-IV") in *Die Aktion* 4 (1914): 345–47; and "Totalität" (for "Totalität V") in *Die Aktion* 4 (1914): 476–78. All five parts were collected and published as "Totalität I-V" in Carl Einstein, *Anmerkungen* (Berlin: Verlag Die Aktion, 1916). See Einstein, *Werke*, 1:229.

20. Einstein, "Totalität" in *Werke*, 1:226.

21. "Now one might say that in the face of everything new (science, for instance) naive human experience still remains the same" (Einstein to Kahnweiler, ca. June 1923, in *Werke*, 4:159).

22. Edmund Husserl, *Philosophy As Rigorous Science*, in *Phenomenology and the Crisis of Philosophy*, trans. Quentin Lauer (New York: Harper and Row, 1965); reprinted in Husserl, *Shorter Works*, ed. Peter McCormick and Frederick A. Elliston (Notre Dame IN: University of Notre Dame Press, 1981), 180. Page references are to the reprinted version.

23. "The qualitative perception of experiences does not allow us to somehow discern a smallest basic unit; that is to say, our experiences would dissolve into a complete chaos and we would lose all means of transforming our experiences into latent determinate functions which would be able to appear in qualititative distinctness at any arbitrary point" (Einstein, "Totalität" in *Werke*, 1:229).

24. "That which separates all of these formations of the mental world and thereby provides them with a determinately formed being is totality" (Einstein, "Totalität" in *Werke*, 1:226).

25. "We would not be capable of imagining and determining anything specific if our memory did not depict the unity of applicable qualitative formations without which time–since totality is a function and contains a temporal determination–would not be able to contain any differentiations for us" (Einstein, "Totalität" in *Werke*, 1:227).

26. Thomas Krämer points out the connection between Einstein's theory of consciousness and Ernst Mach's. See Krämer, *Carl Einsteins "Bebuquin": Romantheorie und Textkonstitution* (Würzburg: Königshausen und Neumann, 1991), 63. The difference between Mach's description and Einstein's that Krämer does not point out is that Mach speaks of association as a constellation of *given* qualities while Einstein describes association as the mechanism by which qualities are themselves constructed. Einstein writes: "closest to me theoretically is perhaps Mach, who, unfortunately however,

fails when he moves beyond the physiological and does not at all bring language into consideration" (Einstein to Kahnweiler, ca. June 1923, in *Werke*, 4:157). This difference between a physiological determination and a linguistic construction of experience is crucial for Einstein's theory because he recognizes the moment in which art, functioning as the conduit for collective forces, determines the construction of the qualities of consciousness.

While it is clearly opposed to Mach's physiological approach, Einstein's linguistic approach turns out to be very similar to the idea of "mythic time" described by Ernst Cassirer. See Diener, *Dichtung als Verwandlung*, 73. See also Kiefer, *Diskurswandel*, 423–24, 443–44. Cassirer writes: "What we have found to be true of mythical space applies also to mythical time—its form depends on the characteristic mythical-religious accentuation, the distribution of the accents of the sacred and the profane. From a religious point of view time is never a simple, uniform process of change but obtains its meaning only through the differentiation of its phases. The gestalt assumed by time as a whole depends on how the religious consciousness distributes the light and shadow, on whether it dwells on and immerses itself in one phase of time or in another upon which it sets a mark of special value" (*The Philosophy of Symbolic Forms*, vol. 2, *Mythical Thought*, trans. Ralph Manheim [New Haven: Yale University Press, 1955], 118–19).

27. "Totality enables the positing of qualitative laws insofar as lawfulness within the single system is no longer based on varied repetition and the return of the same, but rather on the character of specific, elementary formations" (Einstein, "Totalität" in *Werke*, 1:226).

28. "Memory is the pure function of qualitatively differing experiences, which are organized according to their qualities and are *simultaneously* latent in order that they might be able to act within a qualitative experience that incorporates a corresponding or opposing element" (Einstein, "Totalität" in *Werke*, 1:228).

29. Compare Walter Benjamin's similar notion of memory in which he designates "as aura the associations which, at home in the *mémoire involontaire*, tend to cluster around the object of a perception" ("On Some Motifs," 186).

30. Husserl, *Philosophy*, 173.

31. Einstein, "Totalität" in *Werke*, 1:223.

32. The first edition of *Die Kunst des 20. Jahrhunderts* was published as volume 16 of the *Propyläen-Kunstgeschichte* (Berlin: Propyläen, 1926). Both the second edition of 1928 and the third edition of 1931 included revisions of the original 1926 text. Taken together, the three editions provide a clear view of the development of Einstein's thought during this period. The 1931

edition in particular was extensively reworked. The organization was changed to place more emphasis on the work of *Der Blaue Reiter* and to include an important new chapter on *Die Romantische Generation* (André Masson, Joan Miró, Gaston-Louis Roux). See Franke-Gremmelspacher, *"Notwendigkeit der Kunst,"* 69–73; and Kiefer, *Diskurswandel*, 351–54.

33. Though Rhys Williams argues that Wilhelm Worringer's ideas influenced Einstein's early theories, he does not point to any particular passages in Einstein's work where this influence is evident. See Williams, "Primitivism in the Works of Carl Einstein," 255. Neil Donahue provides a more detailed account of the relation of Einstein's early theories to those of Worringer. Though he acknowledges that no documentation of Einstein's knowledge of Worringer's work exists, Donahue goes on to argue that Einstein's interest in the formal in art is sufficient evidence of Worringer's influence. See Donahue, *Forms of Disruption*, 102–8. Liliane Meffre, also recognizing that Einstein does not make any reference to Worringer in his work, suggests that the similarities between Einstein and Worringer stem from their common reception of art theorists such as Theodor Lipps. See Meffre, *Carl Einstein et la problématique des avant-gardes dans les arts plastiques* (Bern: Peter Lang, 1989), 69–70. The connections between Einstein's *Negerplastik* and Worringer's *Abstraction and Empathy* are probably best explained by their common debt to earlier theorists such as Heinrich von Wölfflin and Adolf von Hildebrand. Wölfflin was one of Einstein's professors in Berlin (Penkert, *Carl Einstein: Beiträge*, 45), and Worringer cites Wölfflin repeatedly. See Worringer, *Abstraction and Empathy*, trans. Michael Bullock (1908; reprint, Cleveland: Meridian Books, World Publishing, 1967), 10 n. 4, 28 n. 11, 113 n. 16, 118 n. 18. In addition, both Einstein and Worringer cite Hildebrand's *Das Problem der Form in der bildenden Kunst* (1893; reprint, 3d ed., Strassburg: Heitz, 1901) and base their views on three-dimensionality on Hildebrand's insights. See Einstein, *Negerplastik* in *Werke*, 1:248; Worringer, *Abstraction and Empathy*, 22–23. For an extended discussion of Hildebrand's influence on Einstein, see Michel, *Europe and the Problem of the Other*, 54–61; and Werner E. Drewes, "Max Raphael und Carl Einstein: Konstellationen des Aufbruchs in die 'Klassische Moderne' Im Zeichen der Zeit," *Etudes Germaniques* 53:1 (January-March 1998): 131–33. Rather than a congruence of ideas, Kiefer, citing Ernst Bloch, "Negerplastik," *Die Argonauten* 2 (1915): 14, demonstrates that Einstein argues against Worringer's psychologizing of the primitive art of abstraction as a form of agoraphobia. See Kiefer, *Diskurswandel*, 139.

It is not until he writes *Georges Braque* that elements of Worringer's theories turn up in Einstein's thought, for example, in the argument that closed form is a means of suppressing the complexity of reality. See Einstein, *Georges Braque* in *Werke*, 3:225, 3:283. But even here, Einstein does not limit his idea of "tectonic form" to a discussion of how abstraction isolates objects from the chaos of natural forces, as Worringer does. See Worringer, *Abstraction and Empathy*, 16–17, 20–21. Instead, Einstein also investigates how tectonic form provides a means by which the forces of reality are made collectively accessible to consciousness: "It is now clear that the tectonic does not have anything to do with conceptual abstraction, but is rather the expression of the collective and thus something real which is directly experienced" (*Werke*, 3:283). The work of art becomes the site of a complex play of forces in reality in which the tectonic form both defends consciousness against the violence of these forces and yet enables an immediate experience of these forces.

In Worringer's analysis, form only functions to suppress the horror of nature. Abstraction lies at the beginning (rather than the end) of the development of art, and he assumes that the need to flee from nature's horror is a specific characteristic of an early stage of human development. (See Drewes, "Max Raphael und Carl Einstein," 134.) For Einstein, by contrast, art does not develop in a process of evolution, and abstract form does not provide any indication of the "progressiveness" or "backwardness" of a particular culture. Abstraction simply functions as a means available to any artist who wishes to *convey*, and not to suppress, an experience of the horror of nature.

34. "In the first place one does not actually see in a purely optically direct way, but associates every familiar optical sensation quickly with a composite recollective vision which covers the genetic sensation with a supposedly constant and complete image" (Einstein, *Die Kunst des 20. Jahrhunderts* [1926], 64).

35. "kubische Resultante," Einstein, *Negerplastik* in *Werke*, 1:259.

36. Einstein, *Negerplastik* in *Werke*, 1:255.

37. Einstein, *Negerplastik* in *Werke*, 1:258.

38. "The meaning of cubism: the forming of a three-dimensional experience of movement into a two-dimensional form without imitating depth or modeling with techniques of illusion while the depth dimension, that is, the conception of movement, and the totality of the function of memory is depicted; in the place of a dynamic depth perspective, an image of movement compressed in time, there arises a juxtaposition of two-dimensional forms, which are so arranged that 1) the constructive sections of the image, preserving the integrity of the plane, depict the various views of a body and its volume in two dimensions and 2) the dimension of memory that com-

prises all of this is formed without breaking up the plane of the image illusionistically" (Einstein, *Die Kunst des 20. Jahrhunderts* [1926], 62).

39. Einstein, *Die Kunst des 20. Jahrhunderts* (1926), 60. Einstein uses the term *Gestalt* in *Die Kunst des 20. Jahrhunderts* to describe what, in *Negerplastik*, he calls *das Kubische*, a term he borrows from Hildebrand. See also Einstein, "Diese Aesthetiker veranlassen uns" (early 1930s) in *Werke*, 4:194–221, also published under the title "Gestalt und Begriff" in Sibylle Penkert, *Carl Einstein: Existenz und Ästhetik* (Wiesbaden: Steiner, 1970).

40. Attempting to avoid a reduction of African sculpture to the two-dimensional depictions of cubism, Einstein extends the discussion of African sculpture beyond the specific issue of frontality. He does this by noting that psychologically important elements of an object are given particular emphasis in terms of size or shape in the African sculpture: "Important elements demand an appropriate cubic effect" (Einstein, *Negerplastik* in *Werke*, 1:260). The elongation or flattening of different parts of a sculpture create the spatial equivalent of psychic significance. Einstein also points out that every point in three-dimensional space can be interpreted in two directions, either toward the viewer or away from the viewer (Einstein, *Negerplastik* in *Werke*, 1:260). The fixing of the direction of movement of a particular point or element, for instance, the depiction of the eyes as either a hollowing out or a protrusion, also serves as a tool for recreating in space an aspect of the psychic form of the object. As commentators have often pointed out, Picasso, in his sculpture *Guitar* (1912), borrowed this technique from Grebo masks (in which the eyes are depicted as protrusions) in order to create the hole of a guitar as a protruding cylinder. See Daniel-Henry Kahnweiler, "Negerkunst und Kubismus," *Merkur* 13, no. 8 (August 1959): 728. See also Oehm, *Die Kunsttheorie Carl Einsteins*, 85; and Rubin, "Modernist Primitivism," 19–20.

41. "The task of sculpture is to construct an analogy [*eine Gleichung*] into which the naturalistic impressions of movement and thus the mass are entirely absorbed and their successive differentiation is translated into a formal organization" (Einstein, *Negerplastik* in *Werke*, 1:257).

42. Einstein, *Negerplastik* in *Werke*, 1:256.

43. On this point see Stéphan, "Théorie de la sculpture," 220.

44. "The intuition of space that such a work of art demonstrates must completely absorb cubic space in order to express it as a composite; perspective or the typical frontality are forbidden here, they would be impious. The work of art must provide the total equivalent of space; for only when it excludes every temporal interpretation based on conceptions of movement is it timeless. It absorbs time by integrating what we experience as move-

ment into its form" (Einstein, *Negerplastik* in *Werke*, 1:254). See also Einstein, *Die Kunst des 20. Jahrhunderts* (1926), 67–68.

45. Einstein, *Negerplastik* in *Werke*, 1:256.

46. Einstein, *Negerplastik* in *Werke*, 1:253.

47. On the distinction between normal time and mythical time, see Mircea Eliade, *Myth and Reality*, trans. Willard R. Trask (New York: Harper and Row, 1963), 11–14.

48. Einstein, *Negerplastik* in *Werke*, 1:253. Oehm, avoiding the implication that Einstein equated primitive and modern art, argues that Einstein's theory of art maintains a separation between the two by differentiating between religious and aesthetic mechanisms in art. Quoting Einstein's pronouncement that "the absolute can only be made possible aesthetically" (Einstein, "Von der Kirche und ihren Dienern" in *Werke* 4:129), Oehm does not draw the conclusion that religious art is based on aesthetic forms, but rather interprets this phrase as part of a project of "secularization of religious categories into aesthetic ones" (Oehm, *Die Kunsttheorie Carl Einsteins*, 55). This reading stems from her idea that the techniques of cubism do not presume a reversal of the subject/object split. Instead, she bases the transcendence of African art on the blind belief of the artist in the god while she explains the transcendence of cubism as a broadening of the power of the subject over the object world (Oehm, *Die Kunsttheorie Carl Einsteins*, 85–86). But rather than a secularization of religious categories into an omnipotence of the subject, Einstein's explanation of African art in terms of the aesthetic categories of cubism points toward his affirmation of the identity of aesthetic and religious categories.

49. "Cubism is an example of a subjective realism, i.e., the unmediated experiences of the subject, its conceptions of space, are individualized into objects" (Einstein, *Die Kunst des 20. Jahrhunderts* [1926], 63).

50. Einstein, *Negerplastik* in *Werke*, 1:251.

51. Einstein, *Die Kunst des 20. Jahrhunderts* (1931), 65.

52. Einstein, *Negerplastik* in *Werke*, 1:253.

53. Einstein mentions Freud in *Die Kunst des 20. Jahrhunderts* (1931), 118.

54. Freud, *Totem and Taboo*, in *Standard Edition*, 13:91; Georg Lukács, *The Theory of the Novel: A Historico-philosophical Essay on the Forms of Great Epic Literature*, trans. Anna Bostock (1916; reprint, Cambridge: MIT Press, 1971), 41.

55. Freud, *Standard Edition*, 13:93–94.

56. Einstein, *Negerplastik* in *Werke*, 1:250.

57. Einstein, *Negerplastik* in *Werke*, 1:254.

58. Einstein, *Negerplastik* in *Werke*, 1:255.

59. Einstein, *Negerplastik* in *Werke*, 1:256.

60. Einstein, "Totalität" in *Werke*, 1:223.

61. Oehm, *Die Kunsttheorie Carl Einsteins*, 159ff.

62. Einstein, *Die Kunst des 20. Jahrhunderts* (1926), 57.

63. Einstein, *Die Kunst des 20. Jahrhunderts* (1931), 58.

64. Franke-Gremmelspacher describes this shift as a movement from a cubist model of art to a surrealist one based on a "psychological-ethnographic approach to the theory of art in which the concepts of 'dream,' 'vision,' 'hallucination,' and 'metamorphosis' become central" (*"Notwendigkeit der Kunst,"* 71).

65. Einstein, *Die Kunst des 20. Jahrhunderts* (1931), 70. Einstein does not include this linking of creativity and myth in the 1926 version, which suggests that his work in the early 1920s was less oriented toward myth than at any time before or after. Thomas Krämer reads this passage as Einstein's attempt to create a "new" mythology following Schlegel's conception in "Rede über die Mythologie" (Krämer, *Carl Einsteins "Bebuquin,"* 26). Yet while Krämer speaks of a "new" form of mythology that can only exist after a traditional religious context has been rejected, Einstein speaks not of a "new" mythology but of the return of a mythic stance. His construction of myth depends upon an active community context, which is always created through the totality of the work of art, whether in modern art or African sculpture.

66. Klaus H. Kiefer argues that Einstein's career is punctuated by two "materialist" phases, one in 1917–1920 that centered around his work for the Soldiers' Council of Brussels at the end of World War I and another beginning after the Nazis took power in Germany in 1933 and extending through 1937 and his participation in the Spanish Civil War. See Kiefer, "Carl Einstein and the Revolutionary Soldiers' Councils in Brussels," in *The Ideological Crisis of Expressionism: The Literary and Artistic German War Colony in Belgium 1914–1918*, ed. Rainer Rumold and O. K. Werckmeister (Columbia SC: Camden House, 1990), 110–11. See also Kiefer, *Diskurswandel*, 256. According to Kiefer, these activist phases alternate with his aesthetic modernist phases, in which he develops his theories of art. This constant alternation between two tendencies supports the idea that there is an inherent contradiction in his ideas rather than a consistent evolution. Kiefer also points out that the transformations in Einstein's discourse do not affect the "deep structure" of his thought, which is organized around the idea of community. This concern is common to his enthusiastic participation in World War I, the November Revolution in Brussels, and the Spanish Civil War. See Kiefer, *Diskurswandel*, 206, 213. It is also the factor that unites his early

reflections on totality and African sculpture with his surrealist interest in myth and the critique of intellectuals of the 1930s. In all of these cases particular political goals are always less important than the construction of community.

67. Carl Einstein, *Traité de la Vision*, in *Werke*, 4:255.

68. Einstein, *Die Kunst des 20. Jahrhunderts* (1931), 66. This passage does not appear in the 1926 edition.

69. This shift can also be traced through the different editions of *Die Kunst des 20. Jahrhunderts*. While the 1926 and 1928 editions focus on the innovation of cubism as the most praiseworthy tendency of twentieth-century art, the 1931 edition's new chapter, entitled "Die Romantische Generation" (devoted to André Masson, Joan Miró, and Gaston-Louis Roux), as well as the section on Paul Klee present a vision of modern art in which the construction of the new in cubism is connected to a mimesis of "psychic forces" (Einstein, *Die Kunst des 20. Jahrhunderts* [1931], 123). For an extended discussion of these two crucial sections of *Die Kunst des 20. Jahrhunderts*, see Meffre, *Carl Einstein*, 73–82.

70. Matias Martínez-Seekamp describes this change in Einstein's thought as a shift (taking place around the end of World War I) from an aesthetics of form based on the ideas of the art theorist, Conrad Fiedler, to a psychologically oriented aesthetic based on Einstein's readings of Freud and Jung. See Martínez-Seekamp, "Ferien von der Kausalität?: Zum Gegensatz von 'Kausalität' und 'Form' bei Carl Einstein," in *Text + Kritik* 95 (July 1987): 14. Though Martínez-Seekamp emphasizes the difference between these two phases, I would like to show that these two phases are compatible with each other and make up two essential parts of his theory of art.

71. Einstein, *Die Kunst des 20. Jahrhunderts* (1931), 66.

72. Einstein, *Die Kunst des 20. Jahrhunderts* (1931), 63. This passage does not appear in the 1926 edition.

73. "Totalities differentiate themselves from each other through intensity, that is, the stronger and richer the relationship of their contents are, the more these totalities themselves present many-sided elements" (Einstein, "Totalität" in *Werke*, 1:228).

74. "Cognition is equated with creation and something immediate is created which, though present latently, had not yet been depicted" (Einstein, "Totalität," in *Werke*, 1:226).

75. Einstein, *Die Kunst des 20. Jahrhunderts* (1931), 58. The 1926 version of this passage is very similar and reads: "Intuition and seeing change and exhaust each other, and optical dissatisfaction forces a change, regardless of

whether an inherited intuition is ignored; for it is not a matter of reproduction but production" (*Die Kunst des 20. Jahrhunderts* [1926], 57).

76. Einstein, *Die Kunst des 20. Jahrhunderts* (1931), 128.

7. NARRATIVE FORM AND EXPERIENCE

1. Lukács, *Theory of the Novel*, 34–37.
2. Lukács, *Theory of the Novel*, 71.
3. Lukács, *Theory of the Novel*, 35.
4. Lukacs, *Theory of the Novel*, 37.
5. Lukács, *Theory of the Novel*, 66.
6. Lukács, *Theory of the Novel*, 77–78.
7. Einstein, "Brief über den Roman," in *Werke*, 1:71.
8. "In the exquisiteness of his linguistic creation Goethe often forgets the epic. Homer and Flaubert are different. Here the word serves the epic and is invented, not in order to develop a person, but to mark out an event" (Einstein, "Brief über den Roman," in *Werke*, 1:67).
9. Erich Auerbach, *Mimesis: The Representation of Reality in Western Literature*, trans. Willard R. Trask (Princeton: Princeton University Press, 1953), 15.
10. Husserl, *Philosophy*, 180. Oehm points out the relation to Henri Bergson's theory of time but insists in the end that Einstein understands time as a simultaneity of qualities. See Oehm, *Die Kunsttheorie Carl Einsteins*, 86–88.
11. Einstein, "Brief über den Roman," in *Werke*, 1:69. Compare Freud, *Totem and Taboo*, in *Standard Edition*, 13:116.
12. Thomas Krämer also sees a connection in Einstein between form and a mimesis of fateful forces. See Krämer, *Carl Einsteins "Bebuquin,"* 53, 66. But according to his interpretation, prose for Einstein recreates the diachronic character of experience by creating a flow of impressions whose organization can only be deduced from the text-immanent relations between the different elements. Because this construction of immanent relations extracts the work from a dependence upon empirical reality for the production of its meaning, the work of art escapes the structures of an objectifying rationality in order to create a "mythic" totality. See Krämer, *Carl Einsteins "Bebuquin,"* 69. In this reading, "mythic" implies a separation from reifying outside forces that might affect the construction of the immanent relations within the text. Yet in Einstein's description of form in prose, "mythic" means exactly the opposite, that is, the opening up of the text to outside forces that create the form of the text.

13. Carl Einstein, "Über den Roman," *Die Aktion* 2 (1912), reprinted in *Werke*, 1:129. This demand for the typical forms the basis for Einstein's critique of intellectuals in *Die Fabrikation der Fiktionen*, in which he writes: "The task is now no longer to cultivate exceptions but to create representative types" (Einstein, *Fabrikation der Fiktionen*, 327).

14. "The novel does not present people's lives, but the time in which they move in order to produce their fate" (Einstein, "Brief über den Roman," in *Werke*, 1:71).

15. Carl Einstein, "Über Paul Claudel," *Die weißen Blätter* 1 (1913), reprinted in *Werke*, 1:204.

16. Against this idea, Oehm reads Einstein's theory of prose as being based on an interpretation of time as a simultaneous relation of qualities. See Oehm, *Die Kunsttheorie Carl Einsteins*, 87–88.

17. Einstein, "Brief über den Roman," in *Werke*, 1:67.

18. Einstein, "Brief über den Roman," in *Werke*, 1:66, 71.

19. Einstein, "Über den Roman," in *Werke*, 1:127.

20. "Some of our writers have proceeded in this way. They scorned the singular anecdote, the nuance of descriptive transitions and present a material that has been brought back to the necessary elements; a language that remains within the poetic, the parable; and a writing that has not been subverted by a material principle such as milieu, etc." (Einstein, "Über Paul Claudel," in *Werke*, 1:198–99).

21. "We have ascertained that the objects of true poetry are autonomous and at the same time transcendental structures, that is, structures that surpass an anecdotal, descriptive world, which as 'material' are already creations or dreams. These structures present the elements of our psychic existence and guarantee for us the continuity of psychic processes" (Einstein, "Über Paul Claudel," in *Werke*, 1:200).

22. Einstein, "Über Paul Claudel," in *Werke*, 1:204.

23. Auerbach posits a similar connection: "The concept of god held by the Jews is less a cause than a symptom of their manner of comprehending and representing things" (Auerbach, *Mimesis*, 8). Einstein's description of religious art is from "Über Paul Claudel," in *Werke*, 1:200.

24. Einstein himself was Jewish but not a devout believer. When his play, *Die schlimme Botschaft*, led to a highly publicized trial and eventually conviction on charges of blasphemy in Germany he declared himself at his trial to be "without religion." See Penkert, *Carl Einstein: Beiträge*, 89–91.

25. Einstein, "Über Paul Claudel," in *Werke*, 1:204.

26. Einstein, "Über Paul Claudel," in *Werke*, 1:205.

27. Einstein anticipates here the arguments later made by Auerbach that

mythic stories exercise a tyrannical hold over mundane experience: "The Bible's claim to truth is not only far more urgent than Homer's, it is tyrannical–it excludes all other claims. The world of the Scripture stories is not satisfied with claiming to be a historically true reality–it insists that it is the only real world, is destined for autocracy. All other scenes, issues, and ordinances have no right to appear independently of it, and it is promised that all of them, the history of all mankind, will be given their due place within its frame, will be subordinated to it" (*Mimesis*, 15). Mundane experience needs the myth to constitute itself, and the tyranny of myth is a consequence of this inherent dependency of normal experience on a prior totalization.

28. Einstein, "Über Paul Claudel," in *Werke*, 1:202.

29. The same intertwinement of freedom and fate forms the basis of Nietzsche's example of the Prometheus myth. In addition, Einstein's translations of African myths of creation and original sin in *Afrikanische Legenden* also demonstrate the same dramatic contradiction. See, for example, "Warum die Menschen sterben," "Die Sünde," "Auferstehung," or "Der Gaukler der Ebene" in Einstein, ed. and trans., *Afrikanische Legenden* (Berlin: Rowohlt, 1925); reprinted as *Der Gaukler der Ebene und andere afrikanische Märchen und Legenden* (Frankfurt am Main: Fischer Taschenbuch Verlag, 1983), 9, 17, 131–37.

30. Einstein, "Über Paul Claudel," in *Werke*, 1:202.

31. Einstein, "Über Paul Claudel," in *Werke*, 1:205.

32. Einstein affirms his debt to Nietzsche in one of his earliest documented letters, written about 1910–1911: "the beginning of a new and peculiar version of the Greeks seems to me to have first appeared in the late Hölderlin, with his posthumously published statement that one has overlooked the Asiatic element in the Greeks. The high points of this new direction are Nietzsche's *Birth of Tragedy*, the writings on Homer and the pre-Socratics as well as Rohde's *Psyche*, etc." (quoted in Penkert, *Carl Einstein: Beiträge*, 60–61). Much later in his career, Einstein reaffirms the significance of Nietzsche's ideas for his work on primitive art. In an essay on pre-Hellenic bronze statuettes, he opposes a classical "Goethe-antique" reception of ancient Greek culture to the primitivist "revaluation" carried out by Hölderlin and Nietzsche: "This, let us say Goethe-antique, prized most of all the mannered examples of the decline. A revaluation of these academic plaster conceptions was then made by the mighty Holderlin [*sic*] and Nietzsche. Nietzsche characterized the much famed epoch of Socrates, of Plato and Pericles as an epoch of ignominious decay" ("Preface," in *Werke*, 3:545). The connection between Einstein's primitivism and Nietzsche's *The*

Birth of Tragedy has also been described in Christoph Braun, *Carl Einstein zwischen Ästhetik und Anarchismus: Zu Leben und Werk eines expressionistischen Schriftstellers* (Munich: iudicium verlag, 1987), 37–41, 54–55; Kiefer, *Diskurswandel*, 43, 504–5; and in Williams, "Primitivism in the Works of Carl Einstein," 255–56.

33. Einstein, "Über Paul Claudel," in *Werke*, 1:201.
34. Einstein, "Über Paul Claudel," in *Werke*, 1:205.
35. Einstein, "Über Paul Claudel," in *Werke*, 1:204.
36. Einstein, "Über Paul Claudel," in *Werke*, 1:203.
37. Einstein, "Über Paul Claudel," in *Werke*, 1:203.
38. Einstein, "Über Paul Claudel," in *Werke*, 1:203.
39. Einstein, "Über Paul Claudel," in *Werke*, 1:203.

8. FROM FANTASY TO SACRIFICE

1. Tzvetan Todorov, *The Fantastic: A Structural Approach to a Literary Genre*, trans. Richard Howard (Cleveland: Case Western Reserve University Press, 1973), 171.

2. Auerbach, *Mimesis*, 22–23.

3. Todorov, *The Fantastic*, 173.

4. Oehm, *Die Kunsttheorie Carl Einsteins*, 92–98; and Krämer, *Carl Einsteins "Bebuquin,"* 9–10, use Einstein's theory of prose to understand *Bebuquin or The Dilettantes of Wonder*. Einstein himself designated *Bebuquin* as "a 5 or 6 times miscarried beginning" ("ein 5 6 mal mißglückter Anfang") in a letter to Toni Simon-Wolfskehl (undated, early 1923?), quoted in Penkert, *Carl Einstein: Beiträge*, 98. The prefatory rather than definitive character of the novel is also indicated in the first phrase of Einstein's original title, *Die Dilettanten des Wunders oder die billige Erstarrnis. Ein Vorspiel. Bebuquin*, which designates the novel, not only as a description of a disappointing dilettantism, but also as the "preface" to a future elaboration.

Though the first published version of the complete novel in *Die Aktion* has the title *Bebuquin oder die Dilettanten des Wunders*, the title that Einstein himself wrote on the manuscript he submitted to *Die Aktion* has the longer title in which the first phrase, "Die Dilettanten des Wunders oder die billige Erstarrnis" is very large and the words "ein Vorspiel. Bebuquin." are written relatively small, almost like a footnote. For a facsimile of this page, see Krämer, *Carl Einsteins "Bebuquin,"* plate II. This manuscript serves as the basis for the Reclam edition, and the editor of this edition, Erich Kleinschmidt, argues convincingly for the authority and reliability of this manuscript. See Kleinschmidt, "Nachwort," in Carl Einstein, *Bebuquin*

(Stuttgart: Reclam, 1985), 53–55. The shortened title, *Bebuquin*, first appeared with the second edition in 1917. For a comprehensive discussion of the title, see Dirk Heißerer, *Negative Dichtung: Zum Verfahren der literarischen Dekomposition bei Carl Einstein* (Munich: iudicium verlag, 1992), 111–25, 168–75.

5. Martínez-Seekamp, "Ferien von der Kausalität?," 20.

6. Einstein, *Bebuquin*, 3. Further page references to this book will be noted in parentheses after the quotations. All translations are my own, though I have profited from consulting Angela Mailänder Elston, *Bebuquin or The Dilettantes of Wonder: A Translation* (Ph.D. diss., Kent State University, 1984), 1–76.

7. Nietzsche's text was first published in 1903 (Leipzig: C. G. Naumann). Though it is not certain that Einstein was familiar with it, his later direct reference to Nietzsche in *Bebuquin* (5) demonstrates his familiarity with Nietzsche's ideas and presents strong evidence for their significance in *Bebuquin*.

8. In contrast to Oehm, who reads Bebuquin and Böhm as two different aspects of a single subject (Oehm, *Die Kunsttheorie Carl Einsteins*, 140), I consider Bebuquin and Böhm to be two rivals who compete to define the relation between the real and the miraculous.

9. E. B. Tylor, *Primitive Culture*, vol. 1 (1871; reprint, New York: Henry Holt, 1889), 116.

10. Einstein describes this abstractness of the dilettante in his "Letter Concerning the Novel": "A personality whose stages are not completely objective deeds will always remain a dilettante" ("Brief über den Roman," *Pan* 2 [1911–12], reprinted in *Werke*, 1:71).

11. This interpretation opposes Heidemarie Oehm's thesis that Böhm's model of the fantastic is the basis of Einstein's theory of art. For her, Einstein understands art as its own reality that does not imitate an empirical reality, but rather depends on its own inner organization to guarantee its truth. Following this model, Oehm considers *Bebuquin* as an example of an "absolute prose," which has negated all connection to an empirical reality and whose structure is completely hermetic. Oehm describes this autonomous text as a set of relationships between elements that has its own inner unity. See Oehm, *Die Kunsttheorie Carl Einsteins*, 92–93, 102. Because she interprets Bebuquin and Böhm as two aspects of a single subject, she does not recognize the conflict between them and reads the story based on Böhm's attempt to create an absolute subject that has eliminated all ties to the object world. Like Böhm, Oehm considers form to be the result of a reduction of reality to the subject and an elimination of the empirical

world. She ignores Bebuquin's alternative understanding of form. See Oehm, *Die Kunsttheorie Carl Einsteins*, 109, 123. For a similar reading, see Assenka Oksiloff, *Narratives of Modernism: Readings of Carl Einstein, Franz Kafka, and Walter Benjamin* (Ph.D. diss., University of Minnesota, 1992), 50–84.

Silvio Vietta has a similar reading of the alienation from the world that fantasy creates. However, his interpretation differs from Oehm's in that he reads this fantasy world as a caricature of a scientific order, which replaces the world with a rational construct. This reading demonstrates that the development of an "absolute prose" is simply the logical result of an absolute reason. By reading Einstein's novel as a repetition of the solipsism of rational systems and an absolute prose, however, Vietta overlooks Einstein's attempt to create an art that could provide a mythic alternative to rational constructs. See Vietta, "Carl Einsteins 'Bebuquin': Kritik der absoluten Vernunft," in *Expressionismus*, ed. Vietta and Kemper, 166–67. See also Rainer Rumold, "Carl Einstein: Sprachkrise und gescheitertes Experiment 'Absoluter' Dichtung," in *Erkennen und Deuten: Essays zur Literatur und Literaturtheorie Edgar Lohner in memoriam*, ed. Martha Woodmansee and Walter F. W. Lohnes (Berlin: Erich Schmidt Verlag, 1983), 268.

12. Adorno, *Aesthetic Theory*, 193; Adorno, *Ästhetische Theorie*, 201.

13. Reto Sorg sees the miracle and death to be two different and contradictory goals in the novel rather than inseparably linked. As a consequence, he fails to see the relation between art and transcendence that Einstein attempts to outline in *Bebuquin*, and assumes that such a project is doomed from the very beginning. See Sorg, *Aus den "Gärten der Zeichen": Zu Carl Einsteins Bebuquin* (Munich: Wilhelm Fink, 1998), 254.

14. As Claude Lévi-Strauss writes, "mythical thought always progresses from the awareness of oppositions toward their resolution." Lévi-Strauss, *Structural Anthropology*, vol. 1, trans. Claire Jacobson and Brooke Grundfest Schoepf (New York: Basic Books, 1963), 224.

15. Kiefer, *Diskurswandel*, 62–63. Nietzsche, *The Antichrist*, trans. H. L. Mencken (1895; reprint, Costa Mesa CA: Noontide Press, 1988), 144.

16. This attitude is prominent in Einstein's play, *Die schlimme Botschaft* (Bad tidings)(Berlin: Rowohlt, 1921; reprinted in *Werke*, 2: 147–99), whose title is taken directly from Nietzsche's *The Antichrist*, where Nietzsche differentiates between the "glad tidings" of Christ, in which "anything that puts a distance between God and man, is abolished" (Nietzsche, *The Antichrist*, 102) and the "bad tidings" (112) of Paul and the Christian church, who both emphasize belief and resurrection. As Peter says to Paul in Ein-

stein's play, "You need gods, Paul, and you are too cowardly to be a god yourself" (*Die schlimme Botschaft*, in *Werke*, 2:196).

17. Einstein, "André Masson, étude ethnologique," *Documents* 2 (1929), reprinted in *Werke*, 3:482. Kiefer demonstrates the importance of the idea of metamorphosis for Einstein's later work, reading this interest as part of a primitivist appropriation of mythic forms. See Kiefer, "Fonctions de l'art africain," 159–64. See also Kiefer, *Diskurswandel*, 411–49.

18. Einstein, "Der Traktat vom Wort und dem Kreuz" (ca. 1911) in *Werke*, 4:136.

19. Kiefer points out that the final two words may be read as an act of creation because of the ambiguity between "sagte: Aus" and "sagte aus." The final word is both a speech act and a description of the act of expression. See Kiefer, *Diskurswandel*, 56–57.

9. EXPRESSIONIST MYTH AND AFRICAN LEGEND

1. The French version, entitled "Le Gambadeur-de-la-Plaine," was published in Henri Junod, *Les Ba-Ronga: étude ethnographique sur les indigènes de la baie de Delagoa* (Neuchatel: Imprimerie Attinger Frères, 1898), 353–60. Junod does not document the identity of the original Thonga storyteller. This book is listed in the bibliography of Einstein's collection, *Afrikanische Legenden*, 273. Though the book was first published in 1925, Einstein announced its imminent publication in a letter of 1920 to Moise Kisling (unpublished correspondence, private collection of Jean Kisling). Kiefer mistakenly lists Einstein's source as Henri A. Junod, *Nouveaux Contes Ronga: Transcrits dans la langue indigène avec traduction francaise*. Neuchatel, 1989. Kiefer is correct, however, in noting that Einstein errs in placing the story with those of the Warundi (Urunda) people rather than with other stories of the Thonga (listed as the "Ba Ronga" people in Einstein's book and the French version of Junod's book). See Kiefer, "Fonctions de l'art africain," 157. See also Kiefer, *Diskurswandel*, 190–94.

2. See G. S. Kirk, "On Defining Myths," in *Sacred Narrative*, ed. Alan Dundes (Berkeley: University of California Press, 1984), 57.

3. Compare Kiefer, "Fonctions de l'art africain," 157.

4. "Der Gaukler der Ebene," 131, my translation.

5. As Junod notes, the insulting of the bride and her relations by the bridegroom and his relations is part of the Thonga marriage ceremony. Henri Junod, *The Life of a South African Tribe*, vol. 1, *The Social Life* (Neuchatel: Imprimerie Attinger Frères, 1913), 110–11. In this context, the son's decision to avoid the traditional marriage ritual that includes insult is an

avoidance of exaggerated communication and leads later on in the story to the fatal lack of communication between husband and wife concerning the buffalo. On this opposition between indiscretion and misunderstanding in myth, see Claude Lévi-Strauss, "The Story of Asdiwal," chap. 9 in *Structural Anthropology*, vol. 2, trans. Monique Layton (New York: Basic Books, 1976), 191.

6. The fact that the marriage in the story is contrary to the type normally found in reality accords with Lévi-Strauss's idea that mythical situations do not depict reality but rather its "inherent possibilities and latent potentialities" ("The Story of Asdiwal," 173). His description of the myths of Tsimshian society on the Pacific coast of Canada also reveals marriages that are "contrary to the type found in reality" ("The Story of Asdiwal," 153).

As Marcel Mauss notes concerning Andaman Islanders: "Presents put the seal upon marriage and form a link of kinship between the two pairs of parents" (*The Gift: The Form and Reason for Exchange in Archaic Societies*, trans. W. D. Halls [New York: Norton, 1990], 19).

7. On the importance of the distinction between economic transactions and the social interaction enabled by gifts, see Mauss, *The Gift*, 22. See also Freud, *Totem and Taboo*, in *Standard Edition*, 13:166–68, for a description of the importance of ritual sacrifice and meals for establishing kinship ties. Vincent Crapanzano criticizes Mauss's description of the functioning of the gift because he attempts to locate the spirit of the gift referentially. See Crapanzano, "The Moment of Prestidigitation: Magic, Illusion, and Mana in the Thought of Emile Durkheim and Marcel Mauss," in *Prehistories of the Future*, 105.

Both Mauss and the Maori informant he quotes (from the work of Elsdon Best) describe the gift in terms of the social interactions that it enables rather than for any objective meaning that it might have. However, Crapanzano insists that the "*hau*," or the spiritual force attached to the gift, "demands always another, foundational referent" (Crapanzano, 105). Yet, the purpose of the gift, like the buffalo in "The Wanderer of the Plain," is not to symbolize a referent but to mediate a relationship. The issue of referents is secondary to the issue of creating a common social context, and such mediators do not refer to a "foundational referent" but structure a relationship. As Mauss points out: "What imposes obligation in the present received and exchanged, is the fact that the thing received is not inactive. Even when it has been abandoned by the giver, it still possesses something of him. Through it the giver has a hold over the beneficiary just as, being its owner, through it he has a hold over the thief" (*The Gift*, 11–12). Both the son and his wife in "The Wanderer of the Plain" undermine the relationships established by such gifts.

8. Junod, *Les Ba-Ronga*, 354 n. 1.

9. "Der Gaukler der Ebene," 132.

10. In contrast to Adorno and Horkheimer's interpretation of sacrifice as "the magical pattern of rational exchange, a device of men by which the gods may be mastered," this story demonstrates that exchange must be carefully distinguished from sacrifice. See Horkheimer and Adorno, *Dialectic*, 49.

11. Lévi-Strauss, *Structural Anthropology*, 1:224–25.

12. "[T]he purpose of the myth is to provide a logical model capable of overcoming a contradiction (an impossible achievement if, as it happens, the contradiction is real)" (Lévi-Strauss, *Structural Anthropology*, 1:229).

13. "Der Gaukler der Ebene," 135.

14. "Der Gaukler der Ebene," 135.

15. Antonin Artaud, *The Theater and Its Double*, in *Selected Writings*, trans. Helen Weaver, ed. Susan Sontag (Berkeley: University of California Press, 1976), 238–39.

16. Lévi-Strauss, *Structural Anthropology*, 1:263.

17. "Der Gaukler der Ebene," 137.

18. "Der Gaukler der Ebene," 137.

19. "Le-Gambadeur-de-la-Plaine," in Junod, *Les Ba-Ronga*, 360.

20. "Der Gaukler der Ebene," 137.

21. This reading of myth accords with Lévi-Strauss's idea that the function of myth is to illustrate that the social facts with which a society must live "are marred by an insurmountable contradiction" (Lévi-Strauss, "The Story of Asdiwal," 173).

22. Kiefer, "Fonctions de l'art Africain," 158–59.

23. Nietzsche, BT 33, GT 25.

24. Lévi-Strauss, *Structural Anthropology*, 1:216.

25. Lévi-Strauss, *Structural Anthropology*, 1:216.

26. Freud, *The Interpretation of Dreams*, in *Standard Edition*, 4:263.

27. "[I]t cannot be too strongly emphasized that all available variants should be taken into account. If Freudian comments on the Oedipus complex are a part of the Oedipus myth, then questions such as whether Cushing's version of the Zuni origin myth should be retained or discarded become irrelevant. There is no single 'true' version of which all the others are but copies or distortions. Every version belongs to the myth" (Lévi-Strauss, *Structural Anthropology*, 1:218).

28. Nietzsche, BT 69, GT 67.

29. Lévi-Strauss, *Structural Anthropology*, 1:216.

30. Lévi-Strauss, *Structural Anthropology*, 1:261.

Index

Index

kinship and affinity in, 174–79, 182–83, 227 n.5, 228 n.7, 229 n.10; significance of, for primitivist thought, 186–88; similarity of, to Oedipus myth, 23–24, 182–86; Thonga source for, 173–74, 179–82, 227 n.1; unreality of, 186–87, 228 n.6

Weidmann, August K., 190 n.11

Weiss, Peg, 112; *Kandinsky and Old Russia*, 100–101, 106–7, 205 n.17 n.18 n.19, 206 n.20, 207 n.24 n.27; *Kandinsky in Munich*, 208 n.34

Williams, Rhys W., 211 n.7, 215 n.33, 224 n.32

The Will to Power (Nietzsche), 43, 198 n.37

Wölfflin, Heinrich, 211 n.8, 215 n.33

"The Work of Art in the Age of Mechanical Reproduction" (Benjamin), 9, 14

Worringer, Wilhelm, 215 n.33

Young, Julian, 64, 197 n.20

Zweite, Armin, 208 n.42, 210 n.64